A Livable Future Is Possible

A LIVABLE FUTURE IS POSSIBLE

CONFRONTING THE THREATS TO OUR SURVIVAL

NOAM CHOMSKY

EDITED BY C. J. POLYCHRONIOU

HAYMARKET BOOKS
CHICAGO, ILLINOIS

Published in 2024 by
Haymarket Books
P.O. Box 180165
Chicago, IL 60618
773-583-7884
www.haymarketbooks.org
info@haymarketbooks.org

ISBN: 979-8-88890-262-2

Distributed to the trade in the US through Consortium Book Sales and Distribution (www.cbsd.com) and internationally through Ingram Publisher Services International (www.ingramcontent.com).

This book was published with the generous support of Lannan Foundation and Wallace Action Fund.

Special discounts are available for bulk purchases by organizations and institutions. Please email info@haymarketbooks.org for more information.

Cover design by Steve Leard.

Printed in Canada by union labor.

Library of Congress Cataloging-in-Publication data is available.

10 9 8 7 6 5 4 3 2 1

CONTENTS

PREFACE

The interviews in this volume with the world's greatest public intellectual alive, and one of the most cited scholars in modern history, are a sequel to the collection of interviews that appeared in *Illegitimate Authority: Facing the Challenges of Our Time* and which was published in 2020 by Haymarket Books. They extend and update discussions on some of the most pressing world problems, such as the climate crisis, the consequences of the ongoing war in Ukraine, and the rising nuclear risk, while exploring at the same time the features of the emerging new world order and looking at the dangerous new hot zones around the globe. The fascist threat in the United States and Biden's foreign policy add to concerns both about the future of whatever is left of American democracy and that of the world at large.

However, "optimism over despair" has always been one of Noam Chomsky's mottos, and thus he contends that humanity can avert a climate catastrophe and a nuclear holocaust. He is ninety-five years old and still stresses with the same firm conviction that has characterized his entire extraordinary life that activism is key to building a better world. In terms of the existential threat of the climate crisis, he greatly admires the contributions of the economist Robert Pollin in charting a pathway toward a post–fossil fuel transition that is just and equitable while building at the same time a new and thriving economic environment. There are quite a few joint interviews with Chomsky and Pollin on the climate crisis that are included in this volume, and Noam has always looked forward with great interest and anticipation to these collaborative undertakings as he finds the groundbreaking work that Pollin and his coworkers are doing at the Political Economy Research Institute (PERI) of the University of Massachusetts–Amherst to be of immense significance in the struggle to save the planet from irreversible destruction.

Also addressed in this new collection of interviews is the hot topic of artificial intelligence (AI). As the towering figure in the field of linguistics for many decades, whose work has influenced such fields as cognitive science, psychology, philosophy, and computer science, Chomsky's views on AI are of great import.

A Livable Future Is Possible is the fourth collection of interviews with Noam Chomsky. As with the previous three books, most of the interviews included in this volume originally appeared in *Truthout*, a nonprofit, progressive news organization in the United States providing independent reporting and commentary on a diverse range of social justice issues. And as before, the hope in anthologizing them is that they make the views and ideas of the world's greatest public intellectual as accessible both to a new generation of activists and concerned citizens alike, as well as to his millions of older-generation fans across the globe. As the old saying goes, the struggle continues.

—C. J. Polychroniou

Noam Chomsky and Robert Pollin

JUST TRANSITION CAN STOP EARTH FROM BECOMING UNINHABITABLE

June 7, 2023

C. J. Polychroniou: *Noam, it has been clear for decades that human activities are having a huge impact on the physical environment in many critical ways, and that we are the cause of global warming, with the burning of fossil fuels accounting for nearly 90 percent of all carbon dioxide (CO_2) emissions. It is true, of course, that some concrete actions have been taken over the past three decades or so to stop environmental degradation and reduce carbon emissions, but the gap between what is happening to the planet, which includes a sharp decline in biodiversity, and what is needed in terms of environmental and climate action seems to be growing rather than decreasing. Indeed, one could even argue that our handling of the climate crisis is flawed, as evidenced by the growing emphasis on carbon capture technologies rather than doing away with fossil fuels. Another revealing example of governments constantly advancing highly incomplete courses of action with regard to climate change is the adoption of a historic new law from governments across the European Union today toward deforestation. European governments have agreed to ban the import of goods linked to deforestation, but the new deforestation law does not oblige European banks or investors to stop funding deforestation. So, if it*

1

is the link between policymaking and economic interests that prevents us from implementing fully comprehensive strategies to stop environmental destruction and prevent global warming from becoming worse, what ways are there out of this conundrum?

Noam Chomsky: Two years ago, John Kerry, Biden's special envoy on climate, reported that he'd been "told by scientists that 50 percent of the reductions we have to make (to get to near zero emissions) by 2050 or 2045 are going to come from technologies we don't yet have."

While intended to strike a note of optimism, this forecast was perhaps a little less than reassuring.

A qualification was noted by political economist Adam Tooze: The pledge holds as long as the investments are profitable and "de-risked" by guarantees from the World Bank and International Monetary Fund.

The "technologies we don't yet have" remain technologies we don't yet have or can realistically envision. Some progress has been reported, but it is very far from what would be required to deal with the impending crisis.

The present danger is that what must be done to eliminate fossil fuel use is being set aside on the pretext that some remote technological breakthrough will ride to the rescue. Meanwhile, we can continue to burn up the Earth and pour even more cash into the bulging profits of the fossil fuel industry, now so overflowing that they don't know what to do with their incredible riches.

The industry, of course, welcomes the pretext. It might even spare some cash for carbon capture—maybe as much as a rounding error for their accountants—as long as the usual qualification holds: funded by the friendly taxpayer and de-risked. Meanwhile more federal lands are opened up for fossil fuel production, more gifts are provided to them like the 300-mile-long Mountain Valley Pipeline—Manchin's condition for not tanking the global economy—and other such amenities.

In the background of the euphoria about asset managers and technological miracles lies the Stimson Doctrine, enunciated by Secretary of War Henry Stimson eighty years ago as he was overseeing the huge mobilization for war: "If you are going to try to go to war, or to prepare for war, in a capitalist country, you have got to let business make money out of the process or business won't work."

That's how the system works—as long as we let it.

In the early stages of the war, business was reluctant to accept the bargain. Most hated the reformist New Deal and did not want to cooperate with a government not entirely devoted to their interests. But when the spigot was opened, such reservations disappeared. The government poured huge resources into war production. Keeping to the Stimson Doctrine, policies were structured to ensure great profits for business contractors. That laid the basis for what was much later criticized as the military-industrial complex but might more accurately be described as the not-so-hidden system of US industrial policy, the device by which the public funds the emerging high-tech economy: a highly inefficient system, as elaborated by Seymour Melman and others, but an easy way to gain congressional approval for what approved rhetoric calls a marvelous system of free enterprise that helps the munificent "job creators" labor day and night for the benefit of all.

Eisenhower apparently at first wanted to use the term "military-industrial-congressional complex." That would have been appropriate. Why does Congress go along? One major reason is provided by political economist Thomas Ferguson's well-confirmed "investment theory of politics." In a current updating, once again corroborating the theory, he summarizes the crucial conclusion simply: .

> The dominating fact about American politics is its money-driven character. In our world, both major political parties are first of all bank accounts, which have to be filled for anything to happen. Voters can drive politics, but not easily. Unless they are prepared to invest very substantial time and effort into making the system work or organizations that they control will [sic.]—such as unions or genuine grassroots political organizations—only political appeals that can be financed go live in the system [sic.], unless (of course) as helpful diversions.

That insight into "our world" also offers advice as to ways out of the conundrum. And also, ways to confront the reigning Stimson Doctrine, which is a virtual epitaph for the human species in the context of the awesome and imminent threat of heating the earth beyond the level of recovery.

It is suicidal to look away from the gap between what is happening to the planet, which includes a sharp decline in biodiversity, and what is needed in terms of environmental and climate action, a process which seems to be growing rather than decreasing. When we do look, we find a mixed picture.

One critical case is the Amazon forest. Its central role in global ecology is well understood. It is self-sustaining, but if damaged can shift rapidly to irreversible decline, with catastrophic effects for the region, and the entire world.

During Bolsonaro's term in Brazil, agribusiness, mining, and logging enterprises were unleashed in an assault on the forest and the Indigenous societies that have long lived there in harmony with nature. To take just one measure, "Deforestation across Brazil soared between 2019 and 2022 under the then president, Jair Bolsonaro, with cattle ranching being the number one cause." More than 800 million trees were destroyed for beef export. The main researchers, the Indigenous peoples expert Bruno Pereira and his journalist collaborator Dom Phillips, were murdered while conducting their work in the Amazon.

Brazilian scientists report that some sectors of the forest have already passed the tipping point, transitioning to savannah, permanent destruction.

Lula [da Silva]'s election in 2022 offered hope to limit, perhaps end, the destruction. As minister of the environment, he appointed Marina Silva, a courageous and dedicated environmentalist, with a truly impressive record. But "the masters of mankind" who own the economy (in Adam Smith's phrase) never rest. Their congressional supporters are chipping away at Silva's jurisdiction.

Those who hope to save the world are not resting either. Brazilian ecologists are seeking ways to support Indigenous communities that have been the guardians of the forest, and to extend their reach.

The struggle continues.

It continues on other fronts as well. Some good news from China is summarized in the *Washington Post*. Reviewing many studies, the *Post* reports that China is far in the lead globally in "churn[ing] out batteries, solar panels and other key ingredients of the energy transition" as China has "moved aggressively on renewables," leaving the US far behind—very far behind in per capita terms, the relevant figure. China is "likely on track to meet its goals of peaking its emissions before 2030 and achieving net-zero emissions by 2060. It installed a record amount of solar power capacity last year—and this year alone is set to install more than the entire existing solar capacity of the United States."

I've been mispresenting the article, however. The *Post* does not come to praise China, but to condemn it. Its praise is for the US, which, from its lofty perch on transitioning to renewable energy is seeking ways "to pressure China to help avert climate catastrophe"— the headline of the article. The article warns ominously that China is responsible for more than double US emissions; or to translate from Newspeak, China is far behind the US in per capita emissions, again the relevant figure.

The article discusses the means under consideration to induce China to join us in our noble pursuit of saving the climate, omitting, however, the most important of these: "Commerce Secretary Gina Raimondo said Tuesday that the US will rally allies in order to mount pressure on the world's second-largest economy. 'If we really want to slow down China's rate of innovation, we need to work with Europe,' Raimondo said."

We have to make sure to contain China's innovations in producing the advanced technology that might save the world. The prime method, openly announced and highly praised, is to deny China access to the computer chips that are necessary for advanced technology.

At the same time, Raimondo warned China that the US "'won't tolerate' China's effective ban on purchases of [Idaho corporation] Micron Technology memory chips and is working closely with allies to address such 'economic coercion.'"

More insight into the famed "rules-based international order" and its subtle design, as the world burns.

India has overtaken China as the world's most populous country, and its population is certain to continue to grow in the decades ahead. Do we have to reduce global population to save the planet?

Chomsky: The global population should be reduced, perhaps considerably. Fortunately, there is a method to achieve this result, one that is furthermore humane and should be undertaken irrespective of the goal of saving the planet: education of women. That's been shown to lead to sharp population reduction in both rich countries and poor.

Education of women should be supplemented by other humane methods, such as those prescribed in the 1948 Universal Declaration of Human Rights: "Motherhood and childhood are entitled to special care and assistance. All children, whether born in or out of wedlock, shall enjoy the same social protection."

The Universal Declaration of Human Rights was initiated by the US, but that was in a different era, when New Deal social democracy still had not been undermined by the bitter business assault that finally reached its goals with Reagan. By then, the socioeconomic provisions of the declaration, including the ones just quoted, were ridiculed as "a letter to Santa Claus" (Reagan's UN Ambassador Jeane Kirkpatrick). Kirkpatrick was echoed by Paula Dobriansky, the official in charge of human rights and humanitarian affairs in the Reagan and Bush administrations. Dobriansky sought to dispel "the myth [that] 'economic and social rights' [of the declaration] constitute human rights." These myths are "little more than an empty vessel into which vague hopes and inchoate expectations can be poured." They are "preposterous" and even a "dangerous incitement," in the words of Bush ambassador Morris Abram when he was casting the sole vote against the UN

Right to Development, which closely paraphrased the socioeconomic provisions of the Universal Declaration of Human Rights.

By then dismissal of the letter to Santa Claus had become largely bipartisan, though the GOP has maintained the lead in savagery, as we can see right now in the farcical doings in Congress.

There is a lot more to say about this, but for another time.

Bob, a "just transition" is seen as essential for advancing ambitious climate change policies. Why is a just transition so crucial for effective climate action, and how exactly does it affect average citizens?

Robert Pollin: The term "just transition" has been used in various ways. I will first use it to refer to measures to support workers and communities that are presently dependent on the fossil fuel industry for their incomes and well-being. I will then consider below a second use of the term, considering the ways in which high-income economies need to support the Green New Deal programs advanced by low-income economies.

With respect to the first issue of supporting workers and communities that are now dependent on the fossil fuel industry, the broader context is very important. As we have discussed many times before, investments in energy efficiency and renewable energy to build a global zero-emissions energy infrastructure will be a major engine of overall job creation. That is, overall, saving the planet is very good for jobs. This is, of course, the opposite of the fulminations we hear from [the] likes of Donald Trump, but also much more widely across the political spectrum. The vaguely respectable version of this position is that phasing out fossil fuel consumption might well be beneficial on environmental grounds, but it [is] still going to be a job killer. And everyone other than rich coastal elites care more about jobs than the environment.

Here is how this position can actually resonate. While the clean energy transition is indeed a major engine of job creation overall, it is still also true that phasing out the fossil fuel industry will inevitably mean losses for workers and communities that now depend on the fossil fuel industry. In the absence of generous just transition policies, these workers and communities will indeed be facing layoffs, falling incomes, and declining public-sector budgets to support schools, health clinics, and public safety. Should we be surprised that, without hard commitments to generous just transition policies, a good share of these workers and communities will vehemently oppose the fossil fuel industry phase out?

A viable just transition program for these workers and communities needs to build from the framework first advanced by Tony Mazzocchi, the late great labor movement and environmental leader. Mazzocchi was the person who came up with the term "just transition" in the first place. In considering the phasing out of nuclear plants and related facilities, Mazzocchi wrote in 1993: "Paying people to make the transition from one kind of economy to another is not welfare. Those who work with toxic materials on a daily basis . . . in order to provide the world with the energy and the materials it needs deserve a helping hand to make a new start in life."

Starting from this Mazzocchi perspective, we still need to establish what specifically would constitute a generous set of just transition policies. For the workers, I would argue that, as a first principle, the aim of such policies should be, simply, to truly protect them against major losses in their living standards. To accomplish this, the critical components of a just transition policy should include three types of guarantees for the workers: (1) a guaranteed new job; (2) a guaranteed level of pay with their new job that is at least comparable to their previous fossil fuel industry job; and (3) a guarantee that their pensions will remain intact regardless of whether their employers' business operations are phased out. Just transition policies should also support displaced workers in the areas of job search, retraining, and relocation. These forms of support are important but should be understood as supplementary. This is because, in themselves, they are not capable of protecting workers against major losses in their living standards resulting from the fossil fuel industry phase out.

Among major high-income economies, just transition policies for workers have recently been enacted within the European Union, Germany, and, to a lesser extent, the United Kingdom. Such initiatives are still mainly at the proposal stages in the US, Japan, Canada. But even in the cases of Germany, the UK, and the European Union, these policies remain mostly limited to the areas of job search, retraining, and relocation support. In other words, in none of these cases have policies been enacted that provide workers with the guarantees they need.

The most substantive commitments to just transition policies have been advanced by the European Union, within the framework of the European Green Deal. Thus, Frans Timmermans, executive vice president of the European Commission, has stated that "we must show solidarity with the most affected regions in Europe, such as coal mining regions, and others, to make sure the Green Deal gets everyone's full support and has a chance to become a reality."

In that spirit, the European Commission established a Just Transition Fund in January 2020 to advance beyond broad principles into meaningful concrete policy commitments. Nevertheless, to date, the scope of these programs and the level of funding provided are not close to adequate to achieve the goals, set out by Vice President Timmermans, of "making sure the Green Deal gets everyone's full support." In particular, the categories of support for displaced workers under the Just Transition Fund are limited to skill development, retraining, and job search assistance. The fund does not include any provision for the most critical areas of support for workers who will be facing displacement—that is, the guarantees with respect to reemployment, wage levels, and pensions.

To obtain a sense of what a much more robust just transition program would look like, I have developed, with coworkers, illustrative programs for eight different US states, for the US economy overall, and, most recently, for South Korea. For now, it might be useful to focus on the case of West Virginia, since it is one of the most fossil fuel–dependent state economies in the US. As such, West Virginia provides a highly challenging environment in which to mount a generous just transition program.

It is critical that the just transition policies for West Virginia would be one component of an overall Green New Deal program for the state. Under the overall program, fossil fuel production will fall by 50 percent as of 2030 and clean energy investments will make up the difference in the state's overall energy supply. We estimate that the clean energy investments in West Virginia will generate an average of about 25,000 jobs throughout the state through 2030.

What about the job losses from the state's fossil fuel industry phase out? There are presently roughly 40,000 people employed in West Virginia's fossil fuel industry and ancillary sectors, comprising about 5 percent of the overall West Virginia labor force. But it is critical to recognize that all 40,000 workers are not going to lose their jobs right away. Rather, about 20,000 jobs will be phased out by 2030 as fossil fuel production is cut by 50 percent. This averages to a bit more than 2,000 job losses per year. However, we also estimate that about 600 of the workers holding these jobs will voluntarily retire every year. This means that the number of workers who will face job displacement every year is in the range of 1,400, or 0.2 percent of the state's labor force. This is while the state is also generating about 25,000 new jobs through its clean energy transformation.

In short, there will be an abundance of new job opportunities for the 1,400 workers facing displacement every year. We estimate that to guarantee these workers comparable pay levels and intact pensions, along with retraining, job search, and relocation support, as needed, will cost about $42,000 per worker per year. This totals to an average of about $143 million per year. This is equal to about 0.2 percent of West Virginia's overall level of economic activity, GDP. In short, generous just transition policies for all displaced fossil fuel workers will definitely not create major cost burdens, even in such a heavily fossil fuel dependent state as West Virginia.

For the other seven US states that we have examined, the costs of comparable just transition programs range between 0.001 and 0.02 percent of the state's GDP. For the US economy overall, the just transition program's costs would total to about 0.015 percent of GDP—i.e., one-tenth to one-twentieth of what the West Virginia program would cost relative to the overall economy's size. In short, providing workers with robust just transition support amounts to barely a blip within the

US economy. It is almost certainly the case that similarly robust just transition programs in other high-income economies would generate comparable results.

Now let's consider communities' transitions. In fact, communities that are now dependent on the fossil fuel industry will face formidable challenges adjusting to the decline of the industry. At the same time, it is critical that, as I described for the case of West Virginia, the decline of the fossil fuel industry will be occurring in conjunction with the rapid expansion of the clean energy economy. This will provide a basic supportive foundation for advancing effective community transition policies.

One important example has been the integration of clean renewable energy sources—primarily wind and solar power—into Alaska's long-standing and extensive energy microgrid infrastructure. A microgrid is a localized power grid. Since the 1960s, these grids have been heavily reliant on diesel generators. But since 2005, renewable energy has become an increasingly significant alternative to diesel fuel. As of 2015, the Alaska Center for Energy and Power described this development as follows: "Over the past decade, investment in renewable energy generation has increased dramatically to meet a desire for energy independence and reduce the cost of delivered power. Today, more than 70 of Alaska's microgrids, which represent approximately 12 percent of renewably powered microgrids in the world, incorporate grid-scale renewable generation, including small hydro, wind, geothermal, solar and biomass."

Another important development, primarily, thus far, in Australia, Germany, and the US, is with creating pumped storage hydropower sites in now defunct coal mines. A *Wall Street Journal* article from late 2022 reports as follows:

> Mining operations that contributed to greenhouse-gas emissions could soon help to cut them. Around the world, companies are seeking to repurpose old mines as renewable-energy generators using a century-old technology known as pumped-storage hydropower. The technology, already part

of the energy mix in many countries, works like a giant battery, with water and gravity as the energy source. Water is pumped uphill to a reservoir when energy supply is plentiful. It is released and flows downhill through turbines generating hydroelectric power when electricity demand is high or there are shortages of other types of power. Finally, the water is captured to be pumped uphill again in a repeated cycle. Surface and underground mines hold potential as reservoirs for the water, and could be developed with a lower environmental impact and upfront costs than building such plants from scratch, experts say.

More broadly, there is no shortage of opportunities for revitalizing fossil fuel dependent communities through developing innovative clean energy projects in these very communities. To its credit, the Biden administration's Inflation Reduction Act—which is primarily about financing clean energy investment projects in the US—is providing large-scale funding for such projects. Naturally, the congressional Republicans tried to kill such funding through the farcical and now mercifully concluded debt ceiling debate. Fortunately, they failed.

If moving away from fossil fuels and toward clean energy is the only way forward for the survival of the planet, climate action must be ultimately coordinated on a global level. What does global just transition entail, and what sort of new relationships of power need to be created since the world remains divided by huge differences between rich countries and poor countries?

Pollin: Let's first be clear that there is no such thing as a viable climate stabilization program that applies only to rich countries. All countries, at all levels of development, need to drive their emissions to zero by 2050. It is true that, at present, China, the US, and the European Union together account for 52 percent of all global CO_2 emissions. But that also means that if, miraculously, emissions in China, the US, and the European Union were all to fall to zero tomorrow, we would still be only a bit more than halfway to driving global emissions to zero. Moreover, if large, fast-growing developing economies like India and Indonesia continue to power their growth through a fossil fuel–dominant energy infrastructure, we will not cut global emissions at all by 2050 relative to today, even if emissions in China, the US, and the European Union were to indeed fall to zero. The point is that every place does matter if we really are going to hit the target of zero emissions by no later than 2050.

Thus, recognizing that a Green New Deal program has to be global in scope, the worker-and-community just transitions that I have described above for high-income economies applies equally, if not more so, for low-income economies. For starters, the clean energy investment transition programs will be a major engine of job creation in low-income economies just as it is for high-income economies. For example, research that I have done with coworkers finds that creating a clean energy economy in places like India, Indonesia, and South Africa will generate between two to three times more jobs for a given spending level than maintaining these economies' existing fossil fuel–dominant energy infrastructure. At the same time, phasing out fossil fuels in these economies will still also entail losses for fossil fuel industry–dependent workers and communities. These workers and communities will require just transition support comparable to what we have described above for the US and other high-income economies.

We still need to ask the question: Who pays for the Green New Deal in low-income countries? As a baseline matter of planetary survival, we can start by recognizing that somebody has to pay. How then should we establish fair and workable standards as to who should pay, how much they should pay, and via what financing channels?

Two initial points are critical. First, starting with the early phases of industrial development under capitalism, what are now the globe's high-income countries, including the US, Western Europe, Japan, Canada, and Australia, are primarily responsible for loading up the atmosphere with greenhouse gas emissions and causing climate change. They therefore should be primarily responsible for financing the Global Green New Deal. And second, moving from this historical perspective to the present, high-income people in all countries and regions have massively larger carbon footprints today than everyone else. As documented in a 2020 Oxfam study, the average carbon footprint of people in the richest 1 percent of the global population, for example, is thirty-five times greater than the average emissions level for the overall global population.

Thus, by any minimal standard of fairness, high-income countries and high-income people, no matter where they live, need to cover most of the upfront costs of a global clean energy transformation. At the same time, let's also remember that these upfront costs are investments. They will pay for themselves over time, and then some, by delivering high efficiency and abundant renewable energy at average prices that are already lower today than fossil fuels and nuclear, and falling.

But it is still necessary to mobilize investment funds into low-income economies right now at both a speed and scale that are unprecedented. We are already seeing that, despite various pronouncements and pledges, private capitalists are not about to accomplish this on their own. As Noam described above, private capitalists are rather waiting for their clean energy investment prospects in developing economies to become "de-risked" by public entities. That means, to summarize Noam, that the private investors get big subsidies from public entities to undertake investments, but then pocket all the profits when the investments pay off. The public entities handing out the subsidies can include their own rich country governments, the governments of the low-income countries where they might invest, or international public investment institutions like the World Bank or International Monetary Fund.

It is also the case that the rich country governments have not been fulfilling the pledges they made initially in 2009 to provide $100 billion in annual climate-related support for poor countries. Between 2015 [and] 2020, thirty-five high-income countries reported providing an overall average of $36 billion per year, only one-third of the $100 billion annual pledge. Moreover, even this low-end figure overstates the actual level of climate finance rich countries are providing, given that countries can claim virtually anything as constituting "climate finance." Thus, according to a Reuters story from June 1, 2023:

Italy helped a retailer open chocolate and gelato stores across Asia. The United States offered a loan for a coastal hotel expansion in Haiti. Belgium backed the film "La Tierra Roja," a love story set in the Argentine rainforest. And Japan is financing a new coal plant in Bangladesh and an airport expansion in Egypt. . . .

Although a coal plant, a hotel, chocolate stores, a movie and an airport expansion don't seem like efforts to combat global warming, nothing prevented the governments that funded them from reporting them as such to the United Nations and counting them toward their giving total.

It's obvious that a serious system of monitoring is one necessary step toward moving significant financial resources into legitimate climate projects in developing economies. But in addition, it will also be critical that public investment banks in low-income countries serve as primary conduits in moving specific investment projects forward in their economies. The public investment banks should be managing the financing of clean energy projects in both the public and private sectors, along with mixed public/private projects. We cannot know what the best mix should be between public and private ownership with any specific project in any given low-income country (or for that matter, any high-income country). There is no point in being dogmatic and pretending otherwise. But, in all situations, we need to operate under the recognition that it is not reasonable to allow private firms to profit at rates that they have gotten away with under forty years of neoliberalism. If private firms are happy to accept large public subsidies to support their clean energy investments, they then also need to be willing to accept limits on their profitability. Such regulatory principles are, for example, routine in the private US electric utility sector. Similar standards can be easily established in all regions of the globe.

Noam Chomsky

ON THE STATE OF THE WORLD

This interview was originally published
by Global Policy Journal *on May 27, 2023*

C. J. Polychroniou: *Noam, you have said on numerous occasions that the world is at the most dangerous point in human history. Why do you think so? Are nuclear weapons more dangerous today than they were in the past? Is the surge in right-wing authoritarianism in recent years more dangerous than the rise and subsequent spread of fascism in the 1920s and 1930s? Or is it because of the climate crisis, which you have indeed said represents the biggest threat the world has ever faced. Can you explain in comparative terms why you think that the world is today significantly more dangerous than it used to be?*

Noam Chomsky: The climate crisis is unique in human history and is getting more severe year by year. If major steps are not taken within the next few decades, the world is likely to reach a point of no return, facing decline to indescribable catastrophe. Nothing is certain, but this seems a far too plausible assessment.

Weapons systems steadily become more dangerous and more ominous. We have been surviving under a sword of Damocles since the bombing of Hiroshima. A few years later, seventy years ago, the US, then Russia, tested thermonuclear weapons, revealing that human intelligence had "advanced" to the capacity to destroy everything.

Operative questions have to do with the sociopolitical and cultural conditions that constrain their use. These came ominously close to breaking down in the 1962 missile crisis, described by Arthur Schlesinger as the most dangerous moment in world history, with reason, though we may soon reach that unspeakable moment again in Europe and Asia. The MAD system (mutually assured destruction) enabled a form of security, lunatic but perhaps the best, short of the kind of social and cultural transformation that is still unfortunately only an aspiration.

After the collapse of the Soviet Union, the MAD system of security was undermined by President Bill Clinton's aggressive triumphalism and the Bush II–Trump project of dismantling the laboriously constructed arms control regime. There's an important recent study of these topics by Benjamin Schwarz and Christopher Layne, as part of the background to Russia's invasion of Ukraine. They review how Clinton initiated a new era of international affairs in which the "United States became a revolutionary force in world politics" by abandoning the "old diplomacy" and instituting its preferred revolutionary concept of global order.

The "old diplomacy" sought to maintain global order by "an understanding of an adversary's interests and motives and an ability to make judicious compromises." The new triumphant unilateralism sets as "a legitimate goal [for the US] the alteration or eradication of those arrangements [internal to other countries] if they were not in accord with its professed ideals and values."

The word "professed" is crucial. It is commonly expunged from consciousness here, not elsewhere.

In the background lies the Clinton doctrine that the US must be prepared to resort to force, multilaterally if we can, unilaterally if we must, to ensure vital interests and "uninhibited access to key markets, energy supplies, and strategic resources."

The accompanying military doctrine has led to creation of a far more advanced nuclear weapons system that can only be understood as "a preemptive counterforce capability against Russia and China" (Rand Corporation)—a first-strike capacity, enhanced by Bush's dismantling of the treaty that barred emplacement of anti-ballistic missile systems near an adversary's borders. These systems are portrayed as defensive, but they are understood on all sides to be first-strike weapons.

These steps have significantly weakened the old system of mutual deterrence, leaving in its place greatly enhanced dangers.

How new these developments were, one might debate, but Schwarz and Layne make a strong case that this triumphant unilateralism and open contempt for the defeated enemy has been a significant factor in bringing major war to Europe with the Russian invasion of Ukraine, with the potential to escalate to terminal war.

No less ominous are developments in Asia. With strong bipartisan and media support, Washington is confronting China on both military and economic fronts. With Europe safely in its pocket thanks to Russia's invasion of Ukraine, the US has been able to expand NATO to the Indo-Pacific region, thus enlisting Europe in its campaign to prevent China from developing—a program considered not just legitimate but highly praiseworthy. One of the administration doves, Commerce Secretary Gina Raimondo, expressed the consensus lucidly: "If we really want to slow down China's rate of innovation, we need to work with Europe." It's particularly important to keep China from developing sustainable energy, where it is far in the lead and should reach energy self-sufficiency by 2060 according to Goldman Sachs analysts. China is even threatening to make new breakthroughs in batteries that might help save the world from climate catastrophe.

Plainly a threat that must be contained, along with China's insistence on the one-China policy for Taiwan that the US also adopted fifty years ago and that has kept the peace for fifty years, but that Washington is now rescinding. There's much more to add that reinforces this picture, matters we have discussed elsewhere.

It's hard to say the words in this increasingly odd culture, but it's close to truism that unless the US and China find ways to accommodate, as great powers with conflicting interests often did in the past, we are all lost.

Historical analogies have their limits, of course, but there are two pertinent ones that have repeatedly been adduced in this connection: the Concert of Europe established in 1815 and the Versailles treaty of 1919. The former is a prime example of the "Old Diplomacy." The defeated aggressor (France) was incorporated into the new system of international order as an equal partner. That led to a century of relative peace. The Versailles treaty is a paradigm example of the "revolutionary" concept of global order instituted by the triumphalism of the nineties and its aftermath. Defeated Germany was not incorporated into the postwar international order but was severely punished and humiliated. We know where that led.

Currently, two concepts of world order are counterposed: the UN system and the "rules-based" system, correlating closely with multipolarity and unipolarity, the latter meaning US dominance.

The US and its allies (or "vassals" or "subimperial states" as they are sometimes called) reject the UN system and demand adherence to the rules-based system. The rest of the world generally supports the UN system and multipolarity.

The UN system is based on the UN Charter, the foundation of modern international law and the "supreme law of the land" in the US under the US Constitution, which elected officials are bound to obey. It has a serious defect: it rules out US foreign policy. Its core principle bans "the threat or use of force" in international affairs, except in narrow circumstances unrelated to US actions. It would be hard to find a US postwar president who has not violated the US Constitution, a topic of little interest, the record shows.

What is the preferred rules-based system? The answer depends on who sets the rules and determines when they should be obeyed. The answer is not obscure: the hegemonic power, which took the mantle of global dominance from Britain after World War II, greatly extending its scope.

One core foundation stone of the US-dominated, rules-based system is the World Trade Organization (WTO). We can ask, then, how the US honors it.

As global hegemon, the US is alone in [its] capacity to impose sanctions. These are third-party sanctions that others must obey, or else. And they do obey, even when they strongly oppose the sanctions. One example is the US sanctions designed to strangle Cuba. These are opposed by the whole world, as we see from regular UN votes. But they are obeyed.

When Clinton instituted sanctions that were even more savage than before, the European Union called on the WTO to determine their legality. The US angrily withdrew from the proceedings, rendering them null and void. There was a reason, explained by Clinton's commerce secretary, Stuart Eizenstat: "Mr. Eizenstat argued that Europe is challenging 'three decades of American Cuba policy that goes back to the Kennedy Administration,' and is aimed entirely at forcing a change of government in Havana."

In short, Europe and the WTO have no competence to influence the long-standing US campaign of terror and economic strangulation aimed at forcefully overthrowing the government of Cuba, so they should get lost. The sanctions prevail, and Europe must obey them— and does. A clear illustration of the nature of the rules-based order.

There are many others. Thus, the World Court ruled that US freezing of Iranian assets is illegal. It scarcely caused a ripple.

That is understandable. Under the rules-based system, the global enforcer has no more reason to accede to International Court of Justice (ICJ) judgments than to decisions of the WTO. That much was established years ago. In 1986, the US withdrew from ICJ jurisdiction when it condemned the US for its terrorist war against Nicaragua and ordered it to pay reparations. The US responded by escalating the war.

To mention another illustration of the rules-based system, the US alone withdrew from the proceedings of the tribunal considering Yugoslavia's charges against NATO. It argued correctly that Yugoslavia had mentioned genocide, and the US is self-exempted from the international treaty banning genocide.

It's easy to continue. It's also easy to understand why the US rejects the UN-based system, which bans its foreign policy, and prefers a system in which it sets the rules and is free to rescind them when it wishes. There's no need to discuss why the US prefers a unipolar rather than multipolar order.

All of these considerations arise critically in consideration of global conflicts and threats to survival.

All societies have seen dramatic economic transformations over the past fifty years, with China leading the pack as it emerged in the course of just a few decades from an agrarian society into an industrial powerhouse, lifting in the process hundreds of millions out of poverty. But this is not to say that life is necessarily an improvement over the past. In the US, for instance, the quality of life has declined over the past decade and so has life satisfaction in the European Union. Are we at a stage where we are witnessing the decline of the West and the rise of the East? In either case, while many people seem to think that the rise of the far-right in Europe and the United States is related to perceptions about the decline of the West, the rise of the far-right is a global phenomenon, ranging from India and Brazil to Israel, Pakistan, and the Philippines. In fact, the alt-right has even found a comfortable home on China's internet. So, what's going on? Why are nationalism, racism, and extremism making such a huge comeback on the world stage at large?

There is an interplay of many factors, some specific to particular societies, for example, the dismantling of secular democracy in India as Prime Minister Narendra Modi pursues his project of establishing a harsh racist Hindu ethnocracy. That's specific to India, though not without analogues elsewhere.

There are some factors that have fairly broad scope, and common consequences. One is the radical increase in inequality in much of the world as a consequence of the neoliberal policies emanating from the US and UK and spreading beyond in various ways.

The facts are clear enough, particularly well studied for the US. The Rand Corporation study we've discussed before estimated almost $50 trillion in wealth transferred from workers and the middle class—the lower 90 percent of income—to the top 1 percent during the neoliberal years. More information is provided in the work of

Thomas Piketty and Emmanuel Saez, summarized lucidly by political economist Robert Brenner.

The basic conclusion is that through "the postwar boom, we actually had decreasing inequality and very limited income going to the top income brackets. For the whole period from the 1940s to the end of the 1970s, the top 1 percent of earners received 9–10 percent of total income, no more. But in the short period since 1980, their share, that is the share of the top 1 percent, has gone up to 25 percent, while the bottom 80 percent have made virtually no gains."

That has many consequences. One is reduction of productive investment and shift to a rentier economy, in some ways a reversion from capitalist investment for production to feudal-style production of wealth, not capital—"fictitious capital," as Marx called it.

Another consequence is breakdown of the social order. In their incisive work *The Spirit Level*, Richard Wilkinson and Kate Pickett show a close correlation between inequality and a range of social disorders. One country is off the chart: very high inequality but even greater social disorder than expected by the correlation. That's the country that led the way in the neoliberal assault—formally defined as commitment to small government and the market, in practice radically different, more accurately described as dedicated class war making use of whatever mechanisms are available.

Wilkinson-Pickett's revealing work has been carried forward since, recently in an important study by Stephen Bezruchka. It seems well confirmed that inequality is a prime factor in breakdown of social order.

There have been similar effects in the UK under harsh austerity policies, extending elsewhere in many ways. Commonly, the hardest hit are the weak. Latin America suffered two lost decades under destructive structural adjustment policies. In Yugoslavia and Rwanda such policies in the eighties sharply exacerbated social tensions, contributing to the horrors that followed.

It's sometimes argued that the neoliberal policies were a grand success, pointing to the fastest reduction in global poverty in history—but failing to add that these remarkable achievements were in

China and other countries that firmly rejected the prescribed neoliberal principles.

Furthermore, it wasn't the "Washington consensus" that induced US investors to shift production to countries with much cheaper labor and limited labor rights or environmental constraints, thereby deindustrializing America with well-known consequences for working people.

It is not that these were the only options. Studies by the labor movement and by Congress's own research bureau (OTA [Office of Technology Assessment], since disbanded) offered feasible alternatives that could have benefited working people globally. But they were dismissed.

All of this forms part of the background for the ominous phenomena you describe. The neoliberal assault is a prominent factor in the breakdown of the social order that leaves great numbers of people angry, disillusioned, frightened, and contemptuous of institutions that they see are not working in their interests.

One crucial element of the neoliberal assault has been to deprive the targets of means of defense. President Ronald Reagan and Prime Minister Margaret Thatcher opened the neoliberal era with attacks on unions, the main line of defense of working people against class war. They also opened the door to corporate attacks on labor, often illegal, but that doesn't matter when the state they largely control looks the other way.

A primary defense against class war is an educated, informed public. Public education has come under harsh attack during the neoliberal years: sharp defunding, business models that favor cheap and easily disposable labor (adjuncts, graduate students) instead of faculty, teaching-to-test models that undermine critical thinking and inquiry, and much else. Best to have a population that is passive, obedient, and atomized, even if they are angry and resentful, and thus easy prey for demagogues skilled in tapping ugly currents that run not too far below the surface in every society.

We have heard on countless occasions from both political pundits and influential academics that democracy is in decline. Indeed, the Economist Intelligence Unit (EIU) claimed in early 2022 that just only 6.4 percent of the world's population enjoys "full democracy," though it is anything but clear how the sister company of the conservative weekly magazine The Economist understands the actual meaning and context of the term "full democracy." Be that as it may, I think we can all agree that there are several key indicators pointing to a dysfunction of democracy in the twenty-first century. But isn't it also the case that a perception of a crisis of democracy has existed almost as long as modern democracy itself? Moreover, isn't it also the case that general talk about a crisis of democracy applies exclusively to the concept of liberal democracy, which is anything but authentic democracy? I am interested in your thoughts on these topics.

What exactly is a crisis of democracy? The term is familiar. It was, for example, the title of the first publication of the Trilateral Commission, liberal internationalist scholars from Europe, Japan, and the US. It stands alongside the Powell Memorandum as one of the harbingers of the neoliberal assault that was gathering steam in the Carter administration (mostly trilateralists) and took off with Reagan and Thatcher. The Powell Memorandum, addressing the business world, was the tough side; the Trilateral Commission report was the soft liberal side.

The Powell Memorandum, authored by Justice Lewis Powell, pulled no punches. It called on the business world to use its power to beat back what it perceived as a major attack on the business world— meaning that instead of the corporate sector freely running almost everything, there were some limited efforts to restrict its power. The streak of paranoia and wild exaggerations are not without interest, but the message was clear: launch harsh class war and put an end to the "time of troubles," a standard term for the activism of the 1960s, which greatly civilized society.

Like Powell, the Trilateralists were concerned by the "time of troubles." The crisis of democracy was that sixties activism was bringing about too much democracy. All sorts of groups were calling for greater rights: the young, the old, women, workers, farmers, sometimes called "special interests." A particular concern was the failure of the institutions responsible "for the indoctrination of the young": schools and universities. That's why we see young people carrying out their disruptive activities. These popular efforts imposed an impossible burden on the state, which could not respond to these special interests: a crisis of democracy.

The solution was evident: "more moderation in democracy." In other words, a return to passivity and obedience so that democracy can flourish. That concept of democracy has deep roots, going back to the founding fathers and Britain before them, revived in major works on democratic theory by twentieth-century thinkers, among them Walter Lippmann, the most prominent public intellectual; Edward Bernays, a guru of the huge public relations industry; Harold Lasswell, one of the founders of modern political science; and Reinhold Niebuhr, known as the theologian of the liberal establishment.

All were good Wilson-FDR-JFK liberals. All agreed with the founders that democracy was a danger to be avoided. The people of the country have a role in a properly functioning democracy: to push a lever every few years to select someone offered to them by the "responsible men." They are to be "spectators, not participants," kept in line with "necessary illusions" and "emotionally potent oversimplifications," what Lippmann called the "manufacture of consent," a primary art of democracy.

Satisfying these conditions would constitute "full democracy," as the concept is understood within liberal democratic theory. Others may have different views, but they are part of the problem, not the solution, to paraphrase Reagan.

Returning to the concerns about [the] decline of democracy, even full democracy in this sense is in decline in its traditional centers. In Europe, Prime Minister Viktor Orbán's racist "illiberal democracy" in Hungary troubles the European Union, along with Poland's ruling Law and Justice party and others that share its deeply authoritarian tendencies.

Recently Orbán hosted a conference of far-right movements in Europe, some with neofascist origins. The US National Conservative Political Action Committee (NCPAC), a core element of today's GOP, was a star participant. Donald Trump gave a major address. Tucker Carlson contributed an adoring documentary.

Shortly after, the NCPAC had a conference in Dallas, Texas, where the keynote speaker was Orbán, lauded as a leading spokesman of authoritarian white Christian nationalism.

These are no laughing matters. At both the state and the national level, today's Republican Party in the US, which has abandoned its past role as an authentic parliamentary party, is seeking ways to gain permanent political control as a minority organization, committed to Orbán-style illiberal democracy. Its leader, Trump, has made no secret of his plans to replace the nonpartisan civil service that is a foundation of any modern democracy with appointed loyalists, to prevent teaching of American history in any minimally serious fashion, and in general to end vestiges of more than limited formal democracy.

In the most powerful state of human history, with a long, mixed, sometimes progressive democratic tradition, these are not minor matters.

Countries in the periphery of the global system seem to be trying to break away from Washington's influence and are increasingly calling for a new world order. For instance, even Saudi Arabia is following Iran to join China and Russia's security bloc. What are the implications of this realignment in global relations, and how likely is it that Washington will use tactics to halt this process from going much further?

In March, Saudi Arabia joined the Shanghai Cooperation Organization. It was followed shortly after by the second Middle East petroleum heavyweight, the United Arab Emirates, which had already become a hub for China's Maritime Silk Road, running from Kolkata in Eastern India through the Red Sea and on to Europe. These developments followed China's brokering a deal between Iran and Saudi Arabia, previously bitter enemies, and thus impeding US efforts to isolate and overthrow the regime. Washington professes not to be concerned, but that is hard to credit.

Since the discovery of oil in Saudi Arabia in 1938, and the recognition soon of its extraordinary scale, controlling Saudi Arabia has been a high priority for the US. Its drift toward independence—and even worse, toward the expanding China-based economic sphere—must be eliciting deep concern in policymaking circles. It's another long step toward a multipolar order that is anathema to the US.

So far, the US has not devised effective tactics to counter these strong tendencies in world affairs, which have many sources—including the self-destruction of US society and political life.

Organized business interests have had decisive influence on US foreign policy over the last two centuries. However, there are arguments made today that there is a loosening of business hegemony over US foreign policy, and China is offered as the evidence that Washington is not listening to business anymore. But isn't it the case that the capitalist state, while always working on behalf of the general interests of the business establishment, also possesses a certain degree of independence and that other factors enter into the equation when it comes to the implementation of foreign policy and the management of foreign affairs? It seems to me that US foreign policy toward Cuba, for example, is evidence of the relative autonomy of the state from the economic interests of the capitalist classes.

It may be a caricature to describe the capitalist state as the executive committee of the ruling class, but it's a caricature of something that exists, and has existed for a long time. We may recall again Adam Smith's description of the early days of capitalist imperialism, when the "masters of mankind" who owned the economy of England were the "principal architects" of state policy and ensured that their own interests were properly served no matter how grievous the effects on others. Others included the people of England, but much more so the victims of the "savage injustice" of the masters, particularly in India in the early days of England's destruction of what was then, along with China, the richest society on earth, while stealing its more advanced technology.

Some principles of global order have a long life.

There should be no need to review again how closely US foreign policy has conformed to Smith's maxim, to the present. One guiding doctrine is that the US will not tolerate what State Department officials called "the philosophy of the new nationalism," which embraces "policies designed to bring about a broader distribution of wealth and to raise the standard of living of the masses" along with the pernicious idea "that the first beneficiaries of the development of a country's resources should be the people of that country." They are not. The first beneficiaries are the investor class, primarily from the US.

This stern lesson was taught to backward Latin Americans at a hemispheric conference called by the US in 1945, which established an Economic Charter for the Americas that stamped out these heresies. They were not confined to Latin America. Eighty years ago, it seemed that at last the world would finally emerge from the misery of the Great Depression and fascist horrors. A wave of radical democracy spread throughout much of the world, with hopes for a more just and humane global order. The earliest imperatives for the US and its British junior partner were to block these aspirations and to restore the traditional order, including fascist collaborators, first in Greece (with enormous violence) and Italy, then throughout Western Europe, extending as well to Asia. Russia played a similar role in its own lesser domains. These are among the first chapters of postwar history.

While Smith's masters of mankind quite generally ensure that state policy serves their immediate interests, there are exceptions, which give a good deal of insight into policy formation. We've just discussed one: Cuba. It's not just the world that objects strenuously to the sanctions policy to which it must conform. The same is true of powerful sectors among the masters, including energy, agribusiness, and particularly pharmaceuticals, eager to link up with Cuba's advanced industry. But the executive committee prohibits it. Their parochial interests are overridden by the long-term interest of preventing "successful defiance" of US policies tracing back to the Monroe Doctrine, as the State Department explained sixty years ago.

Any Mafia don would understand.

The very same individual might make different choices as CEO of a corporation and in the State Department, with the same interests in mind but a different perspective on how to further them.

Another case is Iran, in this case going back to 1953, when the parliamentary government sought to gain control of its immense petroleum resources, making the mistake of believing "that the first beneficiaries of the development of a country's resources should be the people of that country." Britain, the longtime overlord of Iran, no longer had the capacity to reverse this deviation from good order, so called on the real muscle overseas. The US overthrew the government, installing the Shah's dictatorship, the first steps in US torture of the people of Iran that has continued without a break to the present, carrying forward Britain's legacy.

But there was a problem. As part of the deal, Washington demanded that US corporations take over 40 percent of the British concession, but they were unwilling, for short-term parochial reasons. To do so would prejudice their relations with Saudi Arabia, where exploitation of the country's resources was cheaper and more profitable. The Eisenhower administration threatened the companies with antitrust suits, and they complied. Not a great burden to be sure, but one the companies didn't want.

The conflict between Washington and US corporations persists to the present. As in the case of Cuba, both Europe and US corporations strongly oppose the harsh US sanctions on Iran, but are forced to comply, cutting them out of the lucrative Iranian market. Again, the state interest in punishing Iran for successful defiance overrides the parochial interests of short-term profit.

Contemporary China is a much larger case. Neither European nor US corporations are happy about Washington's commitment "to slow down China's rate of innovation" while they lose access to the rich China market. It seems that US corporations may have found a way around the restrictions on trade. An analysis by the Asian business press found "a strong predictive relationship between these countries' [Vietnam, Mexico, India] imports from China and their exports to the United States," suggesting that trade with China has simply been re-directed.

The same study reports that "China's share of international trade is rising steadily. Its export volume . . . rose 25 percent since 2018 while the industrial nations' export volume stagnated."

It remains to be seen how European, Japanese, and South Korean industries will react to the directive to abandon a primary market in order to satisfy the US goal of preventing China's development.

It would be a bitter blow, far worse than losing access to Iran or, of course, Cuba.

More than a couple of centuries ago, Immanuel Kant presented his theory of perpetual peace as the only rational way for states to coexist with one another. Yet, perpetual peace remains a mirage, an unattainable ideal. Could it be that a world political order away from the nation-state as the primary unit is a necessary prerequisite for perpetual peace to be realized?

Kant argued that reason would bring about perpetual peace in a benign global political order. Another great philosopher, Bertrand Russell, saw things rather differently when asked about the prospects for world peace: "After ages during which the earth produced harmless trilobites and butterflies, evolution progressed to the point at which it has generated Neros, Genghis Khans, and Hitlers. This, however, I believe is a passing nightmare; in time the earth will become again incapable of supporting life, and peace will return."

I don't presume to enter those ranks. I'd like to think that humans have the capacity to do much better than what Russell forecast, even if not to achieve Kant's ideal.

Noam Chomsky

ARTIFICIAL INTELLIGENCE: MYTH, REALITY, AND FUTURE

This interview was originally published
by Global Policy Journal *on May 3, 2023*

C. J. Polychroniou: *As a scientific discipline, artificial intelligence (AI) dates back to the 1950s, but over the last couple of decades it has been making inroads into all sort of fields, including banking, insurance, auto manufacturing, music, and defense. In fact, the use of AI techniques has been shown in some instance to surpass human capabilities, such as in a game of chess. Are machines likely to become smarter than humans?*

Noam Chomsky: Just to clarify terminology, the term "machine" here means "program," basically a theory written in a notation that can be executed by a computer—and an unusual kind of theory in interesting ways that we can put aside here.

We can make a rough distinction between pure engineering and science. There is no sharp boundary, but it's a useful first approximation. Pure engineering seeks to produce a product that may be of some use. Science seeks understanding. If the topic is human intelligence, or cognitive capacities of other organisms, science seeks understanding of these biological systems.

As I understand them, the founders of AI—Alan Turing, Herbert Simon, Marvin Minsky, and others—regarded it as science, part of the then-emerging cognitive sciences, making use of new technologies and discoveries in the mathematical theory of computation to advance understanding. Over the years those concerns have faded and have largely been displaced by an engineering orientation. The earlier concerns are now commonly dismissed, sometimes condescendingly, as GOFAI—good old-fashioned AI.

Continuing with the question, is it likely that programs will be devised that surpass human capabilities? We have to be careful about the word "capabilities," for reasons to which I'll return. But if we take the term to refer to human performance, then the answer is: definitely yes. In fact, they have long existed: the calculator in a laptop, for example. It can far exceed what humans can do, if only because of lack of time and memory. For closed systems like chess, it was well understood in the fifties that sooner or later, with the advance of massive computing capacities and a long period of preparation, a program could be devised to defeat a grand master who is playing with a bound-on memory and time. The achievement years later was pretty much PR for IBM. Many biological organisms surpass human cognitive capacities in much deeper ways. The desert ants in my backyard have minuscule brains, but far exceed human navigational capacities, in principle, not just performance. There is no Great Chain of Being with humans at the top.

The products of AI engineering are being used in many fields, for better or for worse. Even simple and familiar ones can be quite useful: in the language area, programs like autofill, live transcription, Google Translate, among others. With vastly greater computing power and more sophisticated programming, there should be other useful applications, in the sciences as well. There already have been some: assisting in the study of protein folding is one recent case where massive and rapid search technology has helped scientists to deal with a critical and recalcitrant problem.

Engineering projects can be useful, or harmful. Both questions arise in the case of engineering AI. Current work with Large Language Models (LLMs), including chatbots, provides tools for disinformation, defamation, and misleading the uninformed. The threats are enhanced when they are combined with artificial images and replication of voice. With different concerns in mind, tens of thousands of AI researchers have recently called for a moratorium on development because of potential dangers they perceive.

As always, possible benefits of technology have to be weighed against potential costs.

Quite different questions arise when we turn to AI and science. Here caution is necessary because of exorbitant and reckless claims, often amplified in the media. To clarify the issues, let's consider cases, some hypothetical, some real.

I mentioned insect navigation, which is an astonishing achievement. Insect scientists have made much progress in studying how it is achieved, though the neurophysiology, a very difficult matter, remains elusive, along with evolution of the systems. The same is true of the amazing feats of birds and sea turtles that travel thousands of miles and unerringly return to the place of origin.

Suppose Tom Jones, a proponent of engineering AI, comes along and says: "Your work has all been refuted. The problem is solved. Commercial airline pilots achieve the same or even better results all the time."

If even bothering to respond, we'd laugh.

Take the case of the seafaring exploits of Polynesians, still alive among aboriginal tribes, using stars, wind, currents to land their canoes at a designated spot hundreds of miles away. This too has been the topic of much research to find out how they do it. Tom Jones has the answer: "Stop wasting your time; naval vessels do it all the time."

Same response.

Let's now turn to a real case, language acquisition. It's been the topic of extensive and highly illuminating research in recent years, showing that infants have very rich knowledge of the ambient language (or languages), far beyond what they exhibit in performance. It is achieved with little evidence, and in some crucial cases none at all. At best, as careful statistical studies have shown, available data are sparse, particularly when rank-frequency ("Zipf's law") is taken into account.

Enter Tom Jones: "You've been refuted. Paying no attention to your discoveries, LLMs that scan astronomical amounts of data can find statistical regularities that make it possible to simulate the data on which they are trained, producing something that looks pretty much like normal human behavior. Chatbots."

This case differs from the others. First, it is real. Second, people don't laugh; in fact, many are awed. Third, unlike the hypothetical cases, the actual results are far from what's claimed.

These considerations bring up a minor problem with the current LLM enthusiasm: its total absurdity, as in the hypothetical cases where we recognize it at once. But there are much more serious problems than absurdity.

One is that the LLM systems are designed in such a way that they cannot tell us anything about language, learning, or other aspects of cognition, a matter of principle, irremediable. Double the terabytes of data scanned, add another trillion parameters, use even more of California's energy, and the simulation of behavior will improve, while revealing more clearly the failure in principle of the approach to yield any understanding. The reason is elementary: the systems work just as well with impossible languages that infants cannot acquire as with those they acquire quickly and virtually reflexively.

It's as if a biologist were to say: "I have a great new theory of organisms. It lists many that exist and many that can't possibly exist, and I can tell you nothing about the distinction."

Again, we'd laugh. Or should.

Not Tom Jones—now referring to actual cases. Persisting in his radical departure from science, Tom Jones responds: "How do you know any of this until you've investigated all languages?" At this point the abandonment of normal science becomes even clearer. By parity of argument, we can throw out genetics and molecular biology, the theory of evolution, and the rest of the biological sciences, which haven't sampled more than a tiny fraction of organisms. And for good measure, we can cast out all of physics. Why believe in the laws of motion? How many objects have actually been observed in motion?

There is, furthermore, the small matter of burden of proof. Those who propose a theory have the responsibility of showing that it makes some sense; in this case, showing that it fails for impossible languages. It is not the responsibility of others to refute the proposal, though in this case it seems easy enough to do so.

Let's shift attention to normal science, where matters become interesting. Even a single example of language acquisition can yield rich insight into the distinction between possible and impossible languages.

The reasons are straightforward, and familiar. All growth and development, including what is called "learning," is a process that begins with a state of the organism and transforms it step-by-step to later stages.

Acquisition of language is such a process. The initial state is the biological endowment of the faculty of language, which obviously exists, even if it is, as some believe it is, a particular combination of other capacities. That's highly unlikely for reasons long understood, but it's not relevant to our concerns here, so we can put it aside. Plainly, there is a biological endowment for the human faculty of language. The merest truism.

Transition proceeds to a relatively stable state, changed only superficially beyond: knowledge of the language. External data trigger and partially shape the process. Studying the state attained (knowledge of the language) and the external data, we can draw far-reaching conclusions about the initial state, the biological endowment that makes language acquisition possible. The conclusions about the initial state impose a distinction between possible and impossible languages. The distinction holds for all those who share the initial state—all humans, as far as is known; there seems to be no difference in capacity to acquire language among existing human groups.

All of this is normal science, and it has achieved many results.

Experiment has shown that the stable state is substantially obtained very early, by three to four years of age. It's also well-established that the faculty of language has basic properties specific to humans, hence, that it is a true species property: common to human groups and in fundamental ways a unique human attribute.

A lot is left out in this schematic account, notably the role of natural law in growth and development: in the case of a computational system like language, principles of computational efficiency. But this is the essence of the matter. Again, normal science.

It is important to be clear about Aristotle's distinction between possession of knowledge and use of knowledge (in contemporary terminology, competence and performance). In the language case, the stable state obtained is possession of knowledge, coded in the brain. The internal system determines an unbounded array of structured expressions, each of which we can regard as formulating a thought, each externalizable in some sensorimotor system, usually sound, though it could be sign or even (with difficulty) touch.

The internally coded system is accessed in use of knowledge (performance). Performance includes the internal use of language in thought: reflection, planning, recollection, and a great deal more. Statistically speaking that is by far the overwhelming use of language. It is inaccessible to introspection, though we can learn a lot about it by the normal methods of science, from "outside," metaphorically speaking. What is called "inner speech" is, in fact, fragments of externalized language with the articulatory apparatus muted. It is only a remote reflection of the internal use of language, important matters I cannot pursue here.

Other forms of use of language are perception (parsing) and production, the latter crucially involving properties that remain as mysterious to us today as when they were regarded with awe and amazement by Galileo and his contemporaries at the dawn of modern science.

The principal goal of science is to discover the internal system, both in its initial state in the human faculty of language and in the particular forms it assumes in acquisition. To the extent that this internal system is understood, we can proceed to investigate how they enter into performance, interacting with many other factors that enter into use of language.

Data of performance provide evidence about the nature of the internal system, particularly so when they are refined by experiment, as in standard fieldwork. But even the most massive collection of data is necessarily misleading in crucial ways. It keeps to what is normally produced, not the knowledge of the language coded in the brain, the primary object under investigation for those who want to understand the nature of language and its use. That internal object determines infinitely many possibilities of a kind that will not be used in normal behavior because of factors irrelevant to language, like short-term memory constraints, topics studied sixty years ago. Observed data will also include much that lies outside the system coded in the brain, often conscious use of language in ways that violate the rules for rhetorical purposes. These are truisms known to all field-workers, who rely on elicitation techniques with informants, basically experiments, to yield a refined corpus that excludes irrelevant restrictions and deviant expressions. The same is true when linguists use themselves as informants, a perfectly sensible and normal procedure, common in the history of psychology up to the present.

Proceeding further with normal science, we find that the internal processes and elements of the language cannot be detected by inspection of observed phenomena. Often these elements do not even appear in speech (or writing), though their effects, often subtle, can be detected. That is yet another reason why restriction to observed phenomena, as in LLM approaches, sharply limits understanding of the internal processes that are the core objects of inquiry into the nature of language, its acquisition, and use. But that is not relevant if concern for science and understanding have been abandoned in favor of other goals.

More generally in the sciences, for millennia, conclusions have been reached by experiments—often thought experiments—each a radical abstraction from phenomena. Experiments are theory driven, seeking to discard the innumerable irrelevant factors that enter into observed phenomena—like linguistic performance. All of this is so elementary that it's rarely even discussed. And familiar. As noted, the basic distinction goes back to Aristotle's distinction between possession of knowledge and use of knowledge. The former is the central object of study. Secondary (and quite serious) studies investigate how the internally stored system of knowledge is used in performance, along with the many nonlinguistic factors than enter into what is directly observed.

We might also recall an observation of evolutionary biologist Theodosius Dobzhansky, famous primarily for his work with Drosophila: each species is unique, and humans are the uniquest of all. If we are interested in understanding what kind of creatures we are—following the injunction of the Delphic Oracle 2,500 years ago—we will be primarily concerned with what makes humans the uniquest of all, primarily language and thought, closely intertwined, as recognized in a rich tradition going back to classical Greece and India. Most behavior is fairly routine, hence to some extent predictable. What provides real insight into what makes us unique is what is not routine, which we do find, sometimes by experiment, sometimes by observation, from normal children to great artists and scientists.

One final comment in this connection. Society has been plagued for a century by massive corporate campaigns to encourage disdain for science, topics well studied by Naomi Oreskes among others. It began with corporations whose products are murderous: lead, tobacco, asbestos, later fossil fuels. Their motives are understandable. The goal of a business in a capitalist society is profit, not human welfare. That's an institutional fact: don't play the game and you're out, replaced by someone who will.

The corporate PR departments recognized early on that it would be a mistake to deny the mounting scientific evidence of the lethal effects of their products. That would be easily refuted. Better to sow doubt, encourage uncertainty, contempt for these pointy-headed suits who have never painted a house but come down from Washington to tell me not to use lead paint, destroying my business (a real case, easily multiplied). That has worked all too well. Right now it is leading us on a path to destruction of organized human life on earth.

In intellectual circles, similar effects have been produced by the postmodern critique of science, dismantled by Jean Bricmont and Alan Sokal but still much alive in some circles.

It may be unkind to suggest the question, but it is, I think, fair to ask whether the Tom Joneses and those who uncritically repeat and even amplify their careless proclamations are contributing to the same baleful tendencies.

ChatGPT is a natural-language-driven chatbot that uses artificial intelligence to allow human-like conversations. In a recent article in the New York Times, *in conjunction with two other authors, you shut down the new chatbots as a hype because they simply cannot match the linguistic competence of humans. Isn't it however possible that future innovations in AI can produce engineering projects that will match and perhaps even surpass human capabilities?*

Credit for the article should be given to the actual author, Jeffrey Watumull, a fine mathematician-linguist-philosopher. The two listed coauthors were consultants, who agree with the article but did not write it.

It's true that chatbots cannot in principle match the linguistic competence of humans, for the reasons repeated above. Their basic design prevents them from reaching the minimal condition of adequacy for a theory of human language: distinguishing possible from impossible languages. Since that is a property of the design, it cannot be overcome by future innovations in this kind of AI. However, it is quite possible that future engineering projects will match and even surpass human capabilities, if we mean human capacity to act, performance. As mentioned above, some have long done so: automatic calculators for example. More interestingly, as mentioned, insects with minuscule brains surpass human capacities understood as competence.

In the aforementioned article, it was also observed that today's AI projects do not possess a human moral faculty. Does this obvious fact make AI robots less of a threat to the human race? I reckon the argument can be that it makes them perhaps even more so.

It is, indeed, an obvious fact, understanding "moral faculty" broadly. Unless carefully controlled, AI engineering can pose severe threats. Suppose, for example, that care of patients was automated. The inevitable errors that would be overcome by human judgment could produce a horror story. Or suppose that humans were removed from evaluation of the threats determined by automated missile-defense systems. As a shocking historical record informs us, that would be the end of human civilization.

Regulators and law enforcements agencies in Europe are raising concerns about the spread of ChatGPT while a recently submitted piece of European Union legislation is trying to deal with AI by classifying such tools according to their perceived level of risk. Do you agree with those who are concerned that ChatGPT poses a serious public threat? Moreover, do you really think that the further development of AI tools can be halted until safeguards can be introduced?

I can easily sympathize with efforts to try to control the threats posed by advanced technology, including this case. I am, however, skeptical about the possibility of doing so. I suspect that the genie is out of the bottle. Malicious actors—institutional or individual—can probably find ways to evade safeguards. Such suspicions are, of course, no reason not to try, and to exercise vigilance.

Noam Chomsky and Robert Pollin

IS A LIVABLE FUTURE STILL POSSIBLE?

April 3, 2023

C. J. Polychroniou: *The IPCC has just released a synthesis report that is based on the content of its Sixth Assessment Report, i.e., contributions from the Three Working Groups and the three Special Reports. In sum, we have a synthesis report of scientific assessments on climate change published since 2018, except that the new report paints an even more troubling picture: We are closer than ever before to reaching or surpassing a 1.5-degree Celsius temperature rise and "continued emissions will further affect all major climate system components." Drawing on the findings of hundreds of scientists that have contributed to the IPCC's Sixth Assessment Report (AR6), the IPCC's synthesis report states that "in the near term, every region in the world is projected to face further increases in climate hazards (medium to high confidence, depending on region and hazard), increasing multiple risks to ecosystems and humans (very high confidence)." Accordingly, the authors of the synthesis report assert that limiting global warming requires "net-zero" carbon dioxide emissions and that the window of opportunity "to secure a livable and sustainable future for all" is "rapidly closing" and call for urgent climate action on all fronts. Indeed, in the synthesis report, its authors contend that there are major opportunities "for scaling up climate action" and only lack of political will is holding us back.*

Noam, what are your thoughts on the new IPCC report? I don't suppose you are surprised by any of its findings or policy recommendations.

Noam Chomsky: IPCC reports are consensus documents. Hence, they tend to err on the side of understatement. This one strikes me as different. It seems that desperation within the scientific community has reached such a level that the gloves are off and they feel the time has come to be blunt. Time is brief. Decisive action is an urgent necessity. Opportunities exist. If they are not taken, vigorously, we might as well say: "Too bad, was nice knowing you."

The report highlights the failure of "political will." Fair enough. If we care enough about decent survival to act decisively, we should take a close look at this concept and what it means for existing societies; or better, for societies we have some hope of attaining within the constraints of the time span for necessary action. We must, in short, have a clear understanding of the institutional structures within which political will can have concrete consequences.

Where is political will exercised? In the streets, to adopt the familiar metaphor, meaning among an informed, active, organized public. Insofar as that form of political will is exercised, it may—in this case, must—reach and influence centers of power, private and state, closely linked.

Let's be concrete. Congress just passed "landmark legislation" on climate, the Inflation Reduction Act (IRA) of 2022. It is hailed as the most significant clean energy and climate legislation in the history of the nation, "a new day for climate action in the United States."

That is accurate. It is also a sad commentary on the history and prospects for "climate action."

While not without positive features, the act is a pale shadow of the legislation proposed by the Biden administration under the impetus of intense popular activism, channeled primarily through Bernie Sanders's office. In related developments, similar initiatives reached Congress in the Green New Deal Resolution reintroduced in 2021 by Alexandria Ocasio-Cortez and Ed Markey.

The Biden proposal would indeed have been "landmark legis-lation" had it been enacted. While insufficient in light of the emer-gency we face, it would have been a long step forward. It was cut down step-by-step by 100 percent Republican opposition to anything that might address the most severe crisis of human history—and infringe on their passionate service to extreme wealth and corporate power. Joined by a few right-wing Democrats, GOP radicalism succeeded in removing most of the substance of the original proposal.

To understand our political institutions, it is important to recall that adamant GOP dedication to environmental destruction is not mere sociopathic sadism. In 2008, Republican presidential candidate John McCain introduced a limited climate initiative in his program, and congressional Republicans were also considering some measures.

For years, the huge Koch brothers' energy conglomerate had been working hard to ensure that the GOP would not veer from climate denialism. When they heard of this deviation, they launched a jugger-naut to restore orthodoxy: bribery, intimidation, lobbying, astroturf-ing, all the devices available to unaccountable concentrated economic power. It worked, quickly and effectively. From then until today it's hard to detect any GOP departure from abject service to the demand of concentrated power that we must race to destruction (and profit, during the few years ahead in which it will matter).

This is perhaps an extreme example, but it is not very far from the norm in the reigning form of state capitalism. That is particularly so in the era of savage capitalism called neoliberalism, basically a form of bitter class war disguised in grossly misleading terminology of "free markets," as practice reveals with brilliant clarity.

Returning to the IRA, one basic component is an array of devices to induce the fossil fuel industry and financial institutions that sup-port it to *please act more nicely*. The devices are mainly bribery and subsidy, including the gift of federal lands to exploit for oil extraction for decades to come, long after we pass tipping points for irreversible climate destruction.

The choice of tactics is understandable, given existing institutional structures. It is well understood in the elite culture that all concerns must be subordinated to the welfare of the masters of the private economy. That is Moses and the Prophets, to paraphrase Marx. Unless the masters are happy, we are lost.

During World War II, the whole of society was mobilized for the war effort. But as Secretary of War Henry L. Stimson observed, "If you are going to try to go to war, or to prepare for war, in a capitalist country, you have got to let business make money out of the process or business won't work." Business leaders were called upon "to run the agencies that coordinated production, [but] they remained on company payrolls, still cognizant of the interests of the corporations they ran. A common pattern, which provided an incentive to businesses to cooperate, was the cost-plus-a-fixed-fee system, whereby the government guaranteed all development and production costs and then paid a percentage [of the] profit on the goods produced."

First things first. It is important to win the war, but more important "to let business make money out of the process." That is the real Golden Rule, the rule that must be observed, not only during the most destructive war in history, but even in the far greater war in which human society is now engaged: the war to preserve organized human life on Earth.

The highest principle of our institutional structures also reveals their intrinsic lunacy. It is as if the Mexican government were to appeal to the drug cartels to reduce their mass slaughter by offering them some bribes and payments.

We can hardly be surprised that when oil prices shot up after Putin's invasion of Ukraine, the oil companies politely informed us: Sorry folks, no dice. Their bulging profits could be enhanced even further by curtailing their very limited commitment to sustainable energy and running after the big money, whatever the consequences for life on Earth.

It is all too familiar. We may recall the COP26 Glasgow UN Conference on climate in October 2021. US delegate John Kerry was ecstatic that the market was now on our side. How can we lose? BlackRock and other asset managers were promising to provide tens of trillions of dollars to the cause of sustainable development—with two small provisos: their benevolent investments must be profitable, and accompanied by firm guarantees that they will be risk-free. All thanks to the friendly taxpayer, who is regularly called upon to ride to the rescue in our neoliberal bailout economy, to adopt the phrase of economists Robert Pollin and Gerald Epstein.

I've occasionally cited Adam Smith's observation that in all ages, the "masters of mankind"—those who hold economic power—adhere to their "vile maxim": "All for ourselves, nothing for other people."

In the present context, the observation is a little misleading. Rulers with supreme power can afford some degree of benevolence to their subjects, even at a cost to their immense wealth. Capitalist systems do not permit such deviation from the vile maxim. The basic rules are that you pursue profit and market share, or you're out of the game. Only insofar as an organized public compels bending of the rules can we expect deviation from the vile maxim.

Many have expressed puzzlement that CEOs of fossil fuel companies and the banks that lend to them can consciously sacrifice their grandchildren to amassing even more wealth than what already surpasses the dreams of avarice. They can offer a convincing answer: *Yes, that's what I'm doing, but if I depart from this practice, I will be replaced by someone who keeps to it, and who may not have my goodwill, which might mitigate the tragedy somewhat.*

Again, it is the lunacy of the institutions that prevails.

We can add some of Adam Smith's closely related words of wisdom: thanks to their control of the economy, the masters of mankind become the "principal architects" of state policy and ensure that their own interests are "most peculiarly attended to" no matter how "grievous" the effects on others. Hardly an unfamiliar sight.

The same unaccountable power has a substantial impact on prevailing doctrines, what [Antonio] Gramsci called "hegemonic common sense." Polls show that voters who identify as Republicans have little concern for "climate change"—to adopt the conventional euphemism for boiling the planet. That's not too surprising. What they hear from their leaders and echo chambers like Fox News is that if climate change is even happening, it hardly matters. It's just another concoction of "liberal elites" in their insidious campaigns, along with "grooming" of children by the "sadistic pedophiles" who run the Democratic Party (believed by almost half of GOP voters), fostering the "Great Replacement" to destroy the repressed white race, and whatever may be devised next to keep the rabble in line while legislative programs stab them in the back.

I don't want to suggest that the GOP is alone in the infamy. Far from it. They have just driven class war to extremes that would be comical if the impact were not so ominous.

I mentioned one component of the IRA: gifts and subsidies to the malefactors to induce them to act more nicely. There is a second component: industrial policy, a radical departure from professed neoliberal doctrine. In this case, substantial subsidies to private power to restore a domestic chip industry. That raises further questions: Should the profits from public largesse be directed to the pockets of wealthy shareholders and stock options for the super-rich management class? Or should the social product be distributed differently, including the forgotten general public? Questions that shouldn't be overlooked.

Also not to be overlooked is the broader context of the effort to reconstruct part of the industrial economy that was dispatched abroad by the masters of the economy for their own welfare. The effort is part of the broader commercial war against China, designed to prevent its economic development. One priority in that war is to coerce European, Korean, and Japanese advanced industry to give up their major market and source of raw materials in China in order to serve Washington's campaign to preserve global hegemony. How this will turn out, we do not know. But it merits attention and thought.

These are broad brush strokes, overlooking much of great import. Nevertheless, I think the general picture is a useful framework for thinking about the tasks ahead. One plausible conclusion is that there is little hope within the institutional structure of savage capitalism. Can this be changed sufficiently within a realistic time span, with the savage element of the amalgam reduced or eliminated? It's hardly utopian to think that the savagery can be reversed with a return to something like the capitalism of the Eisenhower years, which, with all its severe flaws, is regarded with some justice as the "golden years" of state capitalism. Taming the worst excesses of the class war of the past decades is surely feasible.

Would that suffice to allow the "political will" of the streets to deter the worst, to open the way to the better future that can realistically be envisioned? There's only one way to find out: Dedication to the task.

Bob, what are your own thoughts on the new IPCC report? Can "net-zero" carbon dioxide emissions be reached across all sectors before midcentury? If so, where do we start, and how? But before you answer this part of the question, does "net zero" mean zero emissions? To be sure, is there such a thing as "net zero" or "zero carbon"?

Robert Pollin: For 2022, total global carbon dioxide (CO_2) emissions reached 40.5 billion tons. Of this total, 36.6 billion tons, or 90 percent of all 2022 CO_2 emissions, were produced by burning oil, coal, and natural gas to produce energy. The remaining 3.9 billion tons, equal to 10 percent of the total, were generated by land use changes, primarily deforestation to clear land for corporate agriculture and mining. The 2022 global emissions total was slightly below the peak figure for 2019, i.e., the year just prior to the COVID lockdown. Global emissions did fall in 2020 due to the lockdown, but only by about 6 percent, and then began rising again in 2021, as the global economy emerged out of the lockdown. Since its landmark 2018 report, the IPCC has become increasingly insistent that, in order to have even a reasonable chance of stabilizing the rise in the average global temperature by 1.5 degrees Celsius relative to pre-industrial levels, global CO_2 emissions need to be cut roughly in half, to 20 billion tons, as of 2030 and then to reach "net-zero" emissions by 2050.

You are absolutely on target to ask what exactly the term "net zero" really means here. In fact, by itself, that one small word "net" in the phrase "net-zero emissions" creates massive opportunities for fudging and outright obfuscation around climate solutions. Fossil fuel producers and anyone else now reaping profits from selling fossil fuels are committed to exploiting these obfuscation opportunities to the maximum.

The point is that the term "net zero" allows for scenarios in which CO_2 emissions remain at some significant positive level by 2050, i.e., that we are still burning oil, coal, and natural gas to produce energy and are still razing forested areas, starting with the Amazon rainforest. The way we would supposedly reach net-zero emissions under such scenarios would entail extracting the ongoing emissions out of the atmosphere through various measures falling under the term "carbon capture" technologies.

What are carbon capture technologies? To date, there is exactly one, and only one, such technology that has been proven to be effective and safe. That is to plant trees. More specifically, I am referring to afforestation—i.e., increasing forest cover or density in previously nonforested or deforested areas. Reforestation, the more commonly used term, is one component of afforestation. Afforestation works for the simple reason that living trees absorb CO_2. This is also why deforestation releases CO_2 into the atmosphere, contributing to global heating.

The big question with afforestation is, realistically, how large can its impact be as a means of counteracting ongoing CO_2 emissions from burning fossil fuels? One careful study by Mark Lawrence and colleagues at the Research Institute for Sustainability in Potsdam, Germany, concludes that afforestation could realistically reduce CO_2 levels by between 0.5 and 3.5 billion tons per year through 2050. As noted above, current global CO_2 levels are at about 40 billion tons. If the estimate by Lawrence and coauthors is even approximately correct, it follows that afforestation can certainly serve as a complementary intervention within a broader climate program. But afforestation cannot bear the major burden of clearing the atmosphere of CO_2 if we continue to burn fossil fuels to any significant extent.

Beyond afforestation are a range of high-tech measures that, according to its fossil fuel industry proponents, will be able to capture CO_2 and then either store it in underground reservoirs for all time or recycle and reuse it as a fuel source. However, none of these technologies are close to being capable of operating on a commercial basis at scale, despite the fact that, for decades, the fossil fuel companies have had huge incentives to make these technologies work.

In fact, in the final drafting of the most recent IPCC report, fossil fuel–producing countries lobbied hard to feature carbon capture technologies as a major climate solution. Still further, the upcoming global climate conference, COP28, will be held in November and December 2023 in the United Arab Emirates (UAE). The COP28 president-designate Sultan [Ahmed] al-Jaber, who is also the head of the UAE's state-owned oil company ADNOC, has been, according to the *Financial Times*, "consistent in stressing the need for a reduction in emissions rather than a reduction in fossil fuel production." In other words, according to al-Jaber, ADNOC and other oil-producing companies should be allowed to keep swimming in oil profits while we gamble the fate of the planet on technologies that don't work now and may never work. The latest IPCC report itself concluded that global rates of carbon capture deployment are "far below" what is needed for any viable climate stabilization project. The IPCC emphasized that implementation of carbon capture and storage "faces technological, economic, institutional, ecological-environmental, and socio-cultural barriers."

Let's now return to the first part of your question: whether net-zero emissions are achievable by 2050 when we allow that afforestation can, at most, extract 5 to 10 percent of the current level of emissions from burning fossil fuels? In other words, is it possible to effectively eliminate fossil fuel consumption throughout the global economy by 2050? The short answer is, yes. I say this even while recognizing that, at present, about 85 percent of current global energy supplies are produced by burning oil, coal, and natural gas. We also need to allow that people are still going to need to consume energy to light, heat, and cool buildings; to power cars, buses, trains, and airplanes, and to operate computers and industrial machinery, among other uses.

Still, purely as an analytic, economic, and policy challenge—i.e., independent of all the forces arrayed to defend fossil fuel profits at all costs—it is entirely realistic to allow that global CO_2 emissions can be driven to net zero by 2050. By my higher-end estimate, it will require an average level of investment spending throughout the global economy of about 2.5 percent of global GDP per year to build a global clean energy infrastructure to supplant our existing fossil fuel–dominant infrastructure. That translates into about $2 trillion in today's global economy, and an average of about $4.5 trillion per year between now and 2050. This is obviously a lot of money. But, as a share of annual GDP, it is about one-tenth of what the US and other high-income countries spent to prevent an economic collapse during the COVID lockdown. These investments should be focused on two areas: (1) dramatically improving energy efficiency standards in the stock of buildings, automobiles, and public transportation systems and industrial production processes; and (2) equally dramatically expanding the supply of clean renewable energy sources—primarily solar and wind power—available to all sectors and in all regions of the globe, at competitive prices relative to fossil fuels.

These investments are centerpieces of the Global Green New Deal. As such, they will also be a major new source of job creation in all regions of the world. This is because building a new global energy infrastructure requires people at work doing their jobs—all kinds of jobs, across the board, including roofers, plumbers, truck drivers, machinists, accountants, office managers, train engineers, researchers, and lawyers. In fact, building a global clean energy infrastructure requires about two to three times more people to do these jobs than to maintain our existing fossil fuel–dominant energy infrastructure.

The global clean energy transition will also deliver cheaper energy. The US Energy Information Administration predicts that the overall cost of generating a kilowatt-hour of electricity from solar or wind power will be roughly half that of coal and nuclear power by 2027. Raising efficiency standards on top of the clean energy investments also means that operating our various types of machinery requires us to buy less energy, any kind of energy—e.g., fewer kilowatt hours to warm, cool, and light buildings, or transport ourselves from one place to the next. Small-scale, low-cost clean energy infrastructures can also be built in the roughly 30 percent of rural areas in developing countries that, to date, still do not have access to electricity.

As we discussed recently, there have been major positive developments over the past year, with clean energy investments having grown rapidly in both the US and Western Europe. Yet, at the same time, the profits of the major oil companies reached an all-time high in 2022 of $200 billion. Moreover, politicians continue to genuflect before the oil companies. President Biden's decision to approve the huge Willow oil drilling project on federally owned land in Alaska is the most recent case in point. This is after Biden had campaigned in 2020 on a pledge of "no more drilling on federal lands, period."

In short, true net-zero emissions—with the "net" referring only to CO_2 absorption through afforestation at a level of perhaps 5 to 10 percent of current emissions—is entirely feasible technically and economically. But it will continue to be a massive political struggle. Rhetoric notwithstanding, the fossil fuel corporations—the public companies like ADNOC in the UAE as well as the private companies like ExxonMobil—have no intention of relinquishing their profits in the name of saving the planet.

Noam, what Bob just said about the transition to a green economy sounds very logical to me, but as the new IPCC report clearly states, such action entails not merely access to major sources of funding and technology but also coordination at all levels of governance, consensus among diverse interests, and, of course, international cooperation. Obviously, humanity has in front of it a herculean task. And I suppose many would say that it is not realistic to expect so much out of human nature and today's political institutions. What would be your reply to such rather pessimistic but not necessarily thoughtless considerations given the political history of the world?

Chomsky: The crucial phrase is "human nature and today's political institutions." On the latter, it's hard to see much hope under today's political institutions, that is, the savage capitalism instituted under the bitter class war misleadingly called "neoliberalism." There is no need to review again its deleterious impact. As usual, the most brutal punishment has been administered to the most vulnerable in the rich societies and particularly beyond. Much of the Global South had to endure harsh structural adjustment programs with effects ranging from the "lost decades" in Latin America to severe disruptions of the social order in Yugoslavia and Rwanda that are a large part of the background for the horrors that followed.

Many defend and even highly praise the "neoliberal" era. Of course, we expect that among the beneficiaries of the highway robbery that transferred an estimated $50 trillion from the working and middle classes in the US to the top 1 percent, according to the Rand Corporation study that we've discussed. But defenders extend to serious analysts, who rightly hail the lifting of hundreds of billions of people from poverty—overwhelmingly in China, not exactly a model of the "free market capitalism" hailed by neoliberal enthusiasts.

Also overlooked is that the methods adopted to bring about this welcome result, along with the great harm it imposed, were not dictated by "sound economics." The driving force was again the vile maxim. The optimal way to pursue it is to set working people in competition with one another while offering enormous gifts to capital. These include the highly protectionist investor rights agreements of the Clinton years, absurdly called "free trade agreements." Detailed alternatives were proposed by the labor movement and Congress's own research bureau, the Office of Technology Assessment (quickly dismantled). These alternative programs aimed to create a high-growth, high-wage international economy in which working people of all countries would benefit. In the era of bitter class war, they were not even considered.

We can reasonably conclude that savage capitalism offers little hope for survival.

The best hope, as mentioned earlier, is to defang the savagery while recognizing that dismantling the anti-human capitalist order is a longer-term and continuing project. That project does not conflict with the urgent task of mitigating the savagery. On the contrary, the two efforts should be mutually reinforcing.

What can we say, then, about the role of human nature? In some domains, quite a lot. A good deal has been learned about fundamental human cognitive nature, but these discoveries at most provide some suggestive hints in the domains that concern us here, where little can be said with much confidence.

If we look over history, we see vast differences in what accords with human nature. Behavior that was considered normal in the past arouses horror today. That's true even of the recent past. A dramatic illustration of the range of options that accord with basic human nature is Germany. In the 1920s, it represented the peak of Western civilization in the arts and sciences, and was also regarded as a model of democracy. A decade later it descended to the depths of depravity. A decade after that it was returning to an earlier course. The same people, the same genes, the same fundamental human nature, differently expressed with changing circumstances.

There are innumerable examples. One case of great relevance to our current discussion is attitudes toward employment. After four decades of the neoliberal assault, it is a high aspiration to find relatively secure employment instead of being left to the precarity designed by contemporary savage capitalism. A century earlier, in the aftermath of World War I, there were major efforts in Western industrial societies to create a very different social order in which working people would be freed from the fetters of capitalist autocracy: guild socialism in England, worker-run enterprises in Italy, many other initiatives. They posed a serious threat to the capitalist order. The initiatives were crushed in many ways. In the US, the extreme violence of Wilson's "red scare" crushed a vibrant labor movement along with social democratic politics, with some revival in the New Deal years but under constant bitter assault.

In earlier years, working people regarded having a job—that is, subordination to a master for most of one's waking life—as an intolerable attack on elementary human rights and dignity, a form of virtual slavery. "Wage slavery" was the conventional term. The slogan of the first great US labor organization, the Knights of Labor, was that "they who work in the mills should own them." Working people should not be subject to the orders of the masters of mankind. At the same time, radical farmers were organizing to free themselves from the grip of northeastern bankers and market managers, seeking to create a "cooperative commonwealth." These were the authentic Populists.

There were promising steps to bring together the agrarian and industrial popular classes. As throughout American history, these efforts were crushed by state and private power. American society is unusual among industrial societies in the power of the masters of the economy and their high level of class consciousness, a feature of American exceptionalism among industrial democracies that has many ramifications.

The transition from regarding subordination to a master as an intolerable attack on basic human dignity and rights to seeking it as the highest aspiration in life involved no change in human nature. Same human nature. Different circumstances.

Progressing to a livable society should enhance many aspects of our fundamental nature: mutual aid, sympathy for others, the right to participate freely in determining social policy, and much else. At the same time, it will inevitably limit other options that for many are important parts of a meaningful existence.

Transition to a sustainable economy is an inescapable necessity. It can be achieved in a manner that will provide a much better life. But it will not be easy, or without significant burdens.

Bob, finance is key to containing global warming. Yet, the world economy is always in the midst of some sort of crisis or another, and nowadays, a new banking crisis may be underway. Is there sufficient global capital and liquidity to overcome political inaction so global emissions can be reduced by over 40 percent by 2030, which seems to be an absolute must if a climate breakdown is to be averted?

Pollin: There are certainly more than sufficient financial resources that could be mobilized to pay for a full-scale clean energy transition. As I noted above, we need to channel about 2.5 percent of global GDP per year into clean energy investments. This compares with the high-income economies having injected about 25 percent of GDP into bailout operations during the COVID lockdown. As it is, global subsidies for fossil fuels doubled in 2022 to $1.1 trillion. Repurposing just these funds into supporting clean energy consumption and investments, as opposed to continuing to underwrite oil company price gouging and profiteering, could itself provide nearly half the funding required in the current global economy.

Under effective policies, the latest banking sector turmoil in the US and Europe should not create any barrier to channeling large-scale funding into clean energy investments. To the contrary, effective policies can enable clean energy investments to become a low-risk safe haven for investors, as they should be. This can then serve to help stabilize the financial system overall.

As one example, the US government could issue green bonds, which would then carry zero risk of default for private holders of these bonds, as with all other US Treasury securities (assuming the US House Republicans still possess the minimal sliver of sanity necessary to enable the federal government's debt ceiling to rise). The government could then utilize these funds, as one example, to procure solar and wind power from private firms to supply the government's electricity consumption needs. Private clean energy suppliers would then operate with long-term guaranteed fixed contracts with the government. This would serve as another source of stability within the financial system. Because the government would be guaranteeing these markets, the profits of the clean energy suppliers would then also be regulated and limited, as they are now for public utilities.

The federal government could also channel a significant share of its green bond funds to developing economies. This would enable those of us in rich countries to meet our obligation to help finance the clean energy transformation in these economies, given that the US and other rich countries are almost entirely responsible for having created the climate crisis in the first place. At the same time, the green bonds used for this purpose would still be US Treasury securities, and would therefore still carry zero default risk.

Similar green bond initiatives could also readily be undertaken in all high-income economies. The overall impact would be to stabilize the global financial system with safe, government-backed investments that also happen to be fulfilling the vital function of advancing the global climate stabilization project, as opposed to feeding yet more useless speculative frenzies on Wall Street.

Noam Chomsky

A STRONGER NATO IS THE LAST THING WE NEED AS RUSSIA-UKRAINE WAR TURNS ONE

February 23, 2023

C. J. Polychroniou: *The war in Ukraine is approaching its one-year anniversary and not only is there no end in sight to the fighting, but the flow of weaponry from the US and Germany to Ukraine is increasing. What's next on the NATO/US agenda, one wonders? Urging the Ukrainian military to retaliate by striking Moscow and other Russian cities? So, what's your assessment, Noam, of the latest developments in the Russia-Ukraine conflict?*

Noam Chomsky: We can usefully begin by asking what is *not* on the NATO/US agenda. The answer to that is easy: efforts to bring the horrors to an end before they become much worse. "Much worse" begins with the increasing devastation of Ukraine, awful enough, even though nowhere near the scale of the US-UK invasion of Iraq or, of course, the US destruction of Indochina, in a class by itself in the post–World War II era. That does not come close to exhausting the highly relevant list. To take a few minor examples, as of February 2023, the UN estimates civilian deaths in Ukraine at about seven thousand. That's surely a severe underestimate. If we triple it, we reach the probable death toll of the US-backed Israeli invasion of Lebanon in 1982. If we multiply it by thirty, we reach the toll of Ronald Reagan's slaughter in Central America, one of Washington's minor escapades. And so it continues.

But this is a pointless exercise, in fact a contemptible one in Western doctrine. How dare one bring up Western crimes when the official task is to denounce Russia as uniquely horrendous! Furthermore, for each of our crimes, elaborate apologetics are readily available. They quickly collapse on investigation, as has been demonstrated in painstaking detail. But that is all irrelevant within a well-functioning doctrinal system in which "unpopular ideas can be silenced, and inconvenient facts kept dark, without the need for any official ban," to borrow George Orwell's description of free England in his (unpublished) introduction to *Animal Farm*.

But "much worse" goes far beyond the grim toll in Ukraine. It includes those facing starvation from the curtailing of grain and fertilizer from the rich Black Sea region; the growing threat of steps up the escalation ladder to nuclear war (which means terminal war); and arguably worst of all, the sharp reversal of the limited efforts to avert the impending catastrophe of global heating, which there should be no need to review.

Unfortunately, there is a need. We cannot ignore the euphoria in the fossil fuel industry over the skyrocketing profits and the tantalizing prospects for decades more of destruction of human life on Earth as they abandon their marginal commitment to sustainable energy as profitability of fossil fuels soars.

And we cannot ignore the success of the propaganda system in driving such concerns from the minds of the victims, the general population. The latest Pew poll of popular attitudes on urgent issues did not even ask about nuclear war. Climate change was at the bottom of the list; among Republicans, 13 percent.

It is, after all, only the most important issue to have arisen in human history, another unpopular idea that has been effectively suppressed.

The poll happened to coincide with the latest setting of the Doomsday Clock, moved forward to ninety seconds to midnight, another record, driven by the usual concerns: nuclear war and envi-

ronmental destruction. We can add a third concern: the silencing of
awareness that our institutions are driving us to catastrophe.

Let's return to the current topic: how policy is being designed to
bring about "much worse" by escalating the conflict. The official reason remains as before: to severely weaken Russia. The liberal commentariat, however, offers more humane reasons: We must ensure
that Ukraine is in a stronger position for eventual negotiations. Or
in a weaker position, an alternative that does not enter into consideration, though it is hardly unrealistic.

In the face of such powerful arguments as these, we must concen-
trate on sending US and German tanks, probably soon jet planes, and
more direct US-NATO participation in the war.

What's probably coming next is not concealed. The press has just
reported that the Pentagon is calling for a top-secret program to insert
"control teams" in Ukraine to monitor troop movements. It has also
revealed that the US has been providing targeting information for
all advanced weapon strikes, "a previously undisclosed practice that
reveals a deeper and more operationally active role for the Pentagon
in the war." At some point there might be Russian retaliation, another
step up the escalation ladder.

Persisting on its present course, the war will come to vindicate the
view of much of the world outside the West that this is a US-Russian
war with Ukrainian bodies—increasingly corpses. The view, to quote
Ambassador Chas Freeman, that the US seems to be fighting Russia
to the last Ukrainian, reiterating the conclusion of Diego Cordovez
and Selig Harrison that in the 1980s the US was fighting Russia to the
last Afghan.

There have been real successes for the official policy of severely
weakening Russia. As many commentators have discussed, for a
fraction of its colossal military budget, the US, via Ukraine, is significantly degrading the military capacity of its sole adversary in this
arena, not a small achievement. It's a bonanza for major sectors of the
US economy, including fossil fuel and military industries. In the geopolitical domain, it resolves—at least temporarily—what has been a
major concern throughout the post–World War II era: ensuring that

Europe remains under US control within the NATO system instead of adopting an independent course and becoming more closely integrated with its natural resource-rich trading partner to the East.

Temporarily. It is not clear how long the complex German-based industrial system in Europe will be willing to face decline, even a measure of deindustrialization, by subordinating itself to the US and its British lackey.

Is there any hope for diplomatic efforts to escape the steady drift to disaster for Ukraine and beyond? Given Washington's lack of interest, there is little media inquiry, but enough has leaked out from Ukrainian, US, and other sources to make it reasonably clear that there have been possibilities, even as recently as last March. We've discussed them in the past and more bits of evidence of varying quality keep trickling through.

Do opportunities for diplomacy still remain? As fighting continues, positions predictably harden. Right now, Ukrainian and Russian stands appear irreconcilable. That is not a novel situation in world affairs. It has often turned out that "peace talks are possible if there is a political will to engage in them," the situation right now, two Finnish analysts suggest. They proceed to outline steps that can be taken to ease the way toward further accommodation. They rightly point out that the political will is there in some circles: among them the chairman of the Joint Chiefs of Staff and senior figures in the Council of Foreign Relations. So far, however, vilification and demonization are the preferred method to deflect such deviation from the commitment to "much worse," often accompanied by lofty rhetoric about the cosmic struggle between the forces of light and darkness.

The rhetoric is all too familiar to those who have paid any attention to US exploits throughout the world. We might, for example, recall Richard Nixon's call to the American people to join him in pulverizing Cambodia: "If, when the chips are down, the world's most powerful nation, the United States of America, acts like a pitiful, helpless giant, the forces of totalitarianism and anarchy will threaten free nations and free institutions throughout the world."

A constant refrain.

Putin's invasion of Ukraine has clearly hit the buffers, but as is the case with any war, there is dishonesty, propaganda, and lies flying left and right from all sides involved. On some occasions, there is also outright madness in the thinking of some commentators, which, unfortunately enough, passes itself off as analytical discourse worth publishing in so-called world-leading opinion pages. "Russia must lose this war and demilitarize" argued the authors of a recent piece that appeared in Project Syndicate. In addition, they claim that the West does not want to see Russia defeated. And they cite you as one of those who is somehow naive enough to believe in the idea that the West bears responsibility for creating the conditions provoking Russia's attack on Ukraine. Your comments and reaction to this piece of "analysis" on the ongoing war in Ukraine, which I presume may in fact be widely shared not only by Ukrainians but also by many others in Eastern Europe and the Baltic states, not to mention the United States?

There's not much point wasting time on "outright madness"—which, in this case, also calls for devastation of Ukraine and great damage far beyond.

But it's not complete madness. They're right about me, though they might add that I share the company of almost all historians and a wide range of prominent policy intellectuals since the nineties, among them leading hawks, as well as the top echelon of the diplomatic corps who know anything about Russia, from George Kennan and Reagan's ambassador to Russia Jack Matlock, to Bush II's hawkish defense secretary Robert Gates, to the current head of the CIA, and an impressive list of others. The list in fact includes any literate person capable of reviewing the very clear historical and diplomatic record with an open mind.

It is, surely, worthwhile to think seriously about the history of the past thirty years since Bill Clinton launched a new Cold War by violating the firm and unambiguous US promise to Mikhail Gorbachev that "we understand the need for assurances to the countries in the East. If we maintain a presence in a Germany that is a part of NATO, there would be no extension of NATO's jurisdiction for forces of NATO one inch to the east."

Those who want to ignore the history are free to do so, at the cost of failure to understand what is happening now, and what the prospects are for preventing "much worse."

Another unfortunate chapter in human mentality in connection with the Russian-Ukraine conflict is the degree of racism manifested by many commentators and policymakers in the Western world. Yes, fortunately enough, Ukrainians fleeing their country have been welcomed with open arms by European countries, which is not, of course, the treatment accorded to those fleeing parts of Africa and Asia (or from Central America in the case of the United States) because of persecution, political instability and conflict, and desire to escape poverty. In fact, it's hard to miss the racism hidden behind the thinking of many who claim that one should not compare US's invasion of Iraq with Russia's invasion of Ukraine because the two events are on a different level. This is, for instance, the position taken by the neoliberal Polish intellectual Adam Michnik, who, incidentally, also cites you as one of those who commits the cardinal sin of failing to draw distinctions between the two invasions! Your reaction to this type of "intellectual analysis"?

Outside the self-protective Western bubble, the racism is perceived in even starker terms, for example, by the distinguished Indian writer and political activist/essayist Arundhati Roy: "Ukraine is certainly not seen here as something with a clear moral tale to tell. When brown or black people get bombed or shocked-and-awed, it does not matter, but with white people it is supposed to be different."

I'll return directly to the "cardinal sin," a most revealing aspect of contemporary high culture in the West, mimicked by loyalists elsewhere.

We should recognize, however, that Eastern Europe is a somewhat special case. For familiar and obvious reasons, Eastern European elites tend to be more susceptible to US propaganda than the norm. That's the basis for Donald Rumsfeld's distinction between Old and New Europe. Old Europe are the bad guys, who refused to join in the US invasion of Iraq, encumbered by antiquated ideas about international law and elementary morality. New Europe, mostly the former Russians satellites, are the good guys, free from such baggage.

Finally, there are even some "leftist" intellectuals out there who have taken the position that the world now, in light of Russia's invasion of Ukraine, needs a stronger NATO and that there shouldn't be any negotiated settlements to the conflict. I find it hard to digest the notion that anyone who claims to be part of the left-radical tradition would be advocating the expansion of NATO and be in favor of the continuation of the war, so what's your take on this particularly strange "leftist" position?

I somehow missed the calls from the left for a revival of the Warsaw Pact when the US invaded Iraq and Afghanistan while also attacking Serbia and Libya—always with pretexts, to be sure.

Those calling for a stronger NATO might want to think about what NATO is doing right now, and also about how NATO depicts itself. The latest NATO summit extended the North Atlantic to the Indo-Pacific, that is, all the world. NATO's role is to participate in the US project of planning for a war with China, already an economic war as the US dedicates itself (and by compulsion, its allies) to preventing Chinese economic development, with steps toward possible military confrontation lurking not far in the distance. Again, terminal war.

We've discussed all of this before. There are new developments as Europe, South Korea, and Japan ponder ways to avoid severe economic decline by following Washington's orders to withhold technology from China, their major market.

It's also of no slight interest to see the self-image that NATO is proudly constructing. One instructive example is the US Navy's latest acquisition, the amphibious assault ship *USS Fallujah*, named to commemorate the two Marine attacks on Fallujah in 2004, among the more atrocious crimes of the US invasion of Iraq. It's normal for imperial states to ignore or seek to explain away their crimes. It's a shade more unusual to see them celebrated.

Outsiders don't always find this amusing, including Iraqis. Reflecting on the commissioning of the *USS Fallujah*, Iraqi journalist Nabil

Salih describes a football field "known as the Martyrs' Cemetery. It is where residents of the once besieged city [of Fallujah] buried the women and children massacred in repeated United States assaults to repress a raging rebellion in the early years of occupation. In Iraq, even playgrounds are now sites for mourning. The war entailed showering Fallujah in depleted uranium and white phosphorus."

"But US savagery didn't end there," Salih continues:

> Twenty years and incalculable birth defects later, the US navy is naming one of its warships the USS Fallujah [*sic*]. . . . This is how the US Empire continues its war against Iraqis. Fallujah's name, bleached in white phosphorus implanted in mothers' wombs for generations, is a spoil of war, too. "Under extraordinary odds," reads a US Empire statement explaining the decision to name a warship after Fallujah, "the Marines prevailed against a determined enemy who enjoyed all the advantages of defending in an urban area." . . . What is left is the haunting absence of family members, homes bombed into nonexistence and photographs incinerated along with the smiling faces. Instead, a lethally corrupt system of cross-sectarian camaraderie-in-theft was bequeathed to us by the unpunished war criminals of Downing Street and the Beltway.

Salih quotes Walter Benjamin in his *Theses on the Philosophy of History*: "Whoever has emerged victorious participates to this day in the triumphal procession in which the present rulers step over those who are lying prostrate."

"Through this historical revisionism," Salih concludes, "the US has launched another assault on our dead. Benjamin had warned us: 'Even the dead will not be safe from the enemy if he wins.' The enemy has won."

That's the true image of NATO, as many victims can testify.

But what do Iraqis know, or other Brown and Black people like them? For "The Truth" one can turn to a Polish writer who obediently repeats the most vulgar American propaganda, echoing many of his counterparts among the commissars at home.

Let's be fair, however. At the time of the massacre, the US media did report what was going on. I can do no better than to quote at length from the damning compilation of much of that reporting that Australian journalist John Menadue published in 2018:

> On October 16, 2004, the *Washington Post* reported that "electricity and water were cut off to the city just as a fresh wave of [bombing] strikes began Thursday night, an action that US forces also took at the start of assaults on Najaf and Samarra." The Red Cross and other aid agencies were also denied access to deliver the most basic of humanitarian aid—water, food, and emergency medical supplies to the civilian population.
>
> On November 7, a *New York Times* front page story detailed how the Coalition's ground campaign was launched by seizing Fallujah's only hospital: "Patients and hospital employees were rushed out of the rooms by armed soldiers and ordered to sit or lie on the floor while troops tied their hands behind their backs." The story also revealed the motive for attacking the hospital: "The offensive also shut down what officers said was a propaganda weapon for the militants: Fallujah General Hospital with its stream of reports of civilian casualties." The city's two medical clinics were also bombed and destroyed.
>
> In a November 2005 editorial denouncing its use, the *New York Times* described white phosphorous, "Packed into an artillery shell, it explodes over a battlefield in a white glare that can illuminate an enemy's positions. It also rains balls of flaming chemicals, which cling to anything they touch and burn until their oxygen supply is cut off. They can burn for hours inside a human body."
>
> In early November 2004, alongside the *New York Times* reports that Fallujah's main hospital had been attacked, the *Nation* magazine referred to "reports that US armed forces killed scores of patients in an attack on a Fallujah health centre and

have deprived civilians of medical care, food and water."

The *BBC* reported on 11 November 2004 "Without water and electricity, we feel completely cut off from every one else. . . . there are dead women and children lying on the streets. People are getting weaker from hunger. Many are dying from their injuries because there is no medical help left in the city whatsoever."

On 14 November 2004, the *Guardian* reported "The horrific conditions for those who remained in the city have begun to emerge in the last 24 hours as it becomes clear that US military claims of 'precision' targeting of insurgent positions were false. . . . *The city has been without power or water for days."* [Italics as original]

That's NATO, for those willing to learn about the world.

But enough of this deplorable whataboutism. Orders from on high are that it is outrageous to compare the new Hitler's assault on Ukraine with the misguided but benign US-UK mercy mission to help Iraqis by ousting an evil dictator—whom the US enthusiastically supported right through his worst crimes, but that's not proper fare for the intellectual class.

Again, however, we should be fair. Not all agree that it's improper to raise questions about the US mission in Iraq. Recently, there was much ado about Harvard's rejection of Human Rights Watch director Kenneth Roth for a position at the Kennedy School, quickly rescinded under protest. Roth's credentials were lauded. He even took the negative position in a debate, moderated by noted human rights advocate Samantha Power, on whether the Iraq invasion qualifies as humanitarian intervention. (Michael Ignatieff, director of the Carr Center for Human Rights, argued it did qualify.)

How lucky we are that at the peak of the intellectual world, our culture is so free and open that we even can have a debate on whether the enterprise was an exercise in humanitarianism.

The undisciplined might ask how we would react to an analogous event at Moscow University.

Noam Chomsky

RIGHT-WING INSURRECTION IN BRAZIL HELD STRONG ECHOES OF JANUARY 6

February 2, 2023

C. J. Polychroniou: *Noam, on January 8, 2023, supporters of former president Jair Bolsonaro stormed government buildings because they wouldn't accept the defeat of their fascist leader—an event, incidentally, that you strongly feared might take place almost from the moment that Luiz Inácio Lula da Silva won the presidential election. The insurrection, of course, has raised a lot of questions inside Brazil, as well as abroad, about the role of the Brazilian police, the failure of the intelligence services to warn Lula about what was going to happen, and who orchestrated the riots. This was undoubtedly an attempted coup, just like the January 6 insurrection at the US Capitol, and should serve as yet another reminder of how fragile liberal democracies have become in the neoliberal era. Can you comment on these matters?*

Noam Chomsky: Fragile indeed. The January 6 attempted coup could have succeeded if a few people had made different decisions and if Trump had succeeded in replacing the top military command, as he was apparently trying to do in his last days in office.

January 6 was unplanned, and the leader was so consumed by narcissistic rage that he couldn't direct what was happening. January 8, clearly modeled on its predecessor, was well-planned and financed. Early inquiries suggest that it may have been financed by small businesses and perhaps by agricultural interests concerned that their free rein to destroy the Amazon would be infringed. It was well advertised in advance. It's impossible that the security services were not aware of the plans. In Brasília itself—pro-Bolsonaro territory—they pretty much cooperated with the marauders. The army watched the coup being well organized and supplied in encampments outside military installations nearby.

With impressive unity that was lacking in the US, Brazilian officials and elites condemned the Bolsonarist uprising and supported newly elected president Lula's decisive actions to suppress it. There is nothing like the US denialist movement in high places. The uprising itself was savage and indiscriminate, as amply portrayed in the extensive TV coverage. The apparent intention was to create sufficient chaos so that the military would have a pretext for taking over and reestablishing the brutal dictatorship that Bolsonaro greatly admired.

International opposition to the insurrection was also immediate and forceful, most importantly, of course, that of Washington. According to the well-informed Brazilian political analyst Liszt Vieira, who shared his thoughts with *Fórum 21* on January 16, President Biden, while no admirer of Lula, "sent 4 diplomats to defend the Brazilian electoral system and send a message to the military: No coup!" His report is confirmed by John Lee Anderson in a judicious account of the unfolding events.

If the January 6 coup attempt had succeeded, or if its copy had taken place during a Republican administration, Brazil might have returned to the grim years of military dictatorship.

I doubt that we've seen the end of this in the US or in "our little region over here" as Latin America was called by Secretary of War Henry Stimson when explaining why all regional systems should be dismantled in the new era of post-war US hegemony, except our own.

The fragility of democracies through the neoliberal era is apparent enough, beginning with the oldest and best established of them, England and the US. It is also no surprise. Neoliberalism, pretensions and rhetoric aside, is basically class war. That goes back to the roots of neoliberalism and its close cousin austerity after World War I, a topic discussed in very illuminating recent work by Clara Mattei.

As such, a core principle is to insulate economic policy from public influence and pressure, either by placing it in the hands of professional experts (as in the liberal democracies) or by violence (as under fascism). The modalities are not sharply distinguished. Organized labor must be eliminated because it interferes with the "sound economics" that transfers wealth to the very rich and corporate sector. Investor rights agreements masked as "free trade" made their own contribution. A range of policies, legislative and judicial, left the political systems even more in the hands of concentrated private capital than the norm, while wages stagnated, benefits declined, and much of the workforce drifted to precarity, living from paycheck to paycheck with little in reserve.

Of course, respect for institutions declines—rightly—and formal democracy erodes, exactly as neoliberal class war dictates.

Brazil, just like the US, is a deeply divided nation, virtually on the verge of a civil war. Having said that, I believe Lula has a very difficult task ahead of him in terms of uniting the nation and pushing forth a new policy agenda based on progressive values. Should we be surprised therefore if his government falls short of carrying out radical reforms, as many seem to expect a leftist president to do?

I don't see any prospect of radical reforms, either in Brazil or in the neighboring countries where there has recently been a new "pink tide" of left political victories. The elected leadership is not committed to radical institutional change, and if they were, they would face the powerful opposition of internal concentrations of economic power and conservative cultural forces, often shaped by the evangelical churches, along with hostile international power—economic, subversive, military—that has not abandoned its traditional vocation of maintaining order and subordination in "our little region over here."

What can realistically be hoped for in Brazil is carrying forward the projects of President Lula's first terms, which the World Bank in a study of Brazil called its "golden decade," with sharp reduction in poverty and significant expansion of inclusiveness in a dramatically unequal society. Lula's Brazil may also recover the international standing it achieved during his first terms, when Brazil became one of the most respected countries in the world and an effective voice for the Global South, all lost during the Bolsonaro regression.

Some knowledgeable analysts are still more optimistic. Jeffrey Sachs, after intense discussions with the new government, concluded that growth and development prospects are favorable and that Brazil's development and international role could "help reform the global architecture—including finance and foreign policy—for the benefit of sustainable development."

Of paramount importance, not just for Brazil but for the whole world, would be resuming and extending the protection of the Amazon that was a highlight of Lula's first terms, and that was reversed by Bolsonaro's lethal policies of enabling mining and agribusiness destruction that were already beginning to turn parts of the forest to savannah, an irreversible process that will turn one of the world's greatest carbon sinks into a carbon producer. With the dedicated environmentalist Marina Silva now in charge of environmental issues, there is some hope of saving this precious resource from destruction, with awesome global consequences.

There is also some hope of rescuing the Indigenous inhabitants of the forests. Some of Lula's first actions on regaining the presidency were to visit Indigenous communities that had been subjected to the terror unleashed by Bolsonaro's assault on the Amazon and its inhabitants. The scenes of misery, of children reduced to virtual skeletons, of disease and destruction, are beyond words to describe, at least mine. Perhaps these hideous crimes will come to an end.

These would be no slight achievements. They might help lay a firmer basis for the more radical institutional change that Brazilians need and deserve—and not Brazil alone. A basis is already there. Brazil is the home of the world's largest left popular movement, the Landless

Workers Movement (MST), which takes over unused lands to form productive communities, often with flourishing cooperatives—to be sure, not without bitter struggle. The MST is establishing links with a major urban left popular movement, the Landless Workers Movement. Its most prominent figure, Guilherme Boulos, is close to Lula, representing tendencies that might be able to forge a path beyond the incremental improvements that are desperately needed in themselves.

The left, no matter where it comes to power, seems to fall short of expectations. In fact, often enough, it ends up carrying out the very neoliberal policy agenda that it challenges while in opposition. Is it because neoliberalism is such a formidable foe, or because today's left lacks both a strategy and a vision beyond capitalism?

There has long been a lively left culture in Latin America, which the northern colossus can learn from. The internal and external barriers, which are formidable quite beyond their neoliberal incarnation, have sufficed to constrain hopes and expectations. Latin America has often seemed on the verge of breaking free from these constraints. It might do so now. That could help propel the developments toward multipolarity that are apparent today and that might, just might, open the way to a much better world. Entrenched power, however, does not just melt away.

We speak of political crises, economic crises, and an ecological and climate crisis, among others, but it seems to me that we should also be talking of a humanity crisis. By that, I mean we may be on the verge of the dawn of an anti-Enlightenment era, with capitalism and irrationality having gone berserk and being at the root of a widespread ontological transition. Do you have any thoughts to share on this matter? Are we confronted with the possibility of the rise of an anti-Enlightenment era?

We should bear in mind that the Enlightenment was not exactly a bed of roses for most of the world. It was accompanied by the unleashing of what Adam Smith called "the savage injustice of the Europeans," a horrific onslaught against most the world. The most advanced societies, India and China, were devastated by European savagery, in its latter stages the world's most awesome narcotrafficking racket, which ravaged India to raise the opium that was rammed down the throats of China by barbarians led by England, with its North American offshoot not far behind, and other imperial powers joining in what China calls the century of humiliation. In the Americas and Africa, the criminal destruction was far worse, in ways too well-known to recount.

There were lofty ideals, with limited, though significant, reach. And it is true that they have been under severe attack.

The fact that unrestrained capitalism is a death sentence for humanity can no longer be concealed with soothing words. Imperial violence, religious nationalism, and accompanying pathologies are running rampant. What is evolving before our eyes raises in ever starker form the question that should have struck all of us with blinding fury seventy-seven years ago: Can humans close the gap between their technological capacity to destroy and their moral capacity to control this impulse?

It is not just a question, but the ultimate question, in that if it does not receive a positive answer, and soon, no one will long care about any others.

Noam Chomsky

ANOTHER WORLD IS POSSIBLE. LET'S BRING IT TO REALITY.

January 4, 2023

C. J. Polychroniou: *Noam, as we enter a new year, I want to start this interview by asking you to highlight the biggest challenges facing our world today and whether you would agree with the claim that human progress, while real and substantial in some regards, is neither even nor inevitable?*

Noam Chomsky: The easiest way to respond is with the Doomsday Clock, now set at one hundred seconds to midnight, likely to advance closer to termination when it is reset in a few weeks. As it should, considering what's been happening in the past year. The challenges it highlighted last January remain at the top of the list: nuclear war, global heating, and other environmental destruction, and the collapse of the arena of rational discourse that offers the only hope for addressing the existential challenges. There are others, but let's look at these.

Washington has just agreed to provide Ukraine with Patriot missiles. Whether they work or not is an open question, but Russia will assume a worst-case analysis and consider them a target. We have few details, but it's likely that US trainers come with the missiles, hence are targets for Russian attack, which might move us a few steps up the escalation ladder.

That's not the only possible ominous scenario in Ukraine, but the threats of escalation to unthinkable war are not just there. It's dangerous enough off the coast of China, particularly as Biden has declared virtual war on China and Congress is seething at the bit to break the "strategic ambiguity" that has maintained peace regarding Taiwan for fifty years, all matters we've discussed before.

Without proceeding, the threat of terminal war has increased, along with foolish and ignorant assurances that it need not concern us.

Let's turn to the environment. On global warming, the news ranges from awful to horrendous, but there are some bright spots. The Biodiversity Convention is a major step toward limiting the lethal destruction of the environment. Support is almost universal, though not total. One state refused to sign, the usual outlier, the most powerful state in world history. The GOP, true to its principles, refuses to support anything that might interfere with private power and profit. For similar reasons, the US refused to sign the Kyoto Protocol on global warming (joined in this case by Andorra), setting in motion a disastrous failure to act that has sharply reduced the prospects for escape from catastrophe.

I don't mean to suggest that the world is saintly. Far from it. But the global hegemon stands out.

Let's turn to the third factor driving the Doomsday Clock toward midnight: the collapse of the arena of rational discourse. Most discussion of this deeply troubling phenomenon focuses on outbursts in social media, wild conspiracy theories, QAnon and stolen elections, and other dangerous developments that can be traced in large part to the breakdown of the social order under the hammer blows of the class war of the past forty years. But at least we have the sober and reasoned domain of liberal intellectual opinion that offers some hope of rational discourse.

Or do we?

What we see in this domain often defies belief—and evokes ridicule outside of disciplined Western circles. For example, the leading establishment journal of international affairs soberly informs us that a Russian defeat "would reinforce the principle that an attack on another country cannot go unpunished."

The journal is referring to the principle that has been upheld so conscientiously when we are the agents of aggression—a thought that surfaces only among those who commit the unpardonable crime of applying to ourselves the principles that we valiantly uphold for others. It's hard to imagine that the thought has never surfaced in the mainstream. But it's not easy to find.

Sometimes what appears is so outlandish that one is entitled to wonder what may lie behind it, since the authors can't believe what they are saying. How, for example, can someone react to a story headlined "No Conclusive Evidence Russia Is behind Nord Stream Attack," going on to explain that "world leaders were quick to blame Moscow for explosions along the undersea natural gas pipelines. But some Western officials now doubt the Kremlin was responsible," even though the Russians probably did it in order to "strangle the flow of energy to millions across the continent"?

It's true enough that much of the West was quick to blame Russia, but that's as informative as the fact that when something goes wrong, Russian *apparatchiks* are quick to blame the US. In fact, as most of the world recognized at once, Russia is about the least likely culprit. They gain nothing from destroying a valuable asset of theirs; Russian state-owned Gazprom is the major owner and developer of the pipelines, and Russia is counting on them for revenue and influence. If they wanted to "strangle the flow of energy," all they would have to do is to close some valves.

As the sane parts of the world also recognized at once, the most likely culprit is the only one that had both motive and capability. US motive is not in question. It has been publicly proclaimed for years. President Biden explicitly informed his German counterparts, quite publicly, that if Russia invaded Ukraine the pipeline would be destroyed. US capability is, of course, not in question, even apart from the huge US naval maneuvers in the area of the sabotage just before it took place.

But to draw the obvious conclusion is as ludicrous as holding that the noble "principle that an attack on another country cannot go unpunished" might apply when the US attacks Iraq or anyone else. Unspeakable.

What then lies beyond the comical headline "No Conclusive Evidence Russia Is behind Nord Stream Attack"—the Orwellian translation of the statement that we have overwhelming evidence that Russia was not behind the attack and that the US was.

The most plausible answer is the "thief, thief" technique, a familiar propaganda device: When you're caught with your hands in someone's pocket, don't deny it and be easily refuted. Rather, point somewhere else and shout "thief, thief," acknowledging that there is a robbery while shifting attention to some imagined perpetrator. It works very well. The fossil fuel industry has been practicing it effectively for years, as we've discussed. It works even better when embellished by the standard techniques that make US propaganda so much more effective than the heavy-handed totalitarian variety: foster debate to show our openness, but within narrow constraints that instill the propaganda message by presupposition, which is much more effective than assertion. So, highlight the fact that there is skepticism about Russian depravity, showing what a free and open society we are while establishing more deeply the ludicrous claim that the propaganda system is seeking to instill.

There is, to be sure, another possibility: perhaps segments of the intellectual classes are so deeply immersed in the propaganda system that they actually can't perceive the absurdity of what they are saying.

Either way, it's a stark reminder of the collapse of the arena of rational discourse, right where we might hope that it could be defended.

Unfortunately, it's all too easy to continue.

In short, all three of the reasons why the clock had been moved to one hundred seconds to midnight have been strongly reinforced in the past year. Not a comforting conclusion, but inescapable.

Scientists are warning us that global warming is such an existential threat to the point that civilization is headed toward a major catastrophe. Are apocalyptic claims or views about global warming helpful? Indeed, what will it take to achieve successful climate action, considering that the most powerful nation in history is actually "a rogue state leading the world toward ecological collapse," as George Monbiot aptly put it in a recent op-ed in The Guardian?

The Yale University Climate program on climate and communication has been conducting studies on how best to bring people to understand the reality of the crisis facing humanity. There are others, from various perspectives.

It is a task of particular importance in the "rogue state leading the world toward ecological collapse." It is also a task of difficulty, given that denialism not only exists in some circles but has been close to official policy in the Republican Party ever since this extremist organization succumbed to the offensive of the Koch energy conglomerate, launched when the party seemed to be veering toward sanity during the 2008 McCain campaign. When party loyalists hear their leaders, and their media echo chamber, assuring them "not to worry," it's not easy to reach them. And though extreme, the GOP is not alone.

It seems to be generally agreed that apocalyptic pronouncements are not helpful. People either tune off or listen and give up: *"It's too big for me."* What seems to be more successful is focusing on direct experience and on steps that can be taken, even if small. All of this is familiar to organizers generally. It's a hard path to follow for those who are aware of the enormity of the crisis. But efforts to reach people have to be tailored to their understanding and concerns. Otherwise, they can descend to self-serving preaching to a void.

Recently, we discussed in another interview the aims and effects of neoliberal capitalism. Now, neoliberalism is often enough conflated with globalization, but it is rather obvious that the latter is a multidimensional process that has existed long before the rise of neoliberalism. Of course, the dominant form of globalization today is neoliberal globalization, but this is not to say that globalization must be structured around neoliberal policies and values, or to think that "there is no alternative." There are indeed continuous struggles across the world for democratic control over states, markets, and corporations. My question, thus, is this: Is it utopian thinking to believe that the status quo can be challenged and that another world is possible?

Globalization simply means international integration. It can take many forms. The neoliberal globalization crafted mostly during the Clinton years was designed in the interest of private capital, with an array of highly protectionist investor-rights agreements masked as "free trade." That was by no means inevitable. Both the labor movement, and Congress's own research bureau (the Office of Technology Assessment, or OTA) proposed alternatives geared to the interests of working people in the US and abroad. They were summarily dismissed. The OTA was disbanded, according to reports, because Newt Gingrich's GOP regarded it as biased against them, though it may be that Clintonite New Democrats shared the sentiment about fact and reason. Capital flourished, including the mostly predatory financial system. Labor was severely weakened, with consequences that reverberate to the present.

Globalization could take a very different form, just as economic arrangements can quite generally. There is a long history of efforts to separate the political from the economic domain, the latter conceived as purely objective, like astronomy, guided by specialists in the economics profession and immune to the agency of ordinary citizens, labor in particular. One very impressive recent study, by Clara Mattei, argues persuasively that this dichotomy, typically taking the form of austerity programs, has been a major instrument of class war for a century, paving the way to fascism, which was indeed welcomed by Western elite opinion, with enthusiasm by "libertarians."

There is, however, no reason to accept the mythology. The political domain in a broad sense, including labor and other popular activism, can shape the economic system in ways that will benefit people, not profit and private power. The rise of social democracy illustrates that well, but there is also no reason to accept its tacit assumption that capitalist autocracy is a law of nature. To quote Mattei, "Either the organizations of people can move beyond capitalist relations [to economic democracy], or the ruling class will reimpose its rule."

The status quo can certainly be challenged. A far better world is surely within reach. There is every reason to honor the slogan of the World Social Forum that "another world is possible," a far better one, and to devote our efforts to bring it to reality.

Noam Chomsky

ADVANCED US WEAPONRY IN UKRAINE IS SUSTAINING BATTLEFIELD STALEMATE

December 22, 2022

C.J. Polychroniou: *Noam, with every passing month, the conflict in Ukraine looks much grimmer. Both the US and the EU are now deeply involved in the war, and Biden has already pledged to support Ukraine for "as long as it takes" to defeat Russia on the battlefield. In the meantime, [Volodymyr] Zelenskyy has made some new demands for peace, but they were quickly rejected by Moscow with the argument that Kyiv must take into account the current reality. Are there any historical analogies that could be useful in seeing how this war might possibly end?*

Noam Chomsky: There are all too many analogues: Afghanistan, Yemen, Libya, Gaza, Eastern Congo, Somalia—just keeping to ongoing horrors where the US and its allies have a primary or at least substantial role in perpetrating and sustaining them. Such examples, however, are not relevant to discussion of Ukraine in polite circles. They suffer from the fallacy of wrong agency: us not them. Therefore, benign intent gone awry and not reincarnation of Hitler. Since this is all a priori truth, it is not subject to discussion any more than 2 + 2 = 4.

The analogues do offer some unhappy suggestions as to how this war might possibly end: by not ending until devastation is so extreme that we wouldn't want to think about it. That unfortunately seems more than likely with each passing day.

I claim no military expertise. I do follow military analysts, and find most of them supremely confident, with opposing conclusions—not for the first time. My suspicion is that General [Mark] Milley, former chair of the joint chiefs, is probably right in concluding that neither side can win a decisive military victory and that the cost of continuing warfare is enormous for both sides, with many repercussions beyond.

If the war goes on, Ukraine will be the primary victim. Advanced US weapons may sustain a battlefield stalemate as Russia pours in more troops and equipment, but how much can Ukrainian society tolerate now that Russia, after many months, has turned to the US-UK style of war, directly attacking infrastructure, energy, communications, anything that allows the society to function? Ukraine is already facing a major economic and humanitarian crisis. As the war persists, Ukrainian central bank officials fear that "People could flee Ukraine in droves, taking their money with them, potentially crashing the national currency as they seek to exchange their Ukrainian hryvnia for euros or dollars."

Fortunately, ethnic Ukrainians who flee are likely to be accepted in the West. They are considered to be (almost) white, unlike those left to drown by the thousands in the Mediterranean while fleeing from Europe's destruction of Africa, or forcefully returned to US-backed terrorist states. While many may be able to flee, as matters now stand destruction of a viable society in Ukraine is likely to continue on its gruesome path.

Talk of nuclear weapons is almost all in the West, though it's all too easy to think of steps up the escalation ladder. The casual talk about nuclear war in the US is shocking, disastrous.

So is the now-standard line about a cosmic struggle between democracy and autocracy—eliciting ridicule outside of Western educated circles. Elsewhere, people are capable of looking at the glaringly obvious facts of past and current history and are not so deeply immersed in doctrinal fabrications that they are rendered blind.

The same is true of the tales concocted in Western propaganda about Putin's plans to conquer Europe, if not beyond, eliciting fears that coexist easily with gloating over the demonstration of Russia's military incompetence and inability even to conquer towns a few miles from its borders. Orwell called it "doublethink": the ability to hold two contradictory ideas in mind and firmly believe them both. Western doublethink is buttressed by the industry of tea leaf reading that seeks to penetrate Putin's twisted mind, discerning all sorts of perversities and grand ambitions. The industry reverses George W. Bush's discoveries when he looked into Putin's eyes, saw his soul, and recognized it to be good. And it is about as well grounded as Bush's insights.

But reality doesn't go away. Apart from the destruction of Ukraine, there is an ever-growing possibility of nuclear war. Millions are facing starvation from disruption of grain and fertilizer shipments from the Black Sea region. Precious resources that are desperately needed to avert climate catastrophe are being wasted in destruction and sharply increased preparation for more. Europe is taking a beating, with its very natural complementary relation with Russia broken, and links to the emerging China-based system harmed as well. It's an open question whether Europe—in particular the German-based industrial system—will agree to decline by subordinating itself to Washington, a topic of far-reaching importance.

That prospect goes beyond Ukraine-Russia. Biden's virtual declaration of war against China, with sanctions against exports to China of technology that makes use of US components or designs, hits European industry hard, particularly the advanced chip-manufacturing industry in the Netherlands. So far it is not clear whether European industry will be willing to pay the costs of the US effort to prevent China's economic development—framed, as usual, in terms of national security, but only the most loyal partisans can take that claim seriously.

Meanwhile the US is gaining enormously in multiple ways: geopolitically by Putin's self-destructive decision to drive Europe into Washington's pocket by ignoring very real possibilities for avoiding criminal aggression, but also in other ways. It is not, of course, the US population that is gaining. Rather, those in charge: fossil fuel industries, financial institutions that invest in them, military producers, the agribusiness semi-monopolies, and masters of the economy generally, who can scarcely control their euphoria over bulging profits (which are feeding inflation with markups) and great prospects for moving on to destroy human society on earth more expeditiously.

It's easy to understand why almost the whole world is calling for negotiations and a diplomatic settlement, including most of Europe, as polls indicate. Ukrainians will decide for themselves. As to what they prefer, we have clear statements by the government, but know little about the general population. The highly regarded correspondent Jonathan Steele brings to our attention a Gallup telephone poll of Ukrainians in September. It found that "although 76 per cent of men wanted the war to continue until Russia is forced to leave all occupied territory including Crimea, and 64 per cent of women had the same view, the rest—a substantial number of people—wanted negotiations." Regional analysis showed that "in areas closest to the front lines where the horror of war is felt most keenly people's doubts about the wisdom of fighting until victory are highest. Only 58 per cent support it in southern Ukraine. In the east the figure is as low as 56 per cent."

Are there possibilities for diplomacy? The US and the UK, the two traditional warrior states, are still insisting that the war must be fought to severely weaken Russia, hence no negotiations, but even in their inner circles there is some softening in this regard.

Right now, the positions of the two adversaries seem irreconcilable, having predictably hardened as hostilities escalate. We don't know whether it is possible to return to the positions of last March, when, according to Ukrainian left sources, "Ukraine had publicly announced proposals to the Istanbul meeting on March 29, which included the withdrawal of Russian troops to the line on February 23 and the postponement of discussion about Crimea and Donbas. At the same time, the Ukrainian side insisted that all disputes should be resolved through transparent referendums held under the supervision of international observers and after the return of all forcibly displaced persons."

The Istanbul negotiations collapsed. The source just quoted places the blame totally on Russia. Little is known, since coverage of diplomatic efforts is so scanty. In particular, we do not know whether a factor in the collapse was Britain's opposition to negotiations, apparently backed by the US. Do possibilities remain? The only way to find out is to facilitate efforts to try.

At the very least we can remove obstacles to diplomacy that the US has placed, topics we've reviewed in detail. And we can try to foster an arena of open discussion about these topics, free from tantrums and heroic posturing about high principles that dismisses the factual record and human consequences.

There are many pitfalls and dangers, but it's hard to see what other course can save Ukraine, and far beyond, from catastrophe.

German chancellor [Olaf] Scholz has described the war in Ukraine as a strategic attempt on the part of Vladimir Putin to recreate the Russian empire and stated that relations with Moscow will be reestablished once the conflict is over and Russia has been defeated. Is there any evidence that Putin's regime is interested in reviving the Russian empire? And what happens if Russia is not defeated in the battlefield? Will Europe be dragged into a new Cold War? Indeed, does the US/NATO-Russia conflict over Ukraine prove that the Cold War perhaps never ended?

Scholz surely knows better. Whatever one thinks of Russian war aims, they were explicit and far narrower, and Scholz, who is well informed, cannot fail to be aware of that.

The tea leaf–reading industry has seized on occasional comments by Putin, generally taken out of context, to conjure up the frightening images of Russia on the march. That requires an impressive subordination to doublethink, as just described.

The Cold War briefly ended when the Soviet Union collapsed. The Gorbachev–Bush I negotiations, supported by Germany, provided a basis for escaping its legacy. The hopes did not long survive.

We should not overlook the fact that the end of the Cold War also lifted the ideological clouds—briefly. Government documents recog-

nized, indirectly, that the Cold War was in large part a tacit agreement between the superpowers to allow each to use violence when
necessary to control its own domains: for Russia, eastern Europe; for
the US, much of the world. Thus, the Bush I administration officially
recognized that we have to maintain intervention forces aimed at
the Middle East, where the serious problems "could not be laid at the
Kremlin's door," contrary to decades of prevarication. Rather, they
were the usual threat: independent nationalism. That didn't change,
apart from the need to design new pretexts, the menacing Russian
hordes having evaporated: "humanitarian intervention" and other
concoctions, lauded at home and bitterly denounced by the Global
South, the traditional victims. All reviewed in detail elsewhere.

The official Cold War briefly ended. Bush I lived up to his promises
to Gorbachev, but Clinton almost immediately rescinded them, initi-
ating the expansion of NATO to Russia's borders in violation of firm
and unambiguous promises. He did so for domestic political reasons
(the Polish vote, etc.) as he explained to his friend Boris Yeltsin. There
should be no need to review again the rest of the sordid story until
today. The hope for a "common European home" with no military alliances—Gorbachev's vision, tolerated by Bush I—was undermined
by Clinton, and a form of Cold War then developed, now becoming
extremely dangerous.

*Former German chancellor Angela Merkel made some revealing remarks
in an interview with the newspaper Die Zeit. She stated that the 2014
Minsk agreements were intended to "give Ukraine time" to make the country stronger, thus admitting that Kyiv was not going to implement the
peace deal and that the plan was to arm Ukraine for a large-scale conflict
with Russia. Is this a case of diplomatic fraud? If so, is it a legitimate claim
for launching an international tribunal?*

What Merkel had in mind we do not know. We do know that there is
no basis in the historical or diplomatic record for her claims. I am in-
clined to agree with the astute commentator who posts under the name
"Moon of Alabama." He points out that "Merkel is under very harsh

critique not only in the US but also in her own conservative party. She is now out to justify her previous decisions as well as the current bad outcome in Ukraine. My hunch is that she is making things up. Unfortunately she also creates serious damage."

He proceeds to a close analysis of the texts to justify this conclusion, which is the most plausible one I've seen. I don't think there's a basis for an international tribunal. More likely it is just a case of a political figure seeking to justify herself in a highly toxic climate.

For the last couple of months or so, Russia has been launching massive attacks on Ukraine's energy infrastructure. What's the strategic incentive behind these hideous types of military operations, which must surely qualify as war crimes? And what might be the implications of Ukrainian strikes inside Russia insofar as diplomatic efforts to end the war are concerned?

As we have discussed before, US-UK strategists expected that Putin would occupy Kyiv in a few days, as Russia did as well, it seems. There were plans reported to set up a Ukrainian government-in-exile. Both sides seriously underestimated Ukrainian will and capacity to resist the aggression, and radically overestimated Russian military power. US-UK military analysts also expressed their surprise that Russia was not launching their kind of war, with immediate resort to the "hideous types of military operations" you mention. It was not hard to predict, as we did over the months, that sooner or later Russia would resort to US-UK-Israeli tactics: quickly destroy everything that sustains a viable society. So they are now doing, arousing justified horror among decent people—joined by those who implement or justify these tactics with the "right agency": us. The strategic incentive is clear enough, especially after Russia's battlefield setbacks: Destroy the economy and the will to resist. All familiar to us.

Quite definitely war crimes, whether in Iraq, or Gaza, or Ukraine.

It's not surprising that Ukraine is seeking to strike back against Russia. So far, the US government, apparently under Pentagon advice, is seeking to restrict those reactions, not sharing the willingness to see the world go up in flames expressed by many commentators in the current crazed environment.

Things could easily go wrong. One new twist is that the US is planning to send Patriot antimissile systems to Ukraine. Whether they work seems to be an open question. They require a substantial military cohort, I think about eighty people, which will presumably include American trainers. Work or not, they're a natural target for Russian attack, even during installation. What then?

Any escalation is very dangerous in itself and can only impede whatever fading chances there may be for diplomatic efforts to fend off worse catastrophe.

Noam Chomsky

"WE'RE ON THE ROAD TO A FORM OF NEOFASCISM"

December 8, 2022

C.J. Polychroniou: *Noam, since neoliberal policies were implemented more than forty years ago, they have been responsible for increasing rates of inequality, destroying social infrastructure, and causing hopelessness and social malaise. However, it has also become evident that neoliberal social and economic policies are breeding grounds for right-wing radicalization and the resurgence of political authoritarianism. Of course, we know that there is an inherent clash between democracy and capitalism, but there is some clear evidence that neofascism emerges from neoliberal capitalism. Assuming that you agree with this claim, what's the actual connection between neoliberalism and neofascism?*

Noam Chomsky: The connection is drawn clearly in the first two sentences of the question. One consequence of the neoliberal social-economic policies is collapse of the social order, yielding a breeding ground for extremism, violence, hatred, search for scapegoats—and fertile terrain for authoritarian figures who can posture as the savior. And we're on the road to a form of neofascism.

The *Britannica* defines neoliberalism as an "ideology and policy model that emphasizes the value of free market competition," with "minimal state intervention." That is the conventional picture. Reality is different. The actual policy model threw open the doors for the masters of the economy, who also dominate the state, to seek profit and power with few constraints. In brief, unconstrained class war.

One component of the policies was a form of globalization that combines extreme protectionism for the masters with search for the cheapest labor and worst working conditions so as to maximize profit, leaving decaying rust belts at home. These are policy choices, not economic necessity. The labor movement, joined by Congress's now-defunct research bureau, proposed alternatives that could have benefited working people here and abroad, but they were dismissed without discussion as Clinton rammed through the form of globalization preferred by those conducting the class war.

A related consequence of "really existing neoliberalism" was rapid financialization of the economy, enabling riskless scams for quick profits—riskless because the powerful state that intervenes radically in the market to provide extreme protections in trade agreements does the same to rescue the masters if something goes wrong. The result, beginning with Reagan, is what economists Robert Pollin and Gerald Epstein call a "bailout economy," enabling the neoliberal class war to proceed without the risk of market punishment for failure.

The "free market" is not missing from the picture. Capital is "free" to exploit and destroy with abandon, as it has been doing, including— we should not forget—destroying the prospects for organized human life. And working people are "free" to try to survive somehow with real wages stagnating, benefits declining, and work being reshaped to create a growing precariat.

The class war took off, very naturally, with an attack on labor unions, the prime means of defense for working people. The first acts of Reagan and Thatcher were vigorous assaults on unions, an invitation to the corporate sector to join in and move beyond, often in ways that are technically illegal, but that is of no concern to the neoliberal state they dominate.

The reigning ideology was expressed lucidly by Margaret Thatcher as the class war was launched: there is no such thing as society, and people should stop whining about "society" coming to their rescue. In her immortal words, "'I am homeless, the Government must house me!' and so they are casting their problems on society and who is society? There is no such thing! There are individual men and women and there are families, and no government can do anything except through people and people look to themselves first."

Thatcher and her associates surely knew very well that there is a very rich and powerful society for the masters, not only the nanny state that races to their rescue when they are in need but also an elaborate network of trade associations, chambers of commerce, lobbying organizations, think tanks, and more. But those less privileged must "look to themselves."

The neoliberal class war has been a grand success for the designers. As we've discussed, one indication is the transfer of some $50 trillion to the pockets of the top 1 percent, mostly to a fraction of them. No slight victory.

Other achievements are "hopelessness and social malaise," with nowhere to turn. The Democrats abandoned the working class to their class enemy by the seventies, becoming a party of affluent professionals and Wall Street donors. In England, Jeremy Corbyn came close to reversing the decline of the Labour Party to "Thatcher lite." The British establishment, across the board, mobilized in force and climbed deep into the gutter to crush his effort to create an authentic participatory party devoted to the interests of working people and the poor. An intolerable affront to good order. In the US, Bernie Sanders has fared somewhat better, but has not been able to break the hold of Clintonite party management. In Europe, the traditional parties of the left have virtually disappeared.

In the midterm elections in the US, the Democrats lost even more of the white working class than before, a consequence of the unwillingness of party managers to campaign on class issues that a moderate left party could have brought to the fore.

The ground is well prepared for the rise of neofascism to fill the void left by unremitting class war and capitulation of the mainstream political institutions that might have combatted the plague.

The term "class war" is by now insufficient. It's true that the masters of the economy and their servants in the political system have been engaged in a particularly savage form of class war for the past forty years, but the targets go beyond the usual victims, now extending even to the perpetrators themselves. As the class war intensifies, the basic logic of capitalism manifests itself with brutal clarity: we have to maximize profit and power even though we know we are racing to suicide by destroying the environment that sustains life, not sparing ourselves and our families.

What's happening calls to mind an often repeated tale on how to catch a monkey. Cut a hole in a coconut of just the right size for a monkey to insert its paw and put some delectable morsel inside. The monkey will reach in to grab the food but will then be unable to extricate its clenched paw and will starve to death. That's us, at least the ones running the sad show.

Our leaders, with their similarly clenched paws, are pursuing their suicidal vocation relentlessly. At the state level, Republicans are introducing "Energy Discrimination Elimination" legislation to ban even release of information on investment in fossil fuel companies. That's unfair persecution of decent folks who are just trying to profit by destroying the prospects for human life, adopting good capitalist logic.

To take one recent example, Republican attorneys general have called on the Federal Energy Regulatory Commission to keep asset managers from purchasing shares in US utility companies if the companies are involved in programs to reduce emissions—that is, to save us all from destruction.

The champion of the lot, BlackRock CEO Larry Fink, calls for investment in fossil fuels for many years ahead, while showing that he is a good citizen by welcoming opportunities to invest in still fanciful ways to get rid of the poisons that are produced and even in green energy—as long as profits are guaranteed to be high.

In short, instead of devoting resources to escape from catastrophe, we must bribe the very rich to induce them to lend a hand in doing so.

The lessons, stark and clear, are helping to invigorate popular movements that are seeking to escape from the shambles of capitalist logic that shine through with brilliant clarity as the neoliberal war against all reaches its latest stages of tragicomedy.

That is the bright and hopeful side of the emerging social order.

With the rise of Donald Trump to power, white supremacy and authoritarianism returned to mainstream politics. But isn't it the case that the US was never immune to fascism?

What do we mean by "fascism"? We have to distinguish what's happening in the streets, very visibly, from ideology and policy, more remote from immediate inspection. Fascism in the streets is Mussolini's Blackshirts and Hitler's Brownshirts: violent, brutal, destructive. The US has surely never been immune from that. The sordid record of "Indian removal" and slavery mutating to Jim Crow needs no recounting here.

A peak period of "street fascism" in this sense just preceded Mussolini's March on Rome. The postwar Wilson-Palmer, post–World War I "red scare" was the most vicious period of violent repression in US history, apart from the two original sins. The shocking story is recounted in vivid detail in Adam Hochschild's penetrating study *American Midnight.*

As usual, Black people suffered the most, including major massacres (Tulsa and others) and a hideous record of lynchings and other atrocities. Immigrants were another target in a wave of fanatic "Americanism" and fear of Bolshevism. Hundreds of "subversives" were deported. The lively Socialist Party was virtually destroyed and never recovered. Labor was decimated, not only the Wobblies but well beyond, including vicious strikebreaking in the name of patriotism and defense against the "reds."

The level of lunacy finally became so outlandish that it self-destructed. Attorney General Palmer and his sidekick J. Edgar Hoover predicted an insurrection led by Bolsheviks on May Day 1920, with feverish warnings and mobilization of police, army, and vigilantes. The day passed with a few picnics. Widespread ridicule and wish for "normalcy" brought an end to the madness.

Not without a residue. As Hochschild observes, progressive options for American society suffered a severe blow. A very different country could have emerged. What took place was street fascism with a vengeance.

Turning to ideology and policy, the great Veblenite political economist Robert Brady eighty years ago argued that the whole industrial capitalist world was moving toward one or another form of fascism, with powerful state control of the economy and social life. On a separate dimension, the systems differed sharply with regard to public influence over policy (functioning political democracy).

Such themes were not uncommon in those years, and to a limited extent beyond both in left and right circles.

The issue becomes mostly moot with the shift from the regulated capitalism of the postwar decades to the neoliberal assault, which forcefully reinstitutes Adam Smith's conception that the masters of the economy are the principal architects of government policy and design it to protect their interests. Increasingly in the course of neoliberal class war, unaccountable concentrations of private power control both the economy and the political domain.

The result is a general sense—not mistaken—that the government is not serving us, but rather someone else. The doctrinal system, also largely in the hands of the same concentrations of private power, deflects attention away from the workings of power, opening the door to what are termed "conspiracy theories," usually founded on some particles of evidence: the Great Replacement, liberal elites, Jews, other familiar concoctions. That in turn engenders "street fascism," drawing on poisonous undercurrents that have never been suppressed and that can easily be tapped by unscrupulous demagogues. The scale and character is by now no small threat to what remains of functioning democracy after the battering of the current era.

Some are arguing that we live in a historic age of protests. Indeed, virtually every region in the world has seen a sharp increase of protest movements over the last fifteen years. Why have political protests become more widespread and more frequent in the age of late neoliberalism? Moreover, how do they compare to the protest movements of the 1960s?

The protests have many different roots. The trucker's strike that almost brought Brazil to a halt protesting the defeat of the neofascist Bolsonaro in the October election had some resemblance to January 6 in Washington, and may be reenacted, some fear, on the day of the inauguration of the elected president Lula da Silva on January 1.

But such protests as these have nothing in common with the remarkable uprising in Iran instigated by the death in police custody of Jina Mahsa Amini. The uprising is led by young people, mostly young women, though it is bringing in much broader sectors. The immediate goal is overturning the rigid controls on women's attire and behavior, though the protesters have gone well beyond, sometimes as far as calling for overthrow of the harsh clerical regime. The protestors have won some victories. The regime has indicated that the Morality Police will be disbanded, though some doubt the substance of the announcement, and it barely reaches the demands of the courageous resistance. Other protests have their own particularities.

Insofar as there is a common thread, it is the breakdown of social order generally in the past decades. Commonalities with sixties protest movements seem to me thin.

Whatever the connection may be between neoliberalism and social unrest, it is nonetheless clear that socialism is still struggling to gain popularity with citizens in most parts of the world. Why is that? Is it the legacy of "actually existing socialism" that hinders progress toward a socialist future?

As with fascism, the first question is what we mean by "socialism." Broadly speaking the term used to refer to social ownership of the means of production, with worker control of enterprises. "Actually existing socialism" had virtually no resemblance to those ideals. In Western usage "socialism" has come to mean something like welfare state capitalism, covering a range of options.

Such initiatives have often been suppressed by violence. The "red scare" mentioned earlier is one example, with long-lasting effects. Not long after, the Great Depression and world war evoked waves of radical democracy throughout much of the world. A primary task of the victors was to suppress them, beginning with the US-UK invasion of Italy, disbanding the partisan-led worker- and peasant-based socialist initiatives and restoring the traditional order, including fascist collaborators. The pattern was followed elsewhere in various ways, sometimes with extreme violence. Russia imposed its iron rule in its own domains. In the Third World, repression of similar tendencies was far more brutal, not excluding church-based initiatives, crushed by US violence in Latin America, where the US army officially claims credit for having helped to defeat liberation theology.

Are the basic ideas unpopular, when extricated from the imagery of hostile propaganda? There is good reason to suspect that they are hardly below the surface and can burst forth when opportunities arise and are exploited.

Noam Chomsky

US SANCTIONS ON IRAN DON'T SUPPORT THE PROTESTS, THEY DEEPEN SUFFERING

November 23, 2022

C.J. Polychroniou: *Noam, Iranian women started these protests over the government's Islamic policies, especially those around dress codes, but the protests seem now to be about overall reform failures on the part of the regime. The state of the economy, which is in a downward spiral, also seems to be one of the forces sending people into the streets with demands for change. In fact, teachers, shopkeepers, and workers across industries have engaged in sit-down strikes and walkouts, respectively, amid the ongoing protests. Moreover, there seems to be unity between different ethnic subgroups that share public anger over the regime, which may be the first time that this has happened since the rise of the Islamic Republic. Does this description of what's happening in Iran in connection with the protests sound fairly accurate to you? If so, is it also valid to speak of a revolution in the making?*

Noam Chomsky: It sounds accurate to me, though it may go too far in speaking of a revolution in the making.

What's happening is quite remarkable, in scale and intensity and particularly in the courage and defiance in the face of brutal repression. It is also remarkable in the prominent leadership role of women, particularly young women.

The term "leadership" may be misleading. The uprising seems to be leaderless, also without clearly articulated broader goals or platform apart from overthrowing a hated regime. On that matter words of caution are in order. We have very little information about public opinion in Iran, particularly about attitudes in the rural areas, where support for the clerical regime and its authoritarian practice may be much stronger.

Regime repression has been much harsher in the areas of Iran populated by Kurdish and Baluchi ethnic minorities. It's generally recognized that much will depend on how Supreme Leader Ali Khamenei will react. Those familiar with his record anticipate that his reaction will be colored by his own experience in the resistance that overthrew the Shah in 1979. He may well share the view of US and Israeli hawks that if the Shah had been more forceful, and had not vacillated, he could have suppressed the protests by violence. Israel's de facto ambassador to Iran, Uri Lubrani, expressed their attitude clearly at the time: "I very strongly believe that Tehran can be taken over by a very relatively small force, determined, ruthless, cruel. I mean the men who would lead that force will have to be emotionally geared to the possibility that they'd have to kill ten thousand people."

Similar views were expressed by former CIA director Richard Helms, Carter high Pentagon official Robert Komer, and other hard-liners. It is speculated that Khamenei will adopt a similar stance, ordering considerably more violent repression if the protests proceed.

As to the effects, we can only speculate with little confidence.

In the West, the protests are widely interpreted as part of a continuous struggle for a secular, democratic Iran but with complete omission of the fact that the current revolutionary forces in Iran are opposing not only the reactionary government in Tehran but also neoliberal capitalism and the hegemony of the US. The Iranian government, on the other hand, which is using brutal tactics to disperse demonstrations across the country, is blaming the protests on "foreign hands." To what extent should we expect to see interaction of foreign powers with domestic forces in Iran? After all, such interaction played a major role in the shaping and fate of the protests that erupted in the Arab world in 2010 and 2011.

There can hardly be any doubt that the US will provide support for efforts to undermine the regime, which has been a prime enemy since 1979, when the US-backed tyrant who was re-installed by the US by a military coup in 1953 was overthrown in a popular uprising. The US at once gave strong support to its then-friend Saddam Hussein in his murderous assault against Iran, finally intervening directly to ensure Iran's virtual capitulation, an experience not forgotten by Iranians, surely not by the ruling powers.

When the war ended, the US imposed harsh sanctions on Iran. President Bush I—the statesman Bush—invited Iraqi nuclear engineers to the US for advanced training in nuclear weapons development and sent a high-level delegation to assure Saddam of Washington's strong support for him. All very serious threats to Iran.

Punishment of Iran has continued since and remains bipartisan policy, with little public debate. Britain, Iran's traditional torturer before the US displaced it in the 1953 coup that overthrew Iranian democracy, is likely, as usual, to trail obediently behind the US, perhaps other allies. Israel surely will do what it can to overthrow its archenemy since 1979—previously a close ally under the Shah, though the intimate relations were clandestine.

Both the US and the European Union imposed new sanctions on Iran over the crackdown on protests. Haven't sanctions against Iran been counterproductive? In fact, don't sanctioned regimes tend to become more authoritarian and repressive, with ordinary people being hurt much more than those in power?

We always have to ask: Counterproductive for whom? Sanctions do typically have the effect you describe and would be "counterproductive" if the announced goals—always noble and humane—had anything to do with the real ones. That's rarely the case.

The sanctions have severely harmed the Iranian economy, incidentally causing enormous suffering. But that has been the US goal for over forty years. For Europe it's a different matter. European business sees Iran as an opportunity for investment, trade, and resource extraction, all blocked by the US policy of crushing Iran.

The same, in fact, is true of corporate America. This is one of the rare and instructive cases—Cuba is another—where the short-term interests of the owners of the society are not "most peculiarly attended to" by the government they largely control (to borrow Adam Smith's term for the usual practice). The government, in this case, pursues broader class interests, not tolerating "dangerous" independence of its will. That's an important matter, which, in the case of Iran, goes back in some respects to Washington's early interest in Iran in 1953. And in the case of Cuba goes back to its liberation in 1959.

One final question: What impact could the protests have across the Middle East?

It depends very much on the outcome, still up in the air. I don't see much reason to expect a major effect, whatever the outcome. Shiite Iran is quite isolated in the largely Sunni region. The Sunni dictatorships of the Gulf are slightly mending fences with Iran, much to the displeasure of Washington, but they are hardly likely to be concerned with brutal repression, their own way of life.

A successful popular revolution would doubtless concern them and might "spread contagion," as Kissingerian rhetoric puts it. But that remains too remote a contingency for now to allow much useful speculation.

Noam Chomsky

OPTIONS FOR DIPLOMACY DECLINE AS RUSSIA'S WAR ON UKRAINE ESCALATES

November 16, 2022

C.J. Polychroniou: *Noam, the war in Ukraine nears its ninth month mark and, instead of de-escalation, it is heading toward "uncontrolled escalation." In fact, it's becoming a war without end as Russia has been targeting Ukraine's energy infrastructure over the last few weeks and stepping up its strikes in the eastern region of the country, while the Ukrainians keep asking for more and more weapons from the West as they believe that they have the potential to defeat Russia on the battlefield. As things stand at the present juncture, can diplomacy end the war? Indeed, how do you de-escalate a conflict when the escalation level is so high, and the warring sides seem to be unable to reach a joint decision about the issues of conflict between them? For example, Russia will never accept rolling back borders to the position they were before February 24, when the invasion was launched.*

Noam Chomsky: Tragedy foretold. Let's briefly look back at what we've been discussing for months.

Prior to Putin's invasion there were options based generally on the Minsk agreements that might well have averted the crime. There is unresolved debate about whether Ukraine accepted these agreements. At least verbally, Russia appears to have done so up until not long before the invasion. The US dismissed them in favor of integrating Ukraine into the NATO (that is, US) military command, also refusing to take any Russian security concerns into consideration, as conceded. These moves were accelerated under Biden. Could diplomacy have succeeded in averting the tragedy? There was only one way to find out: try. The option was ignored.

Putin rejected French president [Emmanuel] Macron's efforts, to almost the last minute, to offer a viable alternative to aggression. Rejected them at the end with contempt—also shooting himself and Russia in the foot by driving Europe deep into Washington's pocket, its fondest dream. The crime of aggression was compounded with the crime of foolishness, from his own point of view.

Ukraine-Russia negotiations took place under Turkish auspices as recently as March-April. They failed. The US and UK opposed them. Due to lack of inquiry, part of the general disparagement of diplomacy in mainstream circles, we don't know to what extent that was a factor in their collapse.

Washington initially expected Russia to conquer Ukraine in a few days and was preparing a government-in-exile. Military analysts were surprised by Russian military incompetence, remarkable Ukrainian resistance, and the fact that Russia didn't follow the expected US-UK model (also the model followed by Israel in defenseless Gaza) of war: go at once for the jugular, using conventional weapons to destroy communications, transportation, energy, whatever keeps the society functioning.

The US then made a fateful decision: continue the war to severely weaken Russia, hence avoiding negotiations and making a ghastly gamble: that Putin will pack up his bags and slink away in defeat to oblivion if not worse, and will not use the conventional weapons, which, it was agreed, he had, to destroy Ukraine.

If Ukrainians want to risk the gamble, that's their business. The US role is our business.

Now Putin has moved on to the anticipated escalation, "targeting Ukraine's energy infrastructure over the last few weeks and stepping up its strikes in the eastern region of the country." Putin's escalation to the US-UK-Israel model has been rightly condemned for its brutality—

condemned by those who have accepted the original with little if any objection, and whose ghastly gamble laid the groundwork for the escalation, exactly as was warned throughout. There will be no accountability, though some lessons may have been learned.

While very mild liberal calls for considering a diplomatic option alongside of full support for Ukraine are at once subjected to a torrent of vilification, and sometimes quickly withdrawn in fear, voices calling for diplomacy from the mainstream establishment are exempted from this treatment, including voices from the major establishment journal *Foreign Affairs*. It may be that such concerns over a destructive war, with increasingly ominous potential consequences, are reaching the neocon war hawks who seem to be driving Biden's foreign policy. So some of their recent statements indicate.

Quite possibly they are hearing other voices, too. While US energy and military corporations are laughing all the way to the bank, Europe is being badly hit by the cutoff of Russian supplies and the US-initiated sanctions. That's particularly true for the German industrial complex that is the base of the European economy. It remains an open question whether European leaders will be willing to supervise Europe's economic decline and increased subordination to the US, and whether their populations will tolerate these outcomes of adhering to US demands.

The most dramatic hit to the European economy is the loss of cheap Russian gas, now partially replaced by far more expensive American supplies (also greatly increasing pollution in transit and distribution). That is, however, not all. Russian supplies of minerals play an essential role in Europe's industrial economy, including efforts to move to renewable energy.

The future of gas supplies to Europe was severely undermined, perhaps permanently, with the sabotage of the Nord Stream pipelines linking Russia and Germany through the Baltic Sea. This is a major blow to both countries. It was enthusiastically welcomed by the US, which had been trying for years to prevent this project. Secretary of State [Antony] Blinken described the destruction of the pipelines as "a tremendous opportunity to once and for all remove the dependence

on Russian energy and thus to take away from Vladimir Putin the weaponization of energy as a means of advancing his imperial designs."

The strong US efforts to block Nord Stream long preceded the
Ukraine crisis and the current fevered constructions about Putin's
long-term imperial designs. They go back to the days when Bush II
was looking into Putin's eyes and perceiving that his soul was good.

President Biden informed Germany that if Russia were to invade
Ukraine, "then there will be no longer a Nord Stream 2. We will bring
an end to it."

One of the most important events of recent months, the sabotage
was quickly dispatched to obscurity. Germany, Denmark, and Sweden have conducted investigations of the sabotage in their nearby
waters but are keeping silent about the results. There is one country
that certainly had the capability and motive to destroy the pipelines.
That is unmentionable in polite society. We can leave it at that.

Is there still an opportunity for the kind of diplomatic efforts that
mainstream establishment voices are calling for? We cannot be sure.
As the conflict has escalated, the options for diplomacy have declined.
At the very least, the US could withdraw its insistence on sustaining
the war to weaken Russia, thus barring the way to diplomacy. A stronger position is that of the establishment voices cited: calls for diplomatic options to be explored before the horrors become even worse,
not only for Ukraine but far beyond.

*Ukrainian officials claim they have a strategy in place to take back
Crimea because it was illegally annexed by Moscow in 2014. Similar
announcements had been made even before Russia's invasion of Ukraine.
While no military strategist believes that Ukraine is in a position to
retake Crimea, isn't this further evidence that there is no endgame in
sight for the Russia-Ukraine war? Isn't this indeed another reason why
the long-range ATACMS weapons that Ukraine says it needs should not
be delivered to them?*

The Biden administration and the Pentagon have been careful to limit the massive flow of weapons to those that are not likely to lead to

a NATO-Russian war, which would be effectively terminal for all. Whether these delicate matters can be kept under control, no one can be sure. All the more reason to try to bring the horrors to an end as soon as possible.

China has warned Russia against threats to use nuclear weapons in the war against Ukraine. Is this a sign that Beijing may be thinking of distancing itself from Putin's military adventures in Ukraine? In either case, it indicates that there are limits to the friendship between China and Russia, doesn't it?

There is little evidence, to my knowledge, of China distancing itself from Russia. It seems, rather, that their relations are becoming closer in common opposition to the entrenchment of a US-run unipolar world, sentiments shared in most of the world. China surely opposes the use of nuclear weapons, as does anyone with a shred of sanity remaining. And like almost all the world, it wants a quick settlement of the conflict.

Talk of nuclear weapons has been mostly in the West. Russia has reiterated the universal position of nuclear states: that they might resort to nuclear weapons in the event of a threat to survival. That stand became more dangerous when Putin annexed parts of Ukraine, extending the universal doctrine to a broader territory.

It's not quite true that the doctrine is universal. The US has a far more extreme position, framed before the invasion of Ukraine but announced only recently: a new nuclear strategy that the Arms Control Association described as "a significant expansion of the original mission of these weapons, namely deterring existential threats against the United States."

The significant expansion is spelled out by Admiral Charles Richard, head of the US Strategic Command (STRATCOM). Under the newly announced Nuclear Posture Review, nuclear weapons provide the "maneuver space" necessary for the United States "to project conventional military power strategically." Nuclear deterrence is therefore a cover for conventional military operations around the globe, deterring others from interfering with US conventional military operations. Nuclear weapons thus "deter all countries, all the time" from interfering with US actions, Admiral Richard continued.

Stephen Young, senior Washington representative at the Union of Concerned Scientists, described the new Nuclear Posture Review as "a terrifying document [that] not only keeps the world on a path of increasing nuclear risk, in many ways it increases that risk," already intolerably high.

A fair assessment.

The press scarcely reported on the Nuclear Posture Review, describing it as not much of a change. They happen to be right, but for reasons of which they are evidently unaware. As STRATCOM commander Richard could doubtless inform them, that has been US policy since 1995, when it was elaborated in a STRATCOM document titled "Essentials of Post–Cold War Deterrence." Under Clinton, nuclear weapons must be constantly available because they "cast a shadow" over conventional use of force, deterring others from interfering. As Daniel Ellsberg put it, nuclear weapons are constantly used, just as a gun is used in a robbery even if it is not fired.

The 1995 STRATCOM document goes on to call for the US to project a "national persona" of "irrationality and vindictiveness," with some elements "out of control." That will frighten those who might have thoughts of interfering. It is the "madman doctrine" attributed to Nixon on thin evidence, but now in an official document.

All of this is within the framework of the overarching Clinton doctrine that the US must be ready to resort to force multilaterally if we can, unilaterally if we must, to ensure "uninhibited access to key markets, energy supplies and strategic resources."

It is, then, true that the new doctrine is not very new, though Americans are unaware of the facts—not because of censorship. The documents have been public for decades and quoted in critical literature that is kept to the margins.

It should be of great concern that talk of nuclear war is being bandied about casually as a possibility to be considered. It is not. It is most definitely not.

Noam Chomsky

MIDTERMS COULD DETERMINE WHETHER US JOINS OMINOUS GLOBAL FASCIST WAVE

November 7, 2022

C. J. Polychroniou: *Midterm elections, in which, typically, about one-third of the seats in the Senate are up for grabs while all 435 seats in the House of Representatives are contested, are yet another peculiar feature of the US political system. However, midterm elections are significant in various ways. First, they are regarded as something of a verdict on the performance of the current president but have lower voter turnout than presidential elections. Secondly, the midterms almost always spell trouble for the party in power. Be that as it may, the upcoming midterm elections, to be held on November 8, are the most critically important elections in recent times both for the country and the rest of the world. Do you agree with this assessment, and, if so, why?*

Noam Chomsky: It's become common in recent years to say that the coming election is the most important ever. There are good reasons. One was laid out starkly by the astute political analyst John Nichols: "The November 8 midterm elections could be the last in which the United States operates as a functional democracy."

Nichols is not exaggerating. There is no need to review again GOP plans to establish permanent rule as a minority party dedicated to the welfare of the super-rich and corporate sector. While legitimate questions can be raised about the extent to which the US is even now a functional democracy, the descent to the Viktor Orbán–style "illiberal democracy" that is openly the ideal of the Trump-owned GOP would institute a qualitative change. It would not only condemn the US to an ugly fate but would be a major impetus to the ominous fascist wave that is threatening global society.

We should note that GOP dedication to the welfare of the ultra-rich—along with pretense to be the party of the little guy—pays off handsomely. Right now, in fact. As the *New York Times* reports: "Fueled by an expanding class of billionaires, political spending on the 2022 midterm elections will shatter records at the state and federal levels, with much of it from largely unregulated super PACs financed with enormous checks written mainly by Republican megadonors."

Critical as are the concerns about the fate of democracy, the issues at stake in the election are still more serious.

As the midterm elections approached, the news delivered a one-two punch, revealing how serious they are.

On October 26 the World Meteorological Organization informed us of new studies showing that "between 1990 and 2021, the warming effect on our climate (known as radiative forcing) by long-lived greenhouse gases rose by nearly 50 percent," reaching new heights, "with carbon dioxide accounting for about 80 percent of this increase." The International Energy Agency reported that the means to avert catastrophe are available and are to some extent being implemented, but "the shift toward cleaner sources of energy still isn't happening fast enough to avoid dangerous levels of global warming, the agency said, not unless governments take much stronger action to reduce their planet-warming carbon dioxide emissions over the next few years."

The following day, October 27, the Pentagon released its 2022 Strategic Reviews. Included is a new nuclear policy, which the Arms Control Association described as "a significant expansion of the original mission of these weapons, namely deterring existential threats against the United States."

The original mission was indeed, at least formally, to deter existential threats. That is the doctrine shared by all nuclear-armed states, arousing great consternation in the US when it has been reiterated by Putin, even before his recent annexation of parts of Ukraine. And it would be highly significant to expand the mission formally to endorsing use of nuclear weapons "in retaliation to a non-nuclear strategic threat to the homeland, US forces abroad or allies."

The "significant expansion" is spelled out by Admiral Charles Richard, head of the US Strategic Command (STRATCOM). Under the new policy, nuclear weapons provide the "maneuver space" necessary for the United States "to project conventional military power strategically." Nuclear weapons thus "deter all countries, all the time" from interfering with US actions, Admiral Richard continued. Nuclear deterrence is therefore a cover for conventional military operations around the globe.

That is a significant expansion of the stated original mission, the shared doctrine. Taking a closer look, we find that there is more to the story: the actual US stance on use of nuclear weapons has gone well beyond the shared doctrine.

The press described the new doctrine as not much of a change. They are right, but for reasons of which they are evidently unaware. As STRATCOM commander Richard could doubtless inform them, the "significant expansion" has been US policy since 1995, when it was spelled out in a STRATCOM document on "Post–Cold War Deterrence." Under Clinton, nuclear weapons must be constantly available because they "cast a shadow" over conventional use of force, deterring others from interfering. As Daniel Ellsberg put it, nuclear weapons are constantly used, just as a gun is used in a robbery even if it is not fired.

The 1995 STRATCOM document goes on to call for the US to project a "national persona" of "irrationality and vindictiveness," with some elements "out of control." That will frighten those who might have thoughts of interfering. All of this is within the framework of the overarching Clinton doctrine that the US must be ready to resort to force multilaterally if we can, unilaterally if we must, to ensure "uninhibited access to key markets, energy supplies and strategic resources."

It is, then, true that the new doctrine is not very new, though Americans are unaware of the facts—not because of censorship. The documents have been public for decades and quoted in critical literature that is kept to the margins.

I have not mentioned the rising threat of nuclear war in Europe, which is very serious, and discussed, though not with sufficient urgency.

How are the most serious questions we face addressed in the current election fever? By silence. That tells us something more about the state of functional democracy.

The US Supreme Court's decision to overturn Roe v. Wade could impact the midterm elections, according to some analysts, although both parties could see a boost in voter turnout. Why has culture become such a menacing force in contemporary US political climate, and how will the economy affect the midterm elections?

Perceptions of the economy will surely affect the elections. According to polls, the economy, and in particular inflation, are a dominant factor in the elections and the basis for likely Republican success.

But we have to distinguish between the economy and perceptions of the economy.

High inflation is blamed on Biden, but there are a few problems with that. One, as frequently observed, is that inflation is worldwide, hence cannot be attributed to Biden. Many of the causes have been discussed: disruption of supply chains by the pandemic, and others. One major cause rarely receives media attention: "rising profit margins have accounted for roughly 40 percent of the rise in prices."

These conclusions are supported in the business press. In the *Financial Times*, UBS Global Wealth Management chief economist Paul Donovan wrote that "today's price inflation is more a product of profits than wages," according to *The Hill*. As usual, "Companies have passed higher costs onto customers. But they have also taken advantage of circumstances to expand profit margins. The broadening of inflation beyond commodity prices is more profit margin expansion than wage cost pressures."

The practice goes back to the opening of the floodgates in the Reagan years. A study in the *Quarterly Journal of Economics* found that "the average profit rate since 1980 has increased from 1 percent to 8 percent and that price markups over that period increased from 21 percent to 61 percent."

Such facts suggest some measures that could be taken to tame the inflationary beast. The Federal Reserve has a different proposal: increase unemployment—the technical term is "raise interest rates."

The choice has ample media support, as general reporting indicates. Another illustration is Fed chair Jerome Powell's November 2 press conference on the latest rate hike. As *Common Dreams* reports, "Powell fielded questions for around 40 minutes on Wednesday following the central bank's decision to impose another large interest rate hike, but not a single reporter asked about the extent to which record-high corporate profits are fueling inflation even as companies openly boast about their pricing power."

Best to let working people bear the burden.

There are prominent figures calling on the Fed to rethink its routine approach to inflation. But they are voices in the wilderness.

Returning to perceptions and reality, Dean Baker [American economist and codirector of the Center for Economic and Policy Research in Washington, DC] has been reporting regularly on the way the liberal media have been constructing a version of the economy that reinforces the "blame Biden" message. "Downplayed or ignored [is the] unprecedented pace of job growth, the unemployment rate reaching a 50-year low, the rise in real wages for workers at the bottom, the sharp drop in the number of uninsured, and savings of thousands of dollars a year in interest costs by tens of millions of homeowners refinancing their mortgages," he writes.

The gloomy press report on the last quarter overlooked the fact that the economy created 1.1 million jobs, reducing unemployment to 3.5 percent, the lowest level since the late 1960s. Also overlooked was "healthy growth in real wages. The average hourly wage rose 1.1 per-

cent over the last three months. That exceeded the 0.4 percent infla-
tion reported by the consumer price index by 0.7 percentage points.
That translates into a 2.8 percent annual rate of real wage growth.
That's really good by any standard."

The October jobs report from the Bureau of Labor Statistics is even
more positive. Justin Wolfers, senior fellow at the Brookings Institution, comments: "This is a very strong economy. And whatever you
read elsewhere, employment growth is motoring along. . . . Indeed, job
growth over the past three months (or indeed, this month) has continued at a rate that exceeds almost any point in the pre-pandemic 2000s."

"In normal times," he adds, "this would be regarded as extremely
rapid growth, and a strong labor market. For some reason people are
shouting 'recession' in a crowded theatre, instead."

These are, however, not normal times. Refracted through the
"information system," facts do not change perceptions. Nor does the
longer record, which reveals that Democrats overall have a far better
record on the economy than the GOP.

True to form, the New York Times lead story on the jobs report portrayed it as more trouble. The report opened by lamenting that "job
growth remained stubbornly robust in October despite higher interest rates, defying policymakers' efforts to dampen the labor market
and curb the fastest inflation in generations." The problems are still
deeper: "American workers are still seeing rapid wage gains, a sign
that a strong labor market is giving them the ability to push for better
pay—potentially worrying news for the Federal Reserve."

The distortions are systematic, Baker has shown. It's understandable that people should be more aware of the prices flashed before
their eyes than by statistics on real wage growth. It's not the proper
task of the media to reinforce these misperceptions.

Like inflation, the menacing role of "culture" in the contemporary
political climate is not limited to the US. It is a global phenomenon,
found in one or another way in diverse societies: India, Israel, Brazil,
Hungary, and many others. It tends to be associated with expansion
of the popular base for repressive authoritarian movements and the
rise of demagogic leaders.

Particularities cannot be ignored, but there are some common threads. One is breakdown of the social order, which has advanced steadily under the neoliberal assault. As intended. Margaret Thatcher helped launch the assault with her dictum that there is no such thing as society. To make sure not to misrepresent her, here are her immortal words:

> "I am homeless, the Government must house me!" and so they are casting their problems on society and who is society? There is no such thing! There are individual men and women and there are families and no government can do anything except through people and people look to themselves first.

As Thatcher knew full well, these strictures do not apply to the wealthy and privileged. They have a rich array of social organizations and associations to sustain and protect them, and even the government that they largely dominate thanks to their ownership of the society is ready to bail them out when they are in trouble. But others are tossed into the market to endure its ravages as best they can, living lives of insecurity and precarity as they face the turbulent world alone.

Thatcher wasn't mistaken about people looking to themselves first. As Adam Smith instructed us 250 years ago, in all ages the "masters of mankind" who own the economy will pursue their "vile maxim": "All for ourselves and nothing for other people"—as long as society will let them get away with it, as it largely has under the neoliberal assault.

When social bonds collapse, or are broken by force, individuals will be easy prey to whatever seems to offer them something. Perhaps a church, perhaps a demagogue who stabs them in the back while professing his eternal love for his victims, or perhaps "cultural issues" to divert their attention to what is being done to them.

The practices are ancient. They became prominent in recent US political culture with Nixon's "Southern strategy," designed to attract Southern Democrats and other white supremacists by not-too-subtle racist appeals. They have flourished since, as the social order has been fragmented by the neoliberal hammers.

The breakdown of the social order has reached quite shocking levels. One grim manifestation is the increase in mortality among the white working class, a sharp departure from the rest of the world, and from history. Other aspects are revealed in studies of public opinion, which find extreme polarization and alienation in a collapsing society.

Almost three-fourths of Republicans and half of the "very liberal" feel that the government is "corrupt and rigged against everyday people like me." Almost half of "strong Republicans" (and one-third of the rest) agree that "it may be necessary at some point soon for citizens to take up arms against the government." Half of Americans—almost 70 percent of "strong Republicans" and 65 percent of the "very conservative"—agree that they "more and more feel like a stranger in my own country." And much more like it.

These are among the many signs that the country is falling apart. One critical factor is the neoliberal assault, which has had similar, if less extreme, impact elsewhere. The rising wave of global neofascism is one consequence.

That consequence has been well documented. Dani Rodrik found

> broad and compelling evidence, from Europe as well the United States, that globalization-fueled shocks in labor markets have played an important role in driving up support for right-wing populist movements. This literature shows that these economic shocks often work through culture and identity. That is, voters who experience economic insecurity are prone to feel greater aversion to outsider groups, deepening cultural and identity divisions in society and enabling right-wing candidates to inflame (and appeal to) nativist sentiment.

These tendencies were particularly strong among "switchers," workers who voted for Obama and switched to Trump after Obama's betrayal. Rodrik found that:

> Switchers viewed their economic and social status very differently from, and as much more precarious than, run-of-the-mill

Republican voters for Trump. In addition to expressing concern about economic insecurity, switchers were also hostile to
all aspects of globalization—trade, immigration, finance.

It should be stressed that none of this is inherent in "globalization."
Alternatives to Clinton's investor-rights version of globalization were
developed by the labor movement and Congress's own research bureau
(the Office of Technology Assessment, dismantled soon after). These
could have directed globalization along very different paths, benefiting working people rather than private capital. But they were quickly
dismissed, a chapter of the nineties that has been too little discussed.

*There are hundreds of candidates across a variety of races who denied the
outcome of the 2020 election results. How important is Trump's role in the
midterms, and is it safe to say that GOP leaders have lost complete control
of the base?*

GOP leaders began to lose control of the base, and even the party management, in 2016, when, to their shock and dismay, they were swept
aside by the Trump crusade. By now they have either succumbed, often
slavishly, or have been expelled, apart from a few relics who are hanging on in silence. By now it's Trump's party. He has managed, skillfully,
to maintain a voting base that he is undermining at every turn along
with dedicated service to the traditional Republican constituency of
extreme wealth and corporate power.

Denialism is one sign of the breakdown of the social order, and
is an element of the undermining of democratic forms. It is rampant
among the GOP voting base, and among those running for election,
amounting to "a majority of Republican nominees on the ballot this
November for the House, Senate and key statewide offices," according
to the *Washington Post*.

"The implications will be lasting," the *Post* analysis continues. The
deniers will "hold enormous sway over the choice of the nation's next
speaker, who in turn could preside over the House in a future contested presidential election" and the winners of state elections "will

hold some measure of power overseeing American elections." Every careful analysis has shown that the charges of election fraud are utterly groundless, but alienation and desperation are so extreme that facts don't matter: "The movement arising from Trump's thwarted plot to overturn the 2020 election is, in many respects, even stronger two years later. Far from repudiating candidates who embrace Trump's false fraud claims, GOP primary voters have empowered them."

"It is a disease that is spreading through our political process, and its implications are very profound," political scientist Larry Jacobs observed: "This is no longer about Donald Trump. This is about the entire electoral system and what constitutes legitimate elections. All of that is now up in the air." No exaggeration.

Again, the phenomenon is not limited to the US. Brazil is an extreme example, despite its having perhaps the world's most efficient and secure voting system. Bolsonaro's pre-election campaign to discredit the results if he did not win even reached the point of his calling in foreign ambassadors to berate them on the matter. Scholarship has shown that more generally, GOP denialism "bears alarming similarities to authoritarian movements in other countries, which often begin with efforts to delegitimize elections. Many of those promoting the stolen-election narrative, they said, know that it is false and are using it to gain power."

There is a huge divide among Democrats over many issues, but there seems to be a consensus among them, at least as reflected on the campaign message, that if the Republicans take power the US could backslide into outright authoritarianism, if not turned into a semi-fascist polity. How likely is this message to resonate with the average American voter, and why do Democrats keep losing the rural vote?

It's primarily in the rural areas that people "more and more feel like a stranger in my own country." Understandably. Apart from ongoing demographic and cultural changes, neoliberal globalization has hit these areas hard. Their small industries have collapsed. Farmers have been edged out by subsidized agribusiness. Stores are closing. Young people are leaving.

Though in the federal system they are supported by the more educated and prosperous urban society they resent, perception is different. As the Democrats have steadily become a party of affluent professionals and Wall Street donors, they have abandoned rural America along with the working class. In these sectors warnings of democratic decline and rights of minorities have little resonance, if any.

The consensus on the drift toward a semi-fascist polity may turn out to be accurate, dooming the world to a bitter fate. It has not been inevitable. Many hands have contributed.

It is not inevitable now, but time is short.

Noam Chomsky and Robert Pollin

PUSHING A VIABLE CLIMATE
PROJECT AROUND COP27

October 23, 2022

C. J. Polychroniou: *The 27th session of the Conference of the Parties (COP27) to the United Nations Framework Convention on Climate Change (UNFCCC) will take place in Egypt from November 6 to 18, 2022. Nearly two hundred countries will come together in yet another attempt to tackle climate breakdown. COP26, held in Glasgow about the same time last year, had been hailed as "our last best hope," but it did not achieve much, as too many compromises were made. The hope for COP27 is that the world will set more stringent greenhouse gas emissions reduction requirements considering the ever-clearer consequences of global warming. Noam, is this a significant climate meeting? Can we expect a breakthrough, or will it end up yet another futile international effort to reverse climate change? Indeed, what's standing in the way of governments' failure to slow or even reverse global warming? Isn't the evidence already overwhelming that the world stands on a climate precipice? What prevents us from stepping back from the abyss?*

Noam Chomsky: Decisions by governments tend to reflect the distribution of power in the society. As Adam Smith phrased this virtual truism in his classic work, "the masters of mankind"—in his day, the merchants and manufacturers of England—are the "principal architects" of government policy and act to ensure that their own interests will be "most peculiarly attended to" no matter how "grievous" the effects on the general welfare. Insofar as governments have failed to act in the ways that will prevent catastrophe, it is because the principal architects of policy have higher priorities.

Let's take a look. The US government has just passed a climate bill, a pale shadow of what was proposed by the Biden administration under the impact of popular climate activism, which in the end could not compete with the power of the true masters in the corporate sector. The final shadow is not meaningless. It is, however, radically insufficient in its reach, and also burdened with measures to ensure that the interests of the masters are "most peculiarly attended to."

The bill that the masters were willing to accept includes vast government subsidies that "are already driving forward large oil and gas projects that threaten a heavy carbon footprint, with companies including ExxonMobil, Sempra and Occidental Petroleum positioned for big payouts," the *Washington Post* reports. One device to satisfy the needs of the masters is "a vast wad of money" for carbon capture—a phrase that means: "Let's keep poisoning the atmosphere freely and maybe someday someone will figure out a way to remove the poisons."

That's too kind. It's much worse. "The irony of carbon capture is that the place it has proven most successful is getting more oil out of the ground. All but one major project built in the United States to date is geared toward fossil fuel companies taking the trapped carbon and injecting it into underground wells to extract crude."

The actual cases would be comical if the consequences were not so grave. Thus, "the subsidies give companies lucrative incentives to drill for gas in the most climate-unfriendly sites, where the concentration of CO_2 in the fuel is especially high. The CO_2, a potent greenhouse gas, is useless for making fuel, but the tax credits are awarded based on how many tons of it companies trap."

It's hard to believe that this is real. But it is. It's Capitalism 101 when the masters are in charge.

Other cases illustrate the same priorities. Arctic permafrost contains huge amounts of carbon and is beginning to melt as the Arctic heats much faster than the rest of the world. Scientists of one oil major, ConocoPhillips, discovered a way to slow the thawing of the permafrost. To what end? "To keep it solid enough to drill for oil, the burning of which will continue to worsen ice melt," according to the *New York Times*.

The exuberant race to destruction is far more general. New fields are being opened to exploration. There is a huge expansion of oil pipelines, with "more than 24,000 km of pipelines planned around world, showing 'an almost deliberate failure to meet climate goals.'"

Corporate lobbyists are even pressing states to punish corporations (by withdrawing pension funds, etc.) that dare even to provide information on environmental impacts of their policies. No stone is left unturned. Every opportunity to destroy must be exploited, no matter how slight, following Marx's script of capitalism going berserk. . . .

There is a certain logic behind it. The rules of the game are that you expand profit and market share, or you lose out. For self-delusion, it suffices to hold out the thin hope that maybe our technical culture will find some answers.

There is an alternative to the resolute march toward suicide. The distribution of power can be changed by an aroused public with its own very different priorities, such as surviving in a livable world. The current masters can be controlled on a path toward elimination of their illegitimate authority. The rules of the game can be changed, in the short term modified sufficiently to enable humankind to adopt the means that have been spelled out in detail to "step back from the abyss."

Bob, can you give us an estimate of where we stand on climate change and what needs to be done for the world to become carbon neutral by 2050?

Robert Pollin: Where we stand with climate change is straightforward and was expressed clearly in the most recent two massive reports, of this past February and April 2022, from the Intergovernmental Panel on

Climate Change (IPCC), the most authoritative mainstream resource on climate change research. In summarizing its February report, the IPCC said that "Human-induced climate change is causing dangerous and widespread disruption in nature and affecting the lives of billions of people around the world, despite efforts to reduce the risks. People and ecosystems least able to cope are being hardest hit." The February report describes how "increased heatwaves, droughts and floods are already exceeding plants' and animals' tolerance thresholds, driving mass mortalities in species such as trees and corals. These weather extremes are occurring simultaneously, causing cascading impacts that are increasingly difficult to manage. They have exposed millions of people to acute food and water insecurity, especially in Africa, Asia, Central and South America, on Small Islands [sic] and in the Arctic." I would note that reputable climate scientists regularly criticize the IPCC for understating our dire ecological condition.

What we need to do to have any chance of stabilizing the climate is also straightforward. By far, the biggest driver of climate change is burning oil, coal, and natural gas to produce energy. This is because burning fossil fuels to produce energy generates CO_2 emissions. These emissions, in turn, are the main cause of heat being trapped in our atmosphere and warming the planet. This is why, in its landmark 2018 special report *Global Warming of 1.5° Celsius*, the IPCC set out the overarching goals of cutting global CO_2 emissions by about 50 percent as of 2030 and for the globe to reach net-zero emissions by 2050. The IPCC concluded in the 2018 report, and emphasized even more emphatically in its 2022 studies, that stabilizing the global climate at 1.5 degrees Celsius [2.7 degrees Fahrenheit] above pre-industrial average temperature levels is imperative for having any chance of reducing significantly, much less preventing, the "dangerous and widespread disruption in nature affecting the lives of billions of people around the world."

It is clear, then, that the single most important project for advancing a viable climate stabilization program is to phase out the consumption of oil, coal, and natural gas for energy production. As the fossil fuel energy infrastructure phases out to zero by 2050, we concurrently have to build an entirely new global energy infrastructure whose centerpieces will be high efficiency and clean renewable energy sources—primarily solar and wind power. People are obviously still going to need to consume energy, from any available source, to light, heat, and cool buildings, to power cars, buses, trains, and airplanes, and to operate computers and industrial machinery, among other uses. Moreover, any minimally decent egalitarian program climate stabilization program—what we may call a Global Green New Deal—will entail a significant increase in energy consumption for lower-income people throughout the world.

The other major driver of climate change is corporate industrial agriculture in its multiple manifestations. This includes the heavy reliance on natural gas–based fertilizers, along with synthetic pesticides and herbicides, to increase land productivity. It also includes deforestation, whose main purpose is to increase available land for cattle grazing and still more industrial farming. Addressing these causes of climate change is, at least in principle, also straightforward. It requires replacing industrial agriculture with organic farming practices that rely on crop rotation, animal manures, and composting for fertilizer and biological pest control. It means humans eating less beef, and thereby freeing up the cattle-grazing land to be used for organic crop cultivation. It then also means stopping deforestation, most especially in the Amazon rainforest, i.e., "the Earth's lungs." This is why, as Noam emphasized in a previous recent interview, it is absolutely imperative, just on the climate issue alone, that Lula defeats Jair Bolsonaro in Brazil's presidential election on October 30. Bolsonaro has no compunctions about obliterating the Amazon rainforest if there is money to be made, while Lula is committed to rainforest preservation and reforestation.

So, in response to both of your questions—where we stand today on climate change and what needs to be done—we will have a clearer picture after Brazil's October 30 election. We can also generalize from Brazil's situation. That is, everywhere in the world, we need to elect people like Lula and to defeat all climate deniers and apologists for the fossil fuel industry, that is, all the Bolsonaros in all regions of the world.

At the same time, electoral politics by itself is never going to be a sufficient action program. Even principled political leaders like Lula can become susceptible to backsliding from a robust Green New Deal program in the face of the enormous pressures from fossil fuel corporations who continue to cash in on destroying the planet. The only solution here is mass organizing that is capable of holding all politicians accountable. There has been tremendous climate activism throughout the world in recent years, led by young people. This activism simply needs to intensify and continue to become increasingly impactful.

In terms of some specifics, the investments required to dramatically increase energy efficiency standards and equally dramatically expand the global supply of clean energy sources will be a major source of new job creation, in all regions of the world. This is excellent news, as far as it goes. But there is no guarantee that these new jobs will be good jobs. After all, we are still operating within capitalism. Climate activists therefore need to join forces with unions and other labor organizers to fight for good wages, benefits, and working conditions for these millions of new clean energy jobs. At the same time, the phasing out of the global fossil fuel industry will mean large-scale losses for workers and communities that are presently dependent on the fossil fuel industry. Providing a just transition for these workers and communities also needs to be at the center of the Global Green New Deal.

There have been some recent positive developments with respect to the energy transition. Clean renewable energy investments have increased for the past two years, at a rate of about 12 percent per year. This contrasts sharply with the five years immediately after the major COP21 conference in Paris in 2015, during which global clean energy investments rose by a paltry 2 percent annual rate.

This recent spike in clean energy investments is being fueled by the fact that the costs of solar and wind power are falling dramatically and are now lower than those for fossil fuels and nuclear. Thus, as of 2020, the average cost for fossil fuel–generated electricity ranged between 5.5 and 4.8 cents per kilowatt hour in the high-income economies. These cost figures then rose sharply in 2021, due to the post COVID lockdown supply-chain breakdowns in the fossil fuel industry and Russia's invasion of Ukraine. By contrast, as of 2021, solar photovoltaic installations generate electricity at 4.8 cents per kilowatt hour and onshore wind is at 3.3 cents. Moreover, average solar costs fell by roughly 90 percent between 2010 and 2021. The average cost figures for solar and wind should continue to decline still further as advances in technology proceed as long as the rapid global expansion of these sectors continues.

At the same time, these positive developments must be weighed against the grim bottom-line reality that, to date, there is still no evidence that global CO_2 emissions have begun falling. A modest reduction did occur in 2020 due to the global COVID lockdown. But as of 2019, global CO_2 emissions stood at 37 billion tons. This is a 50 percent increase relative to 2000 and a 12 percent increase relative to just 2010. Overall, the transition from a fossil fuel–dominant to a high-efficiency- and renewables-dominant global energy infrastructure, to rainforest preservation and an organic farming–dominant agricultural infrastructure needs to be dramatically accelerated for there to be any chance of hitting the IPCC's climate stabilization targets.

We also need to recognize that this transition needs to occur everywhere, in all countries, regardless of their current emissions or income levels. This becomes clear through some simple global emissions accounting. As of now, China and the US are by far most responsible for current total emissions. China's emissions represent 31 percent of the current global total and the United States accounts for another 14 percent. So, adding emissions from China and the US alone gets us to 45 percent of the global total. But we can look at this same statistic from the opposite direction: even after combining the emissions levels for China and the US, we still haven't accounted for fully 55 percent of total global emissions. We can then include the emissions totals for the twenty-seven countries of the European Union along with China and the US. This adds another 8 percent to current total emissions, getting us to 53 percent in total. This means that if we only pay attention to China, the US, and the European

Union countries, we still are neglecting the countries responsible for generating nearly half of current total global emissions. The point is that every place does matter if we really are going to hit the target of net-zero global emissions by no later than 2050. Zero emissions has to really mean *zero*, everywhere.

COP27 has been called Africa's COP. Indeed, Africa contributes only 3 percent to greenhouse gas emissions but suffers disproportionately from its negative effects. To be sure, the issue of who should pay for "loss and damages" from the climate crisis will occupy center stage at COP27. What are your thoughts on this matter? We already know, for instance, that the EU won't back climate damage funds talks at COP, and I don't think we should expect a different attitude from the United States. Is there a case to be made for climate reparations? Is there a better alternative?

Pollin: From an historical perspective, the high-income countries, starting with the US but also including Canada, Western Europe, Europe, and Australia, are almost entirely responsible for loading up the atmosphere with greenhouse gas emissions and causing climate change. They therefore should be primarily responsible for financing the Global Green New Deal. But more recently, as I noted above, China is producing much larger emissions than any other country. China can therefore not be let off the hook as a source of climate financing.

But we also need to recognize that high-income people in all countries and regions have massively larger carbon footprints than everyone else. The average carbon footprint of someone in the richest 10 percent of the global population is sixty times greater than of someone in the poorest 10 percent. From this perspective, the financing of a Global Green New Deal must fall disproportionately on the rich in all countries.

However, more generally, it is not accurate or constructive to consider the issue of financing the energy system transformation as simply a question of who bears how much of the overall burden. We also need to recognize that the overall burden is actually not excessively large and that building a global green economy will also generate huge benefits and opportunities. Consider, for example, just the following:

1. According to my own research and that of others, a global climate stabilization program capable of achieving the zero-emissions goal by 2050 will entail clean energy investment spending of roughly $4.5 trillion per year through 2050. This totals to about $120 trillion over the full period. These are eye-popping numbers from one angle. Yet they amount to an average of only about 2.5 percent of total global income (GDP) between now and 2050. In other words, we can transform the global energy system and save the planet while still spending something like 97 percent of total global income on everything besides clean energy investments. This is also while average incomes are rising over time.

2. Creating a clean global energy infrastructure will pay for itself over time and save money for all energy consumers. This is because energy efficiency investments, by definition, mean spending less money to get the same amount of energy services—like keeping one's home well lit and warm in the winter. Moreover, as I noted above, the costs of delivering a kilowatt of electricity from renewable energy sources is already lower, on average, than getting the same kilowatt from fossil fuels or nuclear power sources, and the costs of renewable energy are falling.

3. Building the clean energy infrastructure will be more decentralized than the current highly capital-intensive and big corporate–dominated fossil fuel infrastructure. Solar energy systems can be installed on rooftops and parking lots and in one's neighborhood. Wind turbines can be located on farmland without sacrificing productivity in crop or livestock cultivation. This, in turn, will create opportunities to expand access to energy into low-income communities throughout the world, including in the rural regions of low-income coun-

tries. Roughly half the people living in these regions do not currently have access to electricity at all.

Overall then, building the global clean energy economy should be understood as a great opportunity for investors and consumers, including, especially, small-scale investors such as both public and private cooperative enterprises.

That said, it will, of course, still be necessary to deliver the up-front money to pay for the initial investments. There is no shortage of big pots [of] money that can be tapped in equitable ways for this purpose. We can start with transferring funds out of military budgets for all countries. Since the US military budget amounts to 40 percent of global military spending, transferring, say, 5 percent of all military spending into global climate investments will mean that the US share of the funds will also amount to about 40 percent of the global total. We can also eliminate existing fossil fuel subsidies in all countries and convert them into clean energy subsidies. The central banks of rich countries can purchase green bonds to support investments both within their own countries as well as globally. They then will receive the revenues that will be generated by these investments. The central banks of rich countries did not hesitate to provide massive bailout funding to financial markets during the COVID lockdown, at levels of 10 percent or more of their countries' respective GDPs. The global green bond fund could amount to perhaps one-tenth the size of these bailout programs. Finally, carbon taxes can be a viable source of funds as long as the tax burden falls mostly on high-income consumers and most of the revenue generated by the tax is rebated back to middle- and low-income energy consumers.

The global financing project will then also need to be supported by private investors, at a level at least equal to that of government funds. Yet, we know that private investors will never deliver sufficient funds without public policies in place that enforce hard limits on profit opportunities through fossil fuel investments, if not eliminating such profit opportunities altogether. The windfall tax on oil company profits proposed in the US Congress by Senator Sheldon Whitehouse and Representative Ro Khanna is one good place to start.

The need for such measures has become ever clearer since the fiasco surrounding the pledges made by major private financial institutions coming out of last year's COP26 climate conference in Glasgow. Perhaps the biggest single story coming out of the Glasgow conference was the formation of the Glasgow Financial Alliance for Net Zero (GFANZ), a group of roughly five hundred financial sector firms holding $130 trillion in overall assets—i.e., something like one-third of total global private financial assets. At the conference, GFANZ members committed their institutions to supporting investments that will deliver a zero-emissions global economy by 2050. But now many of the biggest players in the coalition are abandoning their pledges. The explanation is simple, as reported in *Bloomberg Green*: "The revived fortunes of fossil fuels, especially coal, may explain some of the weakened resolve for decarbonization. Global bank lending to fossil fuel companies is up 15 percent to over $300 billion in the first nine months of this year from the same period in 2021." Justin Guay, director of climate finance strategy at the Sunrise Project summed up the matter perfectly in commenting: "Banks were happy to sign up to a big pageantry contest at COP26 and get a bunch of applause. But when they realized the world expected them to make good on what they said they would do, they have looked for convenient excuses to wiggle out of that responsibility."

Noam, what do you think about this matter? The so-called "triple crisis"— i.e., responsibility, mitigation, and adaptation—need to be addressed by the countries most responsible for climate breakdown, according to both climate activists and various governments of the Global South, including Egypt, the host of COP27.

Chomsky: We can refine the question. More accurately it is the rich in the rich countries who are most responsible for climate breakdown, and much more. Right now, working people in the super-rich United States are suffering from severe inflation, much of which is caused by the sharp rise in oil prices triggered by the Russian invasion of Ukraine. Meanwhile, the profits of the fossil fuel industrial complex are booming. One short-term remedy would be a tax on their rapacious pursuit of the vile maxim, proposed in legislation aimed at oil price gouging introduced by Senators Sherrod Brown and Sheldon Whitehouse, with receipts going directly to consumers. Much more far-reaching steps can easily be envisioned.

These questions should be considered against the background of the neoliberal class war of the past forty years, which has transferred some $50 trillion to the pockets of the super-rich 1 percent. Bob Pollin reminds us that the steady rise in real wages ended in the seventies as the business campaign against working people and the poor was taking shape, with the floodgates opened by Reagan and Thatcher. If real wages had continued to track productivity gains, "the average worker's hourly wage in 2021 would have been $61.94, not $25.18." And if the assault on the public had been curbed, big corporate CEO pay would not have risen "from being 33 times higher than the average worker in 1978 to 366 times higher in 2019—i.e., a more than *tenfold* increase in relative pay." That's only one part of the serious blows against working people and the poor that we expect, on institutional grounds, once the reins are cast off.

All of this is background for considering the "triple crisis." The Global Green New Deal should confront these issues directly and forcefully, not just by proper concern for the countries that have been victimized by global warming but also by dismantling the class basis of the depredations of past centuries, sometimes taking truly savage forms as in the recent neoliberal years.

The immediate crisis is too urgent for the radical social change that we should seek, but efforts to carry it forward should proceed in tandem with addressing urgent demands. If basic capitalist institutions remain in place, the Global Green New Deal will not proceed as far as it must if we are to have a livable world that values freedom and justice.

The Global Green New Deal may represent our only hope for an effective opportunity to address the challenge of global warming while also setting the world economy on a new course of sustainable development. Yet, it wasn't part of COP26's decarbonization concerns and it doesn't figure in the agenda of COP27. Why?

Chomsky: Who meets in the stately halls where agendas are devised?

Let's return to our discussion of the achievements of COP26. The most exciting, eliciting much euphoria, was the commitment of the great private financial institutions to devote up to $130 trillion to such noble projects as wiring Africa for solar power. The market to the rescue!—with a small footnote, as political economist Adam Tooze was unkind enough to add. The giants of finance will gladly make their lavish contribution to the Global Green New Deal if the International Monetary Fund and World Bank "de-risk" the loans by absorbing losses and "there is a carbon price that gives clean energy a competitive advantage."

As long as the vile maxim is firmly in place, their munificence has no bounds.

We return to the same conclusions. The Global Green New Deal cannot be delayed, but it must go hand in hand with raising consciousness and implementing measures to constrain and ultimately dismantle the institutional structures of capitalist autocracy.

Bob, you are one of the leading advocates of [the] Global Green New Deal. Why isn't this project gaining traction? Too idealistic for the taste of the real world where national interests still reign supreme? If so, what needs to be done?

Pollin: As I have tried to convey in my responses above, I don't see the Global Green New Deal as idealistic. I rather see it as the only viable program that can achieve the IPCC's climate stabilization goals in a way that also expands decent job opportunities and raises mass living standards in all regions of the world, at all levels of development. That includes increasing people's access to low-cost energy throughout the world. As such, the Global Green New Deal should attract overwhelming support, both among people who are committed around climate issues as well as those whose primary focus may be paying rent and keeping food on the table.

Achieving this level of support can only be achieved through organizing and educating. To take one example, for over a decade, labor and environment activists, such as those associated with the Labor Network for Sustainability and the BlueGreen Alliance in the US, have been working to build strong coalitions. Against steep odds, they have started to win some significant victories. This includes the endorsement of a robust green investment and just transition program in California by the union representing the state's oil refinery workers.

Of course, these and similar initiatives face relentless opposition from fossil fuel corporations and the full spectrum of interests aligned with them. A clear and coherent Global Green New Deal program will serve as one useful tool in the ongoing struggle to save the planet.

Noam Chomsky

TWENTY YEARS AFTER IRAQ WAR VOTE, US CONTINUES TO FLOUT INTERNATIONAL LAW

October 15, 2022

C. J. Polychroniou: *Noam, twenty years ago, the US Congress authorized the invasion of Iraq despite massive opposition to such an undertaking. Several leading Democratic senators ended up supporting the war authorization, including Joe Biden. For both historical and future purposes, what were the causes and ramifications of the Iraq war?*

Noam Chomsky: There are many kinds of support, ranging from outright to tacit. The latter includes those who regard it as a mistake but no more than that—a "strategic blunder," as in Obama's retrospective judgment. There were Nazi generals who opposed Hitler's major decisions as strategic blunders. We don't regard them as opponents of Nazi aggression. The same with regard to Russian generals who opposed the invasion of Afghanistan as a mistake, as many did.

If we can ever rise to the level of applying to ourselves the standards we rightly apply to others, then we will recognize that there has been little principled opposition to the Iraq War in high places, including the government and the political class. Much as in the case of the Vietnam War and other major crimes.

There was, of course, strong popular opposition. Characteristic was my own experience at MIT. Students demanded that we suspend classes so that they could participate in the huge public protests *before* the war was officially launched—something new in the history of imperialism—later meeting in a downtown church to discuss the impending crime and what it portended.

Much the same was true worldwide, so much so that Donald Rumsfeld came out with his famous distinction between Old and New Europe. Old Europe are the traditional democracies, old-fashioned fuddy-duddies whom we Americans can disregard because they are mired in boring concepts like international law, sovereign rights, and other outdated nonsense.

New Europe in contrast are the good guys: a few former Russian satellites who toe Washington's line, and one Western democracy, Spain, where Prime Minister [José María] Aznar went along with Washington, disregarding close to 100 percent of public opinion. He was rewarded by being invited to join Bush and Blair as they announced the invasion.

The distinction reflects our traditional deep concern for democracy.

It will be interesting to see if Bush and Blair are interviewed on this auspicious occasion. Bush was interviewed on the twentieth anniversary of his invasion of Afghanistan, another act of criminal aggression that was overwhelmingly opposed by international opinion, contrary to many claims, matters we have discussed before. He was interviewed by the *Washington Post*—in the Style section, where he was portrayed as a lovable, goofy grandpa playing with his grandchildren and showing off his portraits of famous people he had met.

There was an official reason for the US-UK invasion of Iraq, the "single question," as it was called from on high: Will Iraq terminate its nuclear weapons programs?

International inspectors had questioned whether there were such programs and asked for more time to investigate, but were dismissed. The US and its UK lackey were aiming for blood. A few months later the "single question" was answered, the wrong way. We may recall the amusing skit that Bush performed, looking under the table, "No not there," maybe in the closet, etc. All to hilarious laughter, though not in the streets of Baghdad.

The wrong answer required a change of course. It was suddenly discovered that the reason for the invasion was not the "single question," but rather our fervent wish to bring the blessings of democracy to Iraq. One leading Middle East scholar broke ranks and described what took place, Augustus Richard Norton, who wrote that "as fantasies about Iraq's weapons of mass destruction were unmasked, the Bush administration increasingly stressed the democratic transformation of Iraq, and scholars jumped on the democratization bandwagon." As did the loyal media and commentariat, as usual.

They did have some support in Iraq. A Gallup poll found that some Iraqis also leaped on the bandwagon: 1 percent felt that the goal of the invasion was to bring democracy to Iraq; 5 percent thought the goal was "to assist the Iraqi people." Most of the rest assumed that the goal was to take control of Iraq's resources and to reorganize the Middle East in US and Israeli interests—the "conspiracy theory" derided by rational Westerners, who understand that Washington and London would have been just as dedicated to the "liberation of Iraq" if its resources happened to be lettuce and pickles and the center of fossil fuel production was in the South Pacific.

By November 2007, when the US sought a status of forces agreement, the Bush administration came clean and stated the obvious: It demanded privileged access for Western energy companies to Iraqi fossil fuel resources and the right to establish US military bases in Iraq. The demands were endorsed by Bush in a "signing statement" the following January. The Iraqi parliament refused.

The ramifications of the invasion were multiple. Iraq has been devastated. What had been in many ways the most advanced country in the Arab world is a miserable wreck. The invasion incited ethnic (Shia-Sunni) conflict that had not existed before, now tearing not only the country but the whole region apart. ISIS emerged from the wreckage, almost taking over the country when the army trained and armed by the US fled at the sight of jihadis in pickup trucks waving rifles. They were stopped just short of Baghdad by Iranian-backed militias. And on, and on.

But none of this is a problem for the lovable, goofy grandpa or the educated classes in the US who now admire him as a serious states-man, called upon to orate about world affairs.

The reaction is much like that of Zbigniew Brzezinski, when asked about his boast to have drawn the Russians into Afghanistan and his support for the US effort to prolong the war and to block UN efforts to negotiate Russian withdrawal. It was a wonderful success, Brzezinski explained to the naive questioners. It achieved the goal of severely harming the USSR, he (dubiously) claimed, while conceding that it left a few "agitated Muslims," not to speak of a million cadavers and a ruined country.

Or like Jimmy Carter, who assured us that we owe "no debt" to the Vietnamese because "the destruction was mutual."

It is all too easy to continue. From a position of supreme power, with a loyal intellectual community, little is beyond reach.

The 2003 Iraq invasion was as criminal an act as Russia's invasion of Ukraine. But the reaction on the part of the Western community was very different than it has been in connection with the Russian invasion of Ukraine. No sanctions were imposed against the US, no freezing of the assets of US oligarchs, no demands that the US be suspended from the UN Security Council. Your comments on this matter?

Comment is hardly needed. The worst crime since World War II was the long US war against Indochina. No censure of the US could be contemplated. It was well understood at the UN that if the horrendous crimes were so much as discussed, the US would simply dismantle the offending institution. The West righteously condemns Putin's an-nexations and calls for punishment of this reincarnation of Hitler, but scarcely dares to utter a chirp of protest when the US authorizes Israel's illegal annexation of the Syrian Golan Heights and Greater Jerusalem, and Morocco's illegal annexation of Western Sahara. The list is long. The reasons are clear.

When the operative rules of world order are violated, reaction is swift. A clear illustration was when the World Court condemned the Holy State [the US] for international terrorism (in legalese, "unlawful use of force") in 1986, ordered it to terminate the crimes and pay substantial reparations to the victim (Nicaragua). Washington reacted by escalating the crimes. The press dismissed the judgment as worthless because the court is a "hostile forum" (according to the *New York Times*), as proven by its judgment against the US. The whole matter has been effectively wiped out of history, including the fact that the US is now the only state to have rejected a World Court decision—of course with total impunity.

It's an old story that "laws are spider webs through which the big flies pass and the little ones get caught." The maxim holds with particular force in the international domain, where the Godfather rules supreme.

By now the contempt for international law—except as a weapon against enemies—is barely concealed. It is reframed as the demand for a "rules-based international order" (where the Godfather sets the rules) to supersede the archaic UN-based international order, which bars US foreign policy.

What would have happened if Congress had refused to go along with the Bush administration's plan to invade Iraq?

One Republican voted against the war resolution ([Lincoln] Chafee). Democrats were split (29–21). If Congress had refused to go along, the Bush administration would have had to find other means to achieve the goals that Cheney-Rumsfeld-Wolfowitz and other hawks had laid out fairly clearly.

Many such means are available: sabotage, subversion, provoking (or manufacturing) some incident that could be used as a pretext for "retaliation." Or simply extending the brutal sanctions regime that was devastating the population. We may recall that both of the distinguished international diplomats who administered Clinton's program (via the UN) resigned in protest, condemning it as "genocidal."

The second, Hans von Sponeck, wrote an extremely illuminating book spelling out the impact in detail, *A Different Kind of War*. There was no need for an official ban of what is arguably the most important book on the build-up to the criminal invasion, and on the US sanctions weapon generally. Silent conformity sufficed. That might have crushed the population sufficiently as to call for "humanitarian intervention."

It is well to remember that there are no limits to cynicism if conformity and obedience prevail.

Noam Chomsky

BRAZIL'S RUNOFF ELECTION WILL HAVE ENORMOUS EFFECTS ON THE GLOBAL CLIMATE CRISIS

October 13, 2022

C. J. Polychroniou: *Noam, the eyes of the world were focused on Brazil's presidential election a couple of weeks ago, which pitted incumbent Jair Bolsonaro, a divisive far-right populist, against former leftist president Luiz Inácio Lula da Silva, who had served years in prison on charges of money laundering and corruption in a controversial trial. Neither candidate managed to win more than 50 percent of the vote, so there is going to be a runoff election at the end of the month. Why does Brazil's election matter so much to the world?*

Noam Chomsky: A century ago, Brazil was declared to be "the Colossus of the South," set to lead the hemisphere along with "the Colossus of the North." Since then, the northern Colossus has replaced Britain as the virtual ruler of the world, extending its power far beyond the dreams of what is now Washington's junior partner. The southern Colossus has stumbled. It is important to understand how.

In the 1950s, decolonization was beginning, and the former colonial societies were not only seeking independence but also advances

toward social justice and peaceful settlement of international disputes. The Non-Aligned Movement was formed. Other initiatives
were beginning. All of this was anathema to the US and its imperial
predecessors.

Brazil was part of the global effort under [Juscelino] Kubitschek
and in the early sixties, [Jânio] Quadros and [João] Goulart. The Kennedy administration was deeply concerned with these global developments, particularly in the traditional US preserve in Latin America.

In 1962, in a decision of historical importance, JFK shifted the role
of the Latin American military from "hemispheric defense" to "internal security," meaning war against the population. The effects were
graphically described by Kennedy-Johnson director of counterinsur-
gency Charles Maechling: the decision led to a shift from toleration
"of the rapacity and cruelty of the Latin American military" to "direct
complicity" in their crimes, to US support for "the methods of Hein-
rich Himmler's extermination squads."

A primary concern was Brazil, Latin America's powerhouse. The
JFK administration helped prepare the ground for a 1964 military
coup that overthrew the flourishing Brazilian democracy shortly after
Kennedy's assassination.

The destruction of democracy was welcomed by Kennedy-Johnson
ambassador to Brazil Lincoln Gordon as a "democratic rebellion," "a
great victory for the free world" that should "create a greatly improved
climate for private investments." This democratic rebellion was "the
single most decisive victory of freedom in the mid-twentieth century,"
Gordon continued, "one of the major turning points in world history"
in this period.

Gordon was right. The vicious military junta in Brazil was the first
of the neo-Nazi terror-and-torture national security states that then
spread over Latin America, a plague that reached Central America
under Reagan's murderous regime.

By the 1980s, the plague was declining in South America, less under
US control. In Argentina and Uruguay, truth commissions exposed
the horrors of the military regimes. Not in Brazil. The democratization process largely evaded the topic, apart from a Church-based

inquiry. The result is that many younger Brazilians are unaware of the terrible crimes, or not concerned. That enables a great admirer of the military regime like Bolsonaro to condemn the Brazilian generals for their "weakness": They did not murder thirty thousand people as their associates in Argentina did.

Plumbing the depths of depravity—a considerable achievement for this Trump admirer—when voting for the fraudulent impeachment of [Workers' Party] Dilma Rousseff, Bolsonaro dedicated his vote to her torturer, the chief torturer of the junta.

All of this passes with little comment, something else we are more than familiar with in the US.

The crushing of Brazilian democracy was one stage of a much broader process that is one of the most important and least discussed features of modern history: beating back the efforts of the former colonies to find a place in the global system. That idea was utterly intolerable to the US, which led the Western campaign to cut off this departure from good order, also virtually wiping it out of history.

Brazil resumed the process in the new century. It became one of the most respected and influential world powers during Lula's term in office (2003–2010), a "golden decade" in Brazil's history in the eyes of the World Bank. Together with his minister of foreign affairs Celso Amorim, Lula also led efforts to gain a voice for the Global South more generally. These positive developments went into reverse during the erratic and authoritarian Bolsonaro years.

The potential remains. The country has abundant resources that the world desperately needs. It is culturally and technologically advanced in many areas. It suffers under the Latin American curse of an ultra-privileged elite that has little commitment to the welfare of the country, a major reason for the sharp divergence in development between resource-rich Latin America and resource-poor East Asia in the past years, as economic historians have discussed.

Cooperating under leadership based on progressive popular movements, the two Colossi could be leading the world toward a brighter future. In a Trump-Bolsonaro alliance, they would be dragging the world to an abyss.

The most compelling immediate concern is the fate of the Amazon forests, mostly in Brazil. It has long been understood that if current trends persist, this core component of the "lungs of the Earth" will turn to savannah, unable to produce enough moisture to sustain itself. A major carbon sink that has been protecting all of us will turn to a carbon producer, impelling us toward catastrophe.

As in many other cases, the timescale of this tragedy has been severely underestimated. Brazilian researchers have shown that it has already begun to happen in some regions, which are reaching irreversible tipping points. The threat to survival has been sharply accelerated by Bolsonaro's support for illegal logging, mining, agribusiness expansion, and destruction of native reserves and the many tribes that inhabit them. Formally, they are protected under laws that are being cast aside in the interests of short-term profit and power.

Though not, of course, confined to Brazil, the crime against humanity is particularly grave there because of the scale. And it is particularly critical right now because the fate of the Amazon, and all that it entails, will be decided on October 30, the runoff for the elections. A Bolsonaro victory would likely doom the Amazon. A Lula victory might be able to save it, averting a disaster for Brazil and a catastrophe for life on earth.

The good news is that in the first round Lula came close to victory, much as polling had predicted. Collaboration with a center-left party rather close to Lula's Workers' Party would have led to victory. This and broader coalitions are now forming and might lead to victory on October 30.

The bad news is dual. Bolsonaro's vote was far beyond what polling predicted, and his candidates swept other offices: governors and parliament particularly, meaning that Lula's hands will be tied even if elected. The far-right surge even included such monstrous figures as Ricardo Salles, the point man for Bolsonaro's campaign to enrich the criminals who were destroying the Amazon under his watch.

A week later, an election will take place in the northern Colossus with similar stakes but of even greater import given power relations. The denialist party is poised to add Congress to its conquests. The most reactionary Supreme Court in memory is already firmly in its hands and is likely to grease the way to the campaign to turn the country into an Orbán-style "illiberal democracy" where a minority party of the far right will be able to maintain power and drive the country to an extremist Christian nationalism. None of this is at all concealed.

That grotesque outcome will, in fact, not matter much as environmental destruction goes out of control under the hands of those dedicated to enhancing corporate profits whatever the human consequences.

In answer to the question, there is a fateful week ahead.

Opinion surveys had shown Lula leading Bolsonaro by more than 10 percentage points, but the race turned out to be much tighter than anticipated, and, in fact, Bolsonaro swept the state and senate races. What happened?

We have to withhold judgment until the facts are in. One possibility is that what happened is similar to what has been studied in depth in the US.

In both countries, the huge evangelical vote is by now fairly solidly in the hands of the far right and its propaganda messages about the fires of hell if the accomplice of the devil triumphs. In the US, that traces back to the GOP campaigns of the seventies to shift to "culture wars" to gain political power.

Trump voters regard pollsters as part of the hated elite that is supposedly leading the "Great Replacement" and grooming children for sexual perversion (not an exaggeration of current right-wing discourse) and therefore do not respond to them accurately, if at all. That is very likely a factor in Brazil as well. There may well be studies of the matter, but I don't know of them.

Another factor is suggested by the fact that many of the right-wingers elected seem to be little known, meaning that voters may have not even been aware of their programs—a fact familiar in the US as well, as extensively documented. Pre-election, Bolsonaro was lavishly distributing state funds to potential voters, using a mysterious "secret budget" of public funds, possibly supplemented by private funds from wealthy supporters in Brazil and the US. What was the impact? We can surmise, but do not know.

What we do know is that the stakes are very high.

The election campaign was marked by a series of violent incidents between supporters of Bolsonaro and Lula, and it's highly unlikely that the climate will be different now that the two candidates are heading to [a] second round. What's the main cause of the extreme polarization that characterizes contemporary Brazilian society?

I should defer here to people who know far more about Brazil than I do.

Some aspects of the polarization are not obscure. One was already mentioned. The polarization goes far back. Inequality is deeply rooted. A very rich, mostly white minority lives in luxury not far from miserable slums, where people lack access even to food and water. Furthermore, the rich have little commitment to the society. They evade taxes, export their capital, import luxury goods, and have second homes in Paris—a pattern increasingly familiar in the US after forty years of the brutal class war misleadingly framed in terms of market worship.

On the surface, Brazil gives the impression of a well-functioning, multiracial society, far more so than the US. That's on the surface. Behind the veil, the white rulers are deeply racist and have harsh class prejudice. One reason for their contempt for Lula, scarcely concealed, is that he is a mere industrial worker lacking formal education. Not the "right kind of person" to be in the presidential palace. Even a white face doesn't protect him from the contempt, in his case class based, and deepened by his initiatives at social inclusion of Afro-Brazilians and Indigenous communities as well as social welfare for the undeserving poor. Again, the resonances in the US are too obvious to discuss.

The polarization may be taking sharper forms today, as is happening in much of the world, but it is drawing from social pathology that runs deep.

Bolsonaro has long raised doubts about Brazil's electoral process. Is it likely that he might refuse to go if he loses the runoff vote at the end of the month, especially with his party having the most seats in both chambers of the congress? How far will Brazil's military back him?

We can speculate idly or devote our efforts to restricting the possibilities. Brazil is not the US, but the questions are not unfamiliar there. Both countries are awash in guns, a recent phenomenon in Brazil as Bolsonaro has opened to arsenals, overwhelmingly to his supporters. There are heavily armed militias that control areas that are barely accessible to the police. Civilian control of the military, and the major police forces, is less firmly institutionalized than in the US—where questions also arise.

In the US, large parts of Republican voters have called for violence if it is necessary to "save the country" from the devils intent on destroying the white race, Christianity, the family. . . . There are similar elements in Brazil. Both countries are plagued by demagogues with the talent to tap the ugliest currents that rot the society from below. They are visible, prominent, influential, close to power.

If power is allowed to fall into their hands, we will be facing the nightmare of a Western Hemisphere in the hands of the two Colossi bent on driving to world to destruction.

Noam Chomsky

US MUST JOIN GLOBAL CALL FOR NEGOTIATIONS AS RUSSIA ESCALATES ACTIONS*

September 28, 2022

C. J. Polychroniou: *Seven months after Putin's criminal invasion of Ukraine, the war has reached a turning point. It has come home to Russia with Putin's call for "partial mobilization," and annexation referendums have been staged. What does the bolstering of Russian forces in Ukraine mean for Russia and Ukraine? Are Putin's orders for military call-up an admission that Russia is no longer conducting a "special military operation" in Ukraine?*

Noam Chomsky: What has come home to Russia is unclear. There are reports of protests and forced conscription, alongside of appeals to defend Mother Russia from yet another Western invasion, which, like those [going] back to Napoleon, will be crushed. Such appeals might have resonance. Historical memories may be deep. What the outcome will be we can only guess.

---

* This interview has been lightly edited for clarity.

From the first day, it was a criminal invasion, never a "special military operation," but the pretense in the Kremlin is still maintained. The mobilization is unlikely to have much effect on the war for some time to come, and what kind of effect is unclear. The failures and incompetence of the Russian military have been a continuing surprise to most well-placed analysts. That may well extend to mobilization, training, and supply of equipment. Any meaningful bolstering of Russian forces from these efforts is likely to be well ahead, probably after the winter months. I suppose Russia could move forces from other regions, but whether the leadership has the capability or will to do that, I don't know.

The mobilization and referenda seem to indicate a plan for a long, drawn-out war of attrition. If the mobilization does succeed in shifting the tide of the war, that increases the risks of inducing the West to up the ante with more advanced weapons, perhaps reaching to Russia itself as President Zelenskyy has requested, so far rebuffed. It's not hard to envision scenarios that lead on to catastrophic consequences.

That's just the beginning. The impact of the war goes far beyond: to the millions facing starvation with the curtailing of grain and fertilizer exports, now partially relieved, though there is little information about how much, and most important of all and least discussed, the sharp reversal of the limited international efforts to address the looming climate crisis, a colossal crime against humanity.

While huge resources are being wasted in destruction and the fossil fuel industries are gleefully celebrating the opening up of new fields for exploitation to poison the atmosphere even more, scientists are regularly informing us that their dire warnings have been far too conservative. Thus, we have recently learned that the Middle East region, not far away from embattled Ukraine, is heating almost twice as fast as the rest of the world, with an estimated 9°F rise by the end of the century, and that sea levels in the Eastern Mediterranean are expected to rise a meter by midcentury and up to 2.5 meters by 2100. Of course, it doesn't stop there. The consequences are almost impossible to envision.

Meanwhile, the region continues to be the global center for heating the world to the brink of survivability and soon beyond. And while Israel and Lebanon may soon be sinking into the sea, they are squabbling about which will have the honor of virtually destroying both of them by producing the fossil fuels at their maritime borders, acts of lunacy duplicated around the world. Escalating the war in Ukraine in the face of such realities reaches levels of imbecility that are hard to capture in words.

Russia hopes to annex four occupied regions of Ukraine with staged referendums. Russia used this tactic before, in 2014, with the Crimean status referendum, although the two situations may be quite different. The voting in the Russian-held Donetsk, Luhansk, Zaporizhzhia, and Kherson regions of Ukraine is clearly illegal under international law, but I suppose this hardly matters to a power that has launched a criminal invasion against an independent country. What does Russia hope to achieve with the "referendums"? And what happens next, especially since Russia has had a difficult time so far establishing order in the occupied territories?

The referenda in this case lack any credibility. It was different in the case of the Crimea referendum in 2014. For one thing, the Russian takeover of Crimea didn't happen in a vacuum. For another, there's reason to suppose that Crimeans looked to Russia more than to Ukraine. Though the referenda were not internationally accepted, it was recognized by many that the results were not very surprising. That's not the case with the current referenda.

Like the mobilization, the staged referenda indicate Russian plans for longtime occupation and a war of attrition. Though they clearly pose another impediment for negotiations over the fate of the regions where they take place, they may not completely close the window, as Anatol Lieven discusses.

It's true that international law means as little to Russia as to the other great powers that launch criminal invasions against independent countries, the US well in the lead. With impunity, thanks to its power.

What does Russia hope to achieve? As we've discussed, there are two ways to approach this question.

One way is to explore the depths of Putin's mind, as George W. Bush did when he looked into Putin's eyes, saw his "soul," and pronounced it good. And as many amateur psychologists do today, with supreme confidence.

A second way is to look at what Putin and his associates are saying. As in the case of other leaders, this may or may not reflect their hidden intentions. What matters, however, is that what they say can be a basis for negotiations if there is any interest in bringing the horrors to an end before they get even worse. That's how diplomacy works.

The second way suggests that what Russia hopes to achieve is primarily neutralization of Ukraine and "demilitarization and denazification." The former means cancellation of the programs of the past years to integrate Ukraine de facto within NATO. That approaches President Zelenskyy's proposals as recently as last March for neutralization with security guarantees. The latter would be a topic for discussion in serious negotiations. It might be spelled out as an agreement to refrain from placing heavy weapons aimed at Russia in Ukraine, no further joint military maneuvers, etc. In short, a status rather like Mexico.

Those are topics for negotiations—if, of course, there is a serious interest in ending the conflict.

We might recall that most of the world, including a large majority of Germans and much of the rest of Europe, is calling for negotiations now, while the US insists that priority must be to severely weaken Russia, hence no negotiations.

There are other issues to be settled, primarily Crimea and the Donbas region. An optimal solution would be internationally sponsored referenda on the various options that have been proposed. That is presumably not possible now, but a serious effort on negotiations might improve the prospects. Recall that we have good evidence that as recently as last April there were serious Ukraine-Russia negotiations under Turkish auspices and that the US-UK opposed them.

As to what happens next, that will depend on choices made by those involved, primarily Ukraine and Russia, of course, but we can hardly pretend to be merely observers from afar. See again Lieven's commentary, just cited.

Lieven is not the only informed analyst who regards peaceful diplomatic settlement as a diminishing but still live option. Another is John Quigley, who has been deeply involved in these issues since the early nineties, when he was the US State Department representative in the OSCE [Organization for Security and Co-operation in Europe] efforts to resolve contested issues in Ukraine after the collapse of the USSR, particularly the status of Crimea and Donbas, his special concern. We have already discussed some of his current thinking, as of June 2022.

Quigley recognizes that though negotiations are currently stalled, "At some point, however, hopefully sooner than later, there will be a negotiated settlement that will need to deal with the Donbas region in Eastern Ukraine" as well as Crimea. On Crimea, he recommends pursuing Zelenskyy's suggestion that perhaps "the two sides could arrange a process of discussion about Crimea, a process that he said could last 15 years." On Donbas, Quigley writes that "if Ukraine does anything even close to implementing the Minsk agreement [the 2015 Ukraine-Russia agreement under French-German sponsorship that called for a degree of autonomy for Donbas within a federal Ukraine], Russia could say that the aim of its invasion has been accomplished," and a settlement could be reached.

Only a few days ago, French president Emmanuel Macron, who has been more closely involved in current negotiation efforts than any other figure, expressed somewhat similar views on CNN. In his opinion, at the time of Zelenskyy's election in 2019, a settlement favorable to Ukraine could have been reached along the lines of the Minsk agreement. He also feels that options for diplomacy remain open.

Whether such assessments are accurate, we do not know. There is one and only one way to find out: try. That won't happen, Quigley concludes, if "the U.S. goal is less to force Russia out of Ukraine than to fight Russia to the last Ukrainian"—a "reasonable" assessment, he reluctantly comments.

That is the one factor in the mix that we can hope to influence, something that cannot be emphasized too strongly.

President Zelenskyy urged the United Nations (UN) to punish Russia for its invasion of Ukraine by stripping it of its security council veto vote. Just a few days ago, the EU president made similar calls. While, technically speaking, a country can be expelled from the UN for "persistent violation" of the principles of the Charter, isn't this a misguided proposal? Isn't it also true that the argument that Russia may not even be a member of the UN is invalid on account of the fact that the continuation of the USSR's membership by the Russian Federation, which Ukraine itself accepted in 1991, is in line with long-established procedures within the UN?

One can easily appreciate President Zelenskyy's sentiments, but whatever the technicalities may be, the very fact that the proposal is being seriously considered is enlightening. Did anyone consider punishing the US in this manner when it invaded Iraq, to take only one example of its "persistent violation" of the core principle of the Charter that bars "the threat or use of force" in international affairs (with exceptions irrelevant here)? These violations are not just persistent but extremely serious, matters we need not review even though they are virtually unspeakable in the US mainstream.

We should, I think, keep our minds focused on what should be the central issue for us: US policy. Should we accept the official US position of fighting the war to severely weaken Russia, precluding diplomatic settlement? Or should we press the US government to join most of the world, including Germans and other Europeans, in seeking a way to end the horrors before they bring further tragedy, not only to Ukraine but also far beyond?

Noam Chomsky

THE US AND ISRAEL ARE STANDING IN THE WAY OF AN IRAN NUCLEAR AGREEMENT

September 24, 2022

C. J. Polychroniou: *Noam, the US and Iran are at odds with each other, having difficulty even talking to each other. Why do they hate each other so much, and how much of a role does Israel's shadow play in this continuous drama?*

Noam Chomsky: At the risk of sounding like a broken record, I'd like to say a few words, once again, on why I feel that the entire framework in which this issue is discussed is seriously distorted—yet another tribute to the enormous power of the US propaganda system.

The US government has been telling us for years that Iranian nuclear programs are one of the gravest threats to world peace. Israeli authorities have made it clear that they will not tolerate this danger. The US and Israel have acted violently to overcome this grave threat: cyberwar and sabotage (which the Pentagon regards as aggression that merits violence in self-defense), numerous assassinations of Iranian scientists, constant threats of use of force ("all options are open") in violation of international law (and if anyone were to care, the US Constitution).

Evidently, it is regarded as a most serious issue. If so, we surely want to see whether there is some way to lay it to rest. There is: establish a nuclear weapons–free zone (NWFZ) in the Middle East, with inspections—which, we know, can work very well. Even US intelligence agrees that before the US dismantled the joint agreement on nuclear weapons ([Joint Comprehensive Plan of Action] JCPOA), international inspections of Iran's nuclear program were successful.

That would solve the alleged problem of Iranian nuclear programs, ending the serious threat of war. What then is the barrier?

Not the Arab states, which have been actively demanding this for decades. Not Iran, which supports the measure. Not the Global South—G-77, 134 "developing nations," most of the world—which strongly supports it. Not Europe, which has posed no objections.

The barrier is the usual two outliers: the US and Israel.

There are various pretexts, which we may ignore. The reasons are known to all: The US will not allow the enormous Israeli nuclear arsenal, the only one in the region, to be subject to international inspection.

In fact, the US does not officially recognize that Israel has nuclear weapons, though, of course, it is not in doubt. The reason, presumably, is that to do so would invoke US law, which, arguably, would render the massive US aid flow to Israel illegal—a door that few want to open.

All of this is virtually undiscussable in the US, outside of arms control circles. On rare occasions, the major media have come close to bringing up the forbidden topic. A year ago, *New York Times* editors proposed "One Way Forward on Iran: A Nuclear-Weapons-Free Persian Gulf."

Note: Persian Gulf, not Middle East. The reason, the editors explain, is that Israel's nuclear weapons are "unacknowledged and nonnegotiable." Filling in the gaps, they are unacknowledged by the US and are nonnegotiable by US fiat.

In brief, there is a straightforward approach to addressing this grave threat to world peace, but it is blocked by the global hegemon, whose power is so enormous that the topic can barely even be discussed. Rather, we must adopt the framework imposed by US power and keep to the deliberations over renewing some kind of agreement over Iranian nuclear weapons.

Another matter that must be sidelined, though it is so obvious that even the grandest propaganda system cannot entirely efface it, is that the current crisis arose when the US unilaterally destroyed the JCPOA, over the strenuous objections of all other signers and the UN Security Council, which had endorsed it unanimously. The US then imposed harsh sanctions on Iran to punish it for the US dismantling of the agreement. Again, other signers strenuously objected, but they obeyed: The threat of US retribution is too awesome, as in many other cases; notoriously the crushing Cuba sanctions, opposed by the whole world apart from the two usual outliers, but obediently observed.

Again, I apologize for continually reiterating all of this. It must, however, be understood. Having made that gesture, let's accept reality, subordinating ourselves to the mighty US propaganda system, and keep to the permitted framework of discussion.

Turning finally to the question, first, Israel's role is more than shadow play. Israel is right at the center of the story, both in its constant violent attacks on Iran and in the "unacknowledged" nuclear arsenal that blocks a path to diplomatic settlement, thanks to its superpower protector.

On mutual hate, we should remember that we are talking about governments. The US and Iranian governments were close allies from 1953, when the US overthrew the parliamentary government of Iran and reinstalled the Shah's dictatorship, until 1979, when a popular uprising overthrew the Shah and Iran switched from favored friend to reviled enemy.

Iraq then invaded Iran and the incoming Reagan administration turned to lavish support for its friend Saddam. Iran suffered huge casualties, many from chemical weapons, while the Reaganites looked away and even tried to shift responsibility to Iran for Saddam's murderous chemical war against Iraqi Kurds. Finally, direct US intervention swung the war in Iraq's favor. After the war, President Bush Sr. invited Iraqi nuclear engineers to the US for advanced training in weapons production, a serious threat to Iran, of course. And the US imposed harsh sanctions on Iran. So, the story continues.

US charges against Iran are too familiar to need reviewing.

Unsurprisingly, nuclear talks between the US and Iran have stalled again and it is unlikely that there will be a deal any time soon—if at all—to restore their 2015 nuclear deal. First, what do you see as the stumbling blocks in these talks? And didn't Iran already make a huge concession when it agreed to the 2015 nuclear agreement without requiring that Israel does away with its own arsenal of nuclear weapons?

Negotiations, through European intermediaries, seem to have been put on hold until after the US November elections, at least. There are outstanding disagreements on a number of issues. The most important, for now, are reported to be Iranian foot-dragging on inspection of traces of uranium that bear on whether Iran had an undeclared weapons program before 2003. In contrast, Israeli nuclear weapons programs are nonnegotiable by US fiat, not even subject to inspection.

Iran's relationship with Russia has been further strengthened since the start of the Ukraine war. Do such moves on the part of Tehran's rulers indicate the possibility of a complete break from the West?

It's hard to see how the break should go much further. Iran's closer relations with Russia are part of a general global realignment, its contours unclear, involving the major Asian states and Russia-China links.

How likely is it that Israel will attack Iran's nuclear facilities? Israel has repeatedly attacked these facilities with sabotage and assassination. It is likely to proceed with further efforts to prevent Iran from gaining the capability to produce nuclear weapons—which many countries have.

Iranian leaders have consistently claimed that they have no intention of producing nuclear weapons. I have no idea what their strategic thinking might be. Perhaps they are thinking along the lines of US nuclear doctrine: that "nuclear weapons must always be available, at the ready, because they 'cast a shadow over any crisis or conflict'" (*Essentials of Post–Cold War Deterrence*, STRATCOM 1995). As Daniel Ellsberg has emphasized, in that respect nuclear weapons are constantly used to enable other aggressive actions with impunity.

Whatever the motives, for Iran or any other state, these weapons must be eliminated from the Earth. NWFZs are a step in this direction. A more far-reaching step is the UN Treaty on the Prohibition of Nuclear Weapons (TPNW), now in force, though without the participation of the nuclear states. Iran was active in negotiation of the TPNW and was one of 122 states that voted in favor its adoption, though it has not yet signed it. These are concerns that should be uppermost in our minds, for all states, for the security of all of life on Earth.

Noam Chomsky

THE WAR IN UKRAINE HAS ENTERED A NEW PHASE

September 22, 2022

C. J. Polychroniou: *Noam, after seven months of conflict, Russia and Ukraine find themselves in a situation that is hard to get out of. Russia is suffering great losses, and a recent Ukrainian counteroffensive has recaptured dozens of towns and villages in the northeast of the country. Under these circumstances, it seems that neither side is eager to pursue a peace settlement. Firstly, are you surprised by Russia's problems on the battlefield, and, secondly, do you agree with the statement made recently by the minister in charge of the Hungarian Prime Minister's Office that Moscow still has a major advantage over Kyiv and that it can declare victory whenever it wants?*

Noam Chomsky: First, let me make it clear that I have nothing original to say about the military situation, and have no expert knowledge in this area. What I know is what's reported, almost entirely from Western sources.

The general picture is that Russia has suffered a devastating defeat, demonstrating the utter incompetence of the Russian military and the remarkable capacities of the Ukrainian army provided with advanced US armaments and detailed intelligence information about the disposition of Russian forces, a tribute to the courage of the Ukrainian fighters and to the intensive US training, organization, and supply of the Ukrainian army for almost a decade.

There's plenty of evidence to support this interpretation, which is close to exceptionless apart from detail. A useful rule of thumb whenever there is virtual unanimity on complex and murky issues is to ask whether something is perhaps omitted. Keeping to mainstream Western sources, we can indeed find more that perhaps merits attention.

Reuters reports a "Western official" whose assessment is that:

> There's an ongoing debate about the nature of the Russian drawdown, however it's likely that in strict military terms, this was a withdrawal, ordered and sanctioned by the general staff, rather than an outright collapse. . . . Obviously, it looks really dramatic. It's a vast area of land. But we have to factor in the Russians have made some good decisions in terms of shortening their lines and making them more defensible, and sacrificing territory in order to do so.

There are varying interpretations of the equipment losses in the Russian flight/withdrawal. There is no need to review the familiar picture. A more nuanced version is given by *Washington Post* journalists on the scene, who report scattered and ambiguous evidence. They also review online video and satellite imagery indicating that the destroyed and abandoned military vehicles may have been at an equipment hub. Examining the videos, Lt. Gen. Ben Hodges, former commander of US Army Europe, concludes that the destruction was mostly at a staging area where "Russian forces stopped for fuel or were waiting for a mission when they fled," the total amounting to a tank company that typically has about ten or eleven tanks.

As one expects in a war zone, there is ample ambiguity, but little doubt that it was a major victory for Ukraine and its US-NATO backers. I don't think that Putin could simply "declare victory" after this humiliating setback, as the Hungarian prime minister suggests. On the prospects for a peace settlement, so little is reported or discussed that there is little to say.

Little, but not nothing. In the current issue of *Foreign Affairs*, the major establishment journal, Fiona Hill and Angela Stent—highly regarded policy analysts with close government connections— report that:

> According to multiple former senior US officials we spoke with, in April 2022, Russian and Ukrainian negotiators appeared to have tentatively agreed on the outlines of a negotiated interim settlement. The terms of that settlement would have been for Russia to withdraw to the positions it held before launching the invasion on February 24. In exchange, Ukraine would promise not to seek NATO membership and instead receive security guarantees from a number of countries.

On dubious evidence, Hill and Stent blame the failure of these efforts on the Russians, but do not mention that British prime minister Boris Johnson at once flew to Kyiv with the message that Ukraine's Western backers would not support the diplomatic initiative, followed by US defense secretary Lloyd Austin, who reiterated the official US position that Washington's goal in the war is to "weaken" Russia, meaning that negotiations are off the table.

Whether such initiatives continue, we do not know. If they do, they would not lack popular support, not only in the Global South but even in Europe, where "77 percent of Germans believe that the West should initiate negotiations to end the Ukraine war." Surprisingly, more than half of Slovaks are reported to favor a Russian victory.

Suppose that negotiations fail or are not even contemplated. What then? The general expert consensus seems to be that there will be a protracted war, with all of its tragic consequences. General Austin and other US officials have held that Ukraine can drive Russia out of all of Ukraine, presumably including Crimea. Suppose the prospect arises.

Then follows the crucial question: Will Putin pack up his bags and slink away silently to obscurity or worse? Or will he use the conventional weapons that all agree he has to escalate the attack on Ukraine? The US is gambling on the former but is not unaware of the nature of this gamble with the lives of Ukrainians, and well beyond. The *New York Times* reports that:

> Some American officials express concern that the most dangerous moments are yet to come, even as Mr. Putin has avoided escalating the war in ways that have, at times, baffled Western officials. He has made only limited attempts to destroy critical infrastructure or to target Ukrainian government buildings. He has not attacked the supply hubs outside Ukraine. While he has directed low-level cyberattacks against Ukrainian targets every week, they have been relatively unsophisticated, especially when compared to capabilities that Russia has shown it has, including in the SolarWinds attack on American government and commercial systems that was discovered just before Mr. Biden took office.

The same report cites Putin's warning that, "if the situation continues to develop in this way—referring to US participation in the recent Ukrainian counter-offensive—the answer will be more serious." To illustrate, Putin "described recent Russian cruise missile attacks against Ukrainian infrastructure as 'warning strikes.'"

The Ukrainian military understands the warning very well. Ukrainian commander-in-chief Gen. Valery Zaluzhny had written that Russian cruise missiles "could strike across the country with 'impunity,'" adding that "limited nuclear war cannot be ruled out."

As we all know, the escalation ladder from limited to terminal nuclear war is all too easy to climb.

To put it simply, the US position that the war must continue to severely weaken Russia, blocking negotiations, is based on a quite remarkable assumption: that facing defeat, Putin will pack his bags and slink away to a bitter fate. He will not do what he easily can: strike across Ukraine with impunity using Russia's conventional weapons, destroying critical infrastructure and Ukrainian government buildings, attacking the supply hubs outside Ukraine, moving on to sophisticated cyberattacks against Ukrainian targets. All of this is easily within Russia's conventional capacity, as US government and the

Ukrainian military command acknowledge—with the possibility of escalation to nuclear war in the not remote background.

The assumption is worth contemplating. It is too quickly evaded.

Also worth contemplating is the fact that "Mr. Putin has avoided escalating the war in ways that have, at times, baffled Western officials." The same puzzlement has been expressed before. The US and UK were baffled by the Russian offensive, severely overestimating its scale from the start. "We assumed they would invade a country the way we would have invaded a country," as one British official put it.

When the US-UK invade a country, they go for the jugular, destroying communications, transportation, energy systems, anything needed to keep the country going. To the surprise of the US-UK planners, Putin didn't do that. The press reports that "in Kyiv and much of the western part of the country, prewar life has largely returned for civilians. People eat in restaurants, drink in bars, dance and enjoy lazy summer days in parks."

Far from the US-UK style of war.

Western military analysts offer reasons why "Putin's Bombers Could Devastate Ukraine, but He's Holding Back." Whatever the reasons, the fact remains.

The gamble with the lives of Ukrainians, and far beyond, remains as well, eliciting little attention. Something else that merits contemplation.

It's also useful finally to reiterate a familiar word of warning. Propaganda never ceases and rises to peaks of intensity at moments of crisis. Triumphant claims are always worth inspection. To take one example, much has been made of India's alleged break with Russia over the war, based on a few words by Prime Minister Modi at a Samarkand meeting with Putin. The quoted words are "I know that today's era is not of war." Omitted is that Modi went on to stress that "the relationship between India and Russia has deepened manifold. We also value this relationship because we have been such friends who have been with each other every moment for the last several decades and the whole world also knows how Russia's relationship with India has been and how India's relationship with Russia has been and therefore the world also knows that it is an unbreakable friendship."

The Ukrainian government is pursuing backroom negotiations for the delivery of advanced American-made weapons, according to some reports. In addition, President Zelenskyy and his government have put forward a document of long-term security guarantees from the West that would link Ukraine's future security directly to the presence of NATO forces in the country. Unexpectedly enough, Moscow immediately shut down the proposal and the vice president of the Russian Security Council called it "a prologue to the third world war." Is the so-called Kyiv Security Treaty a path toward a peace settlement or a sure way not only to keep the conflict going on indefinitely but also to escalate it to a higher level?

It is hard to imagine that any Russian government would tolerate NATO forces in Ukraine. That has been understood for thirty years by high-level US officials who have any knowledge of the region, and it's even more unlikely now. What Russia might tolerate is a weakened version of this demand: long-term security guarantees with what's called in diplomacy "strategic ambiguity," coupled with termination of the plans for NATO membership for Ukraine. In the past, Zelenskyy has suggested something like that. Whether that remains an option, we, of course, cannot know until an effort is undertaken to reach a diplomatic settlement, as apparently it was by Ukraine and Russia as recently as last April.

The Biden administration, the Pentagon particularly, has been careful not to escalate its participation in the war so rapidly as to elicit the Russian reaction that hasn't occurred, baffling Washington and London. Congress is another matter. It seems hell-bent on hurtling to disaster. Calls for no-fly zones and other very dangerous initiatives have been blocked by the Pentagon, but plenty of saber-rattling continues. That extends to China, or to keep to the rules, what we should call the "Indo-Pacific area of the North Atlantic" in the light of the decisions at the recent NATO summit.

Nancy Pelosi's visit to Taiwan was reckless enough, but congressional hawks, a bipartisan collective, are determined to raise the possibility of terminal nuclear war even higher.

A major step in this direction was taken on September 14, when the Senate Foreign Relations Committee approved the Taiwan Policy Act of 2022, cosponsored by Committee Chairman Robert Menendez (D-NJ) and Lindsey Graham (R-SC).

The act calls for Taiwan to be designated as a "major non-NATO ally." Taiwan is to be provided with $4.5 billion in security assistance over the next four years, part of establishing "a comprehensive training program with the Government of Taiwan." The act also seeks "more interoperability between the US and Taiwanese militaries [along with] joint US-Taiwan contingency tabletop exercises, war games and what the bill calls 'robust, operationally relevant, or full-scale' military exercises," *Asia Times* reports.

Furthermore, the act declares US government policy to be "to provide the people of Taiwan with de facto diplomatic treatment equivalent to foreign countries, nations, states, governments, or similar entities" and to remove "any undue restrictions" on the ability of US officials at any level "to interact directly and routinely with their counterparts in the Government of Taiwan."

Former Australian defense official Mike Scrafton observes that "the Chinese cannot but regard this as a provocative de facto recognition of Taiwan's independence." Under international law, which regards Taiwan as part of China, it is "a patent infringement of China's sovereignty and a fundamental weakening of the one-China policy." Once again, the US "rules-based order," in defiance of international law, is seen to be nothing other "than preservation of US hegemony." If passed, "the Act would be a game-changer and reflects the American preparedness to engage in a war that would be disastrous for the region and the world." It should lead Australia to rethink its commitment to the US-dominated regional system.

The wording of the act seems to be modeled on the programs prior to the Russian invasion that were turning Ukraine into a "de facto NATO member," in the words of the US military, matters we have discussed elsewhere.

The Biden administration opposes the measure, as it did Pelosi's action. Even more than that exercise in self-promotion, the Menendez-

Graham measure would be a serious blow to the "strategic ambiguity" of the one-China policy that has kept the peace in a volatile region for half a century.

The European Union is pressuring China and India to support the idea of a price cap on Russian oil. Russia, of course, has said that it will not sell oil to countries that impose a price limit, so the question here is twofold: first, how likely is it that China and India will go along with the EU's suggestion, especially since both countries have not only increased their Russian oil purchases since Moscow's invasion of Ukraine but are buying at discounted prices, and, second, what would be the political ramifications in the event that they succumbed to pressure and did go along?

All of this is part of the reconfiguration of global order that has been going on for some time and was spurred onward by Putin's criminal aggression. A side consequence was to deliver Europe into Washington's hands. This most welcome gift was provided free of charge by Vladimir Putin when he rejected French President Macron's last-minute efforts to avert an invasion, at the end with undisguised contempt, a major contribution to Washington's Atlanticist project of global hegemony.

The core issue at stake, I think, is unipolarity-multipolarity. Since the US took over the reins from Britain eighty years ago, reaching far beyond Britain's dreams, it has sought a unipolar world, and to a substantial extent it has realized that goal, in ways we need not review. There has always been resistance.

In many ways the most significant, and least discussed, form of resistance has been the effort of former colonies to find a place in the international order: UNCTAD [United Nations Conference on Trade and Development], the New International Economic Order, the New International Information Order, and many other initiatives. These were crushed by imperial power, sometimes reaching the level of assassination (the very important case of Patrice Lumumba) if other means did not suffice. Some elements survive, like BRICS [the economic alliance of Brazil, Russia, India, China and South Africa].

Most significantly in the modern global scene, rising China leads the effort to develop a multipolar order.

Right now, the long-term conflict is manifested in many concrete ways. One is the intense US effort to impede China's technological development and to "encircle" it with a ring of heavily armed US satellites. Another is the NATO-based US-run Atlanticist project, now given a shot in the arm by Putin's criminality, and recently extended formally to the Indo-Pacific region. The major competing element is China's huge development and investment project, the Belt and Road Initiative backed by the Shanghai Cooperation Organization, encompassing Central Asia and by now reaching well beyond. At an ideological level, the confrontation sets the UN-based international order against the rules-based international order (with the US setting the rules). The latter is adopted with little controversy or even notice in the US.

The important specific issues raised in the question find their place within this broader framework. Their resolution depends on how the broad process of reorganization of the international order develops. A highly uncertain matter, one of great portent.

Not in the distant background is a more fundamental matter, which cannot be put aside. Unless the great powers find ways to accommodate to confront the most important threats that have arisen in human history—environmental destruction and nuclear war—nothing else will matter.

And time is short.

Noam Chomsky and Robert Pollin

HUMANITY'S FATE ISN'T SEALED—IF WE ACT NOW

September 8, 2022

C J. Polychroniou: *Noam, the systemic impacts of the war in Ukraine are enormous, and they include economic shocks, food and energy security, geopolitical dimensions, and climate change. With regard to the latter, while it is difficult to make an accurate estimate of the climate impact of the war in Ukraine, it is crystal clear that it hinders current efforts to curb global warming and may even alter long-term strategy on climate action and action plan. How exactly are the war in Ukraine and the climate crisis connected, and why are governments doubling down on coal, oil, and gas instead of doubling down on the clean energy transition?*

Noam Chomsky: An independent observer looking at the world today might well conclude that it is being run by the fossil fuel and military industries, or by lunatics. Or both.

The scientific literature is harrowing, regularly showing that earlier dire warnings were too conservative and that we are careening toward disaster at a frightening pace. Even without reading the literature, anyone with eyes open can see that nature is saying "enough": extreme heat, huge floods, devastating drought and severe water crises, large

164

regions of the earth approaching the point where they will soon be uninhabitable.

How are we reacting? The basic character is captured by a clip from the marvelous satirical journal [The] Onion—except that it is perhaps even beyond their imagination. It is real. And reported, with disbelief, in the mainstream [New York Times]:

> In a paradox worthy of Kafka, ConocoPhillips plans to install "chillers" into the permafrost—which is thawing fast because of climate change—to keep it solid enough to drill for oil, the burning of which will continue to worsen ice melt.

In his bitter antiwar essays, Mark Twain wielded his formidable weapon of satire against the perpetrators. But when he reached the renowned General [Frederick] Funston, he threw up his hands in despair: "No satire of Funston could reach perfection," Twain lamented, "because Funston occupies that summit himself. . . . [He is] satire incarnated."

What is happening before our eyes is unleashed savage capitalism as satire incarnated. Even Twain would be silenced.

To see what is at stake, consider some basic facts. "Arctic permafrost stores nearly 1,700 billion metric tons of frozen and thawing carbon. Anthropogenic warming threatens to release an unknown quantity of this carbon to the atmosphere. . . . Carbon dioxide emissions are proportionally larger than other greenhouse gas emissions in the Arctic, but expansion of anoxic conditions within thawed permafrost and soils stands to increase the proportion of future methane emissions. Increasingly frequent wildfires in the Arctic will also lead to a notable but unpredictable carbon flux."

The carbon flux may be unpredictable in detail, but the resulting devastation is all too predictable in its general outline. How then does unleashed savage capitalism respond? Simple. Let's employ our best brains to find ways to slow the melting down a little so that we can pour more poisons into the atmosphere for profit, and as a side effect, release those Arctic permafrost stores into the atmosphere more rapidly so as to make life unlivable.

Unfortunately, the observation generalizes. We find satire incarnate wherever we turn, even in marginal corners. Thus, one argument against solar energy is land use. A real problem, especially in the UK, where golf courses take up over four times as much space as solar power, so we learn from political economist Adam Tooze's invaluable *Chartbook*.

Satire incarnate is just the cutting edge. It brings out dramatically the elements of dominant economic institutions that are lethal if unleashed. It would be hard to conjure up a more fitting epitaph for the species—or more accurately, for the institutions that have become dominant as what we call civilization marches forward.

The Ukraine war finds its natural place in this collective madness. One outcome of Putin's criminal aggression and the consequent sanctions regime is to restrict the fossil fuel flow from Russia on which Europe relies, particularly the German-based system that is its economic powerhouse. Economic consequences for Europe are severe, though not for the US, which is largely immune; or for that matter for Russia, which at least for now is profiting handsomely from rising oil prices and has many eager customers outside of Europe.

Europe is seeking alternative sources of oil and gas, a bonanza for the US fossil fuel industry, rewarded with new markets and expansive drilling opportunities to enable it to destroy life on Earth more effectively. And the military industry could hardly be more ecstatic as the killing and destruction mount.

People seem to have a different view. In Germany, for example, where 77 percent of the population "believe that the West should initiate negotiations to end the Ukraine war."

One can think of other reasons to bring the horrors to a quick end, but the fate of organized human society is surely one. The Ukraine war has reversed the limited efforts to address the mounting crisis of environmental destruction. While it should have accelerated efforts to move rapidly toward sustainable energy, that was not the path chosen by the political leadership. Rather, the choice has been to accelerate the race to the abyss.

What should be done at this critical moment is outlined percep-
tively by economist and political analyst Thomas Palley: "The European Union must build trade and commerce with Russia. That is an
economic marriage made in heaven. Russia has resources and needs
technology and capital goods. Europe has technology and capital
goods and needs resources."

And more generally, "what should be done is a profound recalibra-
tion that diminishes the influence of the US in Europe, strengthens
the European Union, and aims for inclusion of Russia in the European
family as envisaged by President Mikhail Gorbachev in 1990," in his
call for a "common European home" from Lisbon to Vladivostok with
no military alliances, no victors or defeated, and a common effort to
move toward a more just social democratic future—if not beyond.

"Getting there is beginning to look impossible," Palley adds. But
accommodation among the great powers must be achieved, and soon,
if there is to be any hope for decent survival. The madness of devoting
scarce resources to slaughter and destruction when cooperation to
meet major crises is an absolute necessity simply cannot be tolerated.

Unleashed savage capitalism is a death sentence for the species.
That has long been obvious, even before it reached the level of satire
incarnated. The crucial word is "unleashed." The leash should be, and
can be, in the hands of those who have higher aims in life than enriching private power and enhancing the political forces that prefer global
dominance to the Gorbachev vision.

We should not underestimate the barriers in economic and political realms, and also in the doctrinal systems that articulate and protect the structures of power. The matter is of particular importance in
the US, for reasons too obvious to elaborate.

The barriers within the reigning doctrinal system are illustrated
in a very revealing current essay in the major establishment journal ["The World Putin Wants," in *Foreign Affairs*]. The authors are
two well-informed foreign policy analysts at the more liberal end of
received opinion, Fiona Hill and Angela Stent.

Their article illustrates graphically the extraordinary subordination
to official doctrine that confines US elites to an "alternative reality"

that has little resemblance to the world. Confined within their self-re-
inforcing cocoon, they are simply incapable of comprehending the
global reaction to their vocation of endless criminality.

Hill-Stent harshly condemn the Global South—most of the
world—for its failure to join the US in its profound distress "that Russia has violated the UN Charter and international law by unleashing
an unprovoked attack on a neighbor's territory." The Global South
even sinks so low as to "argue that what Russia is doing in Ukraine
is no different from what the United States did in Iraq or Vietnam."

Hill-Stent attribute this failure to rise to our level of nobility and
understanding of global reality to Putin's machinations. What else
could account for such blindness?

Could there be a different reason, for example, the fact that outside
the cocoon people actually look at the world and quickly discover that
the US is far and away the world leader in violating the Charter and
international law by unleashing unprovoked attacks—worldwide,
even thousands of miles away? And could it be that they see that US
aggression in Iraq and Vietnam is an incomparably graver crime even
than Putin's aggression in Ukraine?

And as a minor footnote, perhaps these "backward" peoples are
well aware that the Russian aggression, which they, in fact, harshly
condemn, was in fact extensively provoked—as Western commentators tacitly acknowledge in their own curious way by conjuring up
for this case alone the novel phrase "unprovoked attack," which has
become *de rigeur* in polite circles for the plainly provoked Russian
aggression.

Given the climate of irrationality and subordination to doctrine
that reigns in the US, it is necessary to reiterate, once again, that
extensive provocation does not provide any justification for criminal
aggression.

The Hill-Stent exercise in obfuscation is, regrettably, an instructive example of prevailing mentality among the more liberal sectors
of doctrinal orthodoxy, amplified by conformist media and journals
of opinion. These sectors, of course, play a prominent role in shaping
the climate in which policy is designed and implemented, a matter of

overwhelming significance in the most powerful state in world history, with no close competitor.

The realities of the modern world impose unique responsibility on Americans. Ludwig Wittgenstein described the task of philosophy as "to show the fly the way out of the fly-bottle," the flies being philosophers who buzz about in conventional confusions. Analogously, one task for those concerned about the future is to try to help educated elites find their way out of the doctrinal cocoon in which they have confined themselves, and to liberate the general public from the "alternative reality" that elite circles have constructed.

No small task, but an essential one.

Military operations produce enormous amounts of greenhouse gas emissions as capacity for and use of military force depend on energy that comes in the form of fossil fuels. In fact, the US military emits more carbon into the atmosphere than some countries do and has a long history of fighting wars for oil. Is it realistic therefore to expect serious climate action on the part of the world's major powers if they continue to ignore how militarism fuels the climate crisis?

Chomsky: And, we may add, if they continue to ignore how the climate crisis fuels militarism. The climate crisis engenders conflicts. We've already witnessed that in Syria and Darfur, where migrations caused by unprecedented droughts provided a large part of the background for the horrors that ensued. There are looming crises that may put even these awful events in the shade.

India and Pakistan are at sword's point, engaged in constant armed confrontations. Both are suffering severely from global warming. One-third of Pakistan is under water, sometimes many feet deep, following an intense heatwave and a long monsoon that has dumped a record amount of rain. In neighboring India, poor peasants in mud huts are trying to survive drought and heat reaching 50 degrees Celsius [122 degrees Fahrenheit], virtually unlivable, of course, without air conditioning. Meanwhile, the governing authorities race to produce more and better means of destruction. Another grim case of satire incarnates, perhaps. The sources of their water supplies are shared and diminishing. The rest can be left to the imagination.

What isn't left to the imagination is that both are armed to the teeth, including huge nuclear arsenals, an unsustainable arms race for much smaller Pakistan. For both, it is an unconscionable waste of resources that are desperately needed to face their shared and devastating problems of global warming and other forms of destruction of the environment.

India-Pakistan is only one of many such examples of impending disaster. The US, though unusually privileged, is not immune, as we have seen in the past months.

As usual, the crises are not just human destruction of the environment. Scandals proliferate. The city that has been worst hit is Jackson, Mississippi, the state capital. The water system has been failing for years, and now its residents are literally without potable water—in a country with unparalleled wealth and natural advantages.

"Experts say this crisis was years in the making, a result of inadequate funding for essential infrastructure upgrades. For the past year, leaders of this majority-Black, Democrat-led city have pushed for additional funding from the white Republicans who run the state. Little has come of those appeals."

Deeply rooted social pathologies make their own contributions to human misery, exacerbating those produced by destroying the environment and radical misuse of resources. The US is, furthermore, far in the lead in accelerating the militarization of the world.

More tasks for Americans, and not them alone.

Bob, the world was falling short of meeting its climate goals even before the outbreak of the Ukraine war. Indeed, it's obvious by now that climate goals cannot be reached without fast and radical action. In that context, can you talk a bit about the role that carbon tax and cap-and-trade play as strategies for reducing carbon emissions?

Robert Pollin: Let's first be clear on what we mean by the world's "climate goals." The most basic goals were set out in 2018 by the Intergovernmental Panel on Climate Change (IPCC), the leading global organization that brings together and synthesizes climate change research. In its landmark 2018 special report *Global Warming of 1.5°*, the IPCC established two primary goals: to reduce global carbon dioxide (CO_2) emissions by about 45 percent in 2030 relative to the 2010 level and to achieve net-zero emissions by around 2050. The IPCC argued that these goals must be achieved to have a reasonable chance of limiting global warming to 1.5°C above pre-industrial levels. The IPCC had concluded that limiting global warming to 1.5°C above pre-industrial levels is needed to dramatically lower the likely negative consequence of climate change.

Just since the IPCC's 2018 report came out, we have been seeing much more severe impacts of climate change than what the IPCC had anticipated in terms of heat extremes, heavy rains and flooding, droughts, sea level rise, and biodiversity losses. To take just one recent example, average daily temperatures were sustained at over 110°F during the heat wave in India this past May. The intensifying climate crisis is making such episodes increasingly frequent. As Noam discusses, the war in Ukraine is only worsening the situation. It is therefore fair to conclude that the IPCC's 2018 targets should be understood as what is minimally necessary to move on to a viable global climate stabilization path. This conclusion has been affirmed by the IPCC itself in its even more extensive 2022 follow-up studies.

Where does the world stand today in terms of achieving the IPCC's emission reduction targets? As of the most recent data from the International Energy Agency (IEA)—the best-known and thoroughly mainstream organization that develops global energy models—global CO_2 emissions were at around 36 billion tons in 2019. This represents a roughly 70 percent emissions increase since 1990 and a 14 percent increase just since 2010. More to the point, according to the IEA's projections for future emissions under alternative realistic scenarios, emissions will fall barely at all by 2030 and will not come close to achieving the zero-emissions target by 2050.

Specifically, in its 2021 *World Energy Outlook* report, the IEA developed two scenarios for future CO_2 emissions levels based on what it considers to be realistic assessments of the current global policy environment. One is what the IEA terms a "Stated Policies Scenario." This scenario "explores where the energy system might go without additional policy implementation." It is based on taking "a granular, sector-by-sector look at existing policies and measures and those under development." In short, this scenario aims to project what CO_2 emissions will be through 2050 if global policies remain basically fixed along their current trajectory. In this scenario, global CO_2 emissions will not fall *at all* by 2030 and will decline by only 6 percent, to 33.9 billion tons, by 2050. In short, assuming we take climate science seriously, this is nothing less than a doomsday scenario.

Under a second "Announced Pledges Scenario," the IEA "takes account of all of the climate commitments made by governments around the world, including Nationally Determined Contributions as well as longer term net-zero targets, and assumes that they will be met in full and on time." Under this more aggressive scenario, the IEA projects that emissions will still fall by only 7 percent as of 2030, and that by 2050, the emissions level will be at 20.7 billion tons—i.e., well less than halfway to achieving the zero-emissions goal by 2050. In other words, even this more aggressive IEA scenario also is not too far from a doomsday scenario, assuming we take climate science seriously.

The IEA does also develop a scenario through which the world can reach zero emissions by 2050. The difference between the IEA's stated policies and announced pledges scenarios relative to their net-zero emissions by 2050 scenario is what the IEA terms an "ambition gap." The question for getting to zero emissions is therefore to figure out how to close this "ambition gap," i.e., how to avoid, somehow, a full-scale global climate catastrophe.

How much can carbon tax or carbon cap policies contribute here? Both of these measures aim to directly reduce the consumption of oil, coal and natural gas. This is critical, since CO_2 emissions from burning coal, oil, and natural gas to produce energy is, by far, the largest source of overall CO_2 emissions, and thus, the major cause of climate change.

In principle at least, a carbon cap establishes a firm limit on the allowable level of emissions for major polluting entities, such as utilities. Such measures will also raise the prices of oil, coal, and natural gas by limiting their supply. A carbon tax, on the other hand, will directly raise fossil fuel prices to consumers, and aim to reduce fossil fuel consumption through the high prices. Either approach can be effective as long as the cap is strict enough, or tax rate high enough, to significantly reduce fossil fuel consumption and as long as exemptions are minimal to none. Raising the prices for fossil fuels will also create increased incentives for both energy efficiency and clean renewable investments, as well as a source of revenue to help finance these investments.

However, significant problems are also associated with both approaches. The first is their impact on the budgets of middle- and lower-income people. All else equal, increasing the price of fossil fuels would affect middle- and lower-income households more than affluent households, since gasoline, home-heating fuels, and electricity absorb a higher share of lower-income households' consumption. There is an effective solution here, developed initially by my PERI coworker Jim Boyce. That is to rebate to lower-income households a large share, if not most, of the revenues generated either by the cap or tax to offset the increased costs of fossil-fuel energy. Boyce termed this a "cap-and-dividend" program.

Another major problem with carbon caps is with enforcement. In particular, when these cap programs are combined with a carbon permit option—as in "cap-and-trade" policies—the enforcement of a hard cap becomes difficult to sustain or even monitor. So instead of measures that could be major contributors to fighting climate change, we end up with a mess of accounting tricks and exceptions. For the most part, this has been the experience thus far with cap-and-trade policies, both in the US and Europe.

There are some easy fixes for this problem, as we have discussed in previous interviews. The most straightforward is to establish hard caps, such as utilities being required to reduce their fossil fuel consumption by, say, 5 percent per year, every year, with no exceptions and no cap-and-trade escape hatches. The CEOs of corporations who fail to hit these hard caps would face serious criminal liability.

Arguments in favor of the deployment of negative-emissions technologies, such as direct air capture and bioenergy with carbon capture and storage, are gaining ground these days in spite of their technological immaturity. Same goes for nuclear power plants and even geo-engineering in spite of the inherent risks that they entail. What role can such strategies play in the effort to make a complete break from reliance on fossil fuels?

Pollin: Neither negative-emissions technologies nor nuclear power can likely contribute significantly to building an alternative global clean energy infrastructure. Indeed, it is more likely that they will create still more severe problems.

Let's start with nuclear. It does have the important benefit that it generates electricity without producing CO_2 emissions. But nuclear also creates major environmental and public safety concerns, which only intensified after the March 2011 meltdown at the Fukushima Daiichi power plant in Japan, and still more, after Russia seized control of the Chernobyl and Zaporizhzhia nuclear power plants in the early stages of its invasion of Ukraine six months ago. Nuclear disasters at both Chernobyl and Zaporizhzhia became active threats immediately. Just over the past month, the Zaporizhzhia plant has come under intense siege. Thus, as of August 3, the director general of the International Atomic Energy Agency Rafael Grossi stated that conditions at Zaporizhzhia are "completely out of control," underlying "the very real risk of a nuclear disaster." By mid-August, the BBC described "the growing concern over safety at the site . . . as both sides accuse each other of shelling the area." The BBC article quotes UN Secretary-General António Guterres's warning that "any potential damage to Zaporizhzhia is suicide."

Negative-emissions technologies include a range of measures whose purpose is either to remove existing CO_2 or to inject cooling forces into the atmosphere to counteract the warming effects of CO_2 and other greenhouse gases. One category of removal technologies is carbon capture and sequestration. A category of cooling technologies is stratospheric aerosol injections.

Carbon capture technologies aim to remove emitted carbon from the atmosphere and transport it, usually through pipelines, to sub-surface geological formations, where it would be stored permanently. The general class of carbon capture technologies has not been proven at a commercial scale, despite decades of efforts to accomplish this. After all, as we have discussed in previous interviews, carbon capture would be the savior for the oil, coal, and natural gas industries if the technology could be made to work commercially at scale. However, even if carbon could be successfully captured at reasonable costs, the technology would still face the threat of carbon leakages that would result under flawed transportation and storage systems. These dangers will only increase to the extent that carbon capture becomes commercialized and operates under an incentive structure in which maintaining safety standards cuts into corporate profits.

The idea of stratospheric aerosol injections builds from the results that followed from the volcanic eruption of Mount Pinatubo in the Philippines in 1991. The eruption led to a massive injection of ash and gas, which produced sulfate particles, or aerosols, which then rose into the stratosphere. The impact was to cool the Earth's average temperature by about 0.60°C for fifteen months. The technologies being researched now aim to artificially replicate the impact of the Mount Pinatubo eruption through deliberately injecting sulfate particles into the stratosphere. Some researchers contend that doing so would be a cost-effective method of counteracting the warming effects of CO_2 and other greenhouse gases.

However, the viability of stratospheric aerosol injections as a major climate solution has been refuted repeatedly by leading researchers in the field. For example, the Oxford University climate scientist Raymond Pierrehumbert, a major contributor to various IPCC studies, is emphatic in his 2019 paper, "There is No Plan B for Dealing with the Climate Crisis," that this type of geo-engineering—what he refers to [as] "albedo hacking"—does not offer a viable solution to the climate crisis. Pierrehumbert writes:

The excess carbon dioxide that human activities inject into the atmosphere has a warming effect that extends essentially forever, whereas the stratospheric aerosols meant to offset that warming fall out of the atmosphere in about a year. It's just a matter of gravity—stuff denser than its surroundings falls—aided a bit by atmospheric circulations that enhance the removal. This is why the cooling effects of even a major volcanic eruption like Pinatubo dissipate after two years or so. Hence, whatever level of albedo hacking is needed to avoid a dangerous level of warming must be continued essentially forever.

Pierrehumbert further writes that "We simply do not know the way the climate will respond to these novel forcings, or how our social and political systems will respond to these disruptive and possibly ungovernable technologies."

Renewable energy critics argue that wind and solar are not reliable sources because of their variability. Others argue that wind farms encroach on pristine environment and destroy a country's natural habitat, as is the case with the installation of thousands of wind turbines on scores of Greek islands in the Aegean Sea. How would you respond to such concerns, and are there ways around them?

Pollin: Three major sets of challenges arise in building a high-efficiency/renewable energy–dominant global energy infrastructure. They include the two you mentioned, i.e., (1) intermittency with solar and wind energy; and (2) the land use requirements for renewables, especially solar and wind. The third major challenge is the heavy mineral requirements as inputs for the clean energy infrastructure. In the interests of space, I will focus on just the first two.

Intermittency refers to the fact that the sun does not shine, and the wind does not blow, twenty-four hours a day. Moreover, on average, different geographical areas receive significantly different levels of sunshine and wind. As such, the solar and wind power that are generated in the sunnier and windier areas of the globe will need to be stored and transmitted at reasonable costs to the less sunny and windy areas. In fact, these issues around transmission and storage of wind and solar power will not become pressing for many years into the clean energy transition, probably for at least a decade. This is because fossil fuels, along with nuclear energy, will continue to provide a baseload of nonintermittent energy supply as these energy sectors proceed toward their phaseout while the clean energy industry rapidly expands. Fossil fuels and nuclear energy now provide roughly 85 percent of all global energy supplies. Even with a phaseout to zero by 2050 trajectory, fossil fuels will continue to provide most of the overall energy demand through about 2035. Meanwhile, fully viable solutions to the technical challenges with transmission and storage of solar and wind power—including around affordability—should not be more than a decade away, certainly as long as the market for clean energy grows at the rapid rate that is necessary. For example, the International Renewable Energy Agency (IRENA) estimates that global battery storage capacity could expand between 17- and 38-fold as of 2030.

The issue of land use requirements is frequently cited to demonstrate that building a 100 percent renewable energy global economy is unrealistic. But these claims are not supported by evidence. Thus, the Harvard University physicist Mara Prentiss shows, in her 2015 book *Energy Revolution: The Physics and the Promise of Efficient Technology*, as well as in her more recent follow-up discussions, that well below 1 percent of the total US land area would be needed through solar and wind power to meet 100 percent of US energy needs.

Most of this land use requirement could be met, for example, by placing solar panels on rooftops and parking lots, then operating wind turbines on about 7 percent of current agricultural land. Moreover, the wind turbines can be sited on existing operating farmland with only minor losses of agricultural productivity. Farmers should mostly welcome this dual use of their land, since it provides them with a major additional income source. At present, the US states of Iowa, Kansas, Oklahoma, and South Dakota all generate more than 30 percent of their electricity supply through wind turbines. The remaining supplemental energy needs could then be supplied by geothermal, hydro and low-emissions bioenergy, which are all nonintermittent renewable sources. This particular scenario includes no further contributions from solar farms in desert areas, solar panels mounted on highways or offshore wind projects, among other supplemental renewable energy sources. However, if handled responsibly, all of these options are also viable possibilities.

It is true that conditions for renewable energy production in the United States are more favorable than those in some other countries. Germany and the UK, for example, have population densities seven to eight times greater than the US and also receive less sunlight over the course of a year. As such, these countries, operating at high efficiency levels, would need to use about 3 percent of their total land area to generate 100 percent of their energy demand through domestically produced solar energy. But using cost-effective storage and transmission technologies, the UK and Germany can also import energy generated by solar and wind power in other countries, just as, in the United States, wind power generated in Iowa could be transmitted to New York City. Any such import requirements are likely to be modest.

What about Greece? With coauthors, I am currently working on a study that considers the land use issues in Greece within the framework of achieving a zero-emissions economy there by 2050. I hope to be able to give more details on our results soon. For now, suffice it to say that there is no need for Greece to be installing wind farms on pristine sites. As with the US, there is more than sufficient land area in Greece to meet 100 percent of the country's energy demand through investments in high efficiency and building a renewable infrastructure situated on artificial surfaces like rooftops, parking lots, highways and commercial locations, as well as, to a relatively modest extent, agricultural lands.

Noam, we are the only species to evolve a higher intelligence, but we are not making the right decisions over climate and the environment. Is it because of politics and the way the world economy functions, or perhaps because of fears that the challenge of global warming is too overwhelming so we might as well go on with business as usual, make some alterations along the way and just hope for the best?

Chomsky: Evolution of higher intelligence is an intriguing scientific problem. It is even possible that we are the only species in the accessible universe to have evolved what we call higher intelligence, or at least to have sustained it without self-destruction. Yet.

As for why the existential crises that may soon end sustainable life on Earth receive far too little attention, one can think of many possible reasons. There is also a deeper question lingering in the not too remote background. The question burst into consciousness with dramatic intensity seventy-seven years ago, on August 6, 1945. Or should have.

On that fateful day we learned that human intelligence had registered a grand achievement. It had devised the means to destroy everything. Not quite yet, in fact, though it was clear that further technological progress would soon reach that point. It did, in 1952, when the US exploded the first thermonuclear weapon, and the Doomsday Clock advanced to two minutes to midnight. It did not become that close to terminal disaster again until Trump's term, then moving on to seconds as analysts abandoned minutes.

The question that arose with stark clarity seventy-seven years ago was whether human moral intelligence could rise to the level where it could control the impulse to destruction. Can the gap be overcome? The record so far is not promising.

The game is not over unless we choose to end it. The choice is unavoidable. How humans will decide is by far the most important question that has arisen in the brief sojourn of humans on Earth. We will soon provide the answer.

Noam Chomsky

MAINTAINING CLASS INEQUALITY AT ANY COST IS GOP'S GUIDING MISSION

August 27, 2022

C. J. Polychroniou: *Noam, the Republican Party has become an unabashedly anti-democratic political organization steering the US toward authoritarianism. In fact, most GOP voters continue to support a political figure that sought to overturn a presidential election and seem to be enamored with Hungary's strongman Viktor Orbán, who dismantled democracy in his own country. It is also of little surprise the way Republicans have responded to the FBI raid on Mar-a-Lago. The rule of law is of no consequence to them, yet conservatives charge that it is the Democrats who are moving the country toward authoritarianism. What's shaping the character of the current Republican Party?*

Noam Chomsky: What is unfolding before our eyes is a kind of classical tragedy, the grim conclusion foreordained, the march toward it seemingly inexorable. The origins are deep in the history of a society that has been free and bountiful for the privileged, awful for those who were in the way or cast aside.

A century ago, a stage was reached that has some similarity to today. In his classic study, *The Fall of the House of Labor*, labor historian David Montgomery writes that in the 1920s "corporate mastery of American life seemed secure. . . . Rationalization of business could then proceed with indispensable government support." Inequality was soaring, along with corruption and greed. The vibrant labor movement had been crushed by Woodrow Wilson's "red scare," after decades of violent repression.

"Modern America had been created over its workers' protests," Montgomery continued, "even though every step in its formation had been influenced by the activities, organizations, and proposals that had sprung from working class life." In the late nineteenth century, it seemed possible that the Knights of Labor, with its demand that those who work in the mills should own them, might link up with the radical farmers movement, the Populists, who were seeking a "cooperative commonwealth" that would free farmers from the tyranny of northeastern bankers and market managers. That could have led to a very different America. But it could not withstand state-corporate repression and violence.

A few years after the fall of the house of labor came the Great Depression. The labor movement revived and expanded, moving to large-scale industrial organization and militant actions. Crucially, there was a sympathetic administration, and a lively and often radical political environment. All of this laid the basis for the New Deal reforms that enormously improved American life and had repercussions in European social democracy.

The business world was split. Thomas Ferguson's research shows that capital-intensive, internationally oriented business accepted New Deal policies, while labor-intensive, domestically oriented business was bitterly opposed. Their publications warned ominously of the "hazard facing industrialists" from labor action backed by "the newly realized political power of the masses," topics explored in depth in Alex Carey's *Taking the Risks out of Democracy*, which inaugurated the study of corporate propaganda.

As soon as the war ended, the business world launched a major assault on labor. It was impressive in scale, ranging from forced indoctrination sessions for the workforce even to taking over sports leagues. This was all part of the project of "selling free enterprise," while the salesmen were happily gorging at the public trough where the hard and creative work of constructing the new high-tech economy was on the account of the friendly taxpayer.

Violent repression was no longer adequate to restoring the glory days of the twenties. More subtle means of indoctrination were devised, including "scientific methods of strike-breaking," by now honed to a high art with the support of administrations since Reagan that barely pay attention to such labor laws as still exist.

The business campaign was expedited by the attack on civil liberties called "McCarthyism," which led to expulsion of many of the most effective labor activists and organizers. Unions entered into a compact with capital to gain benefits for members (though not the public) in return for abandoning any significant role on the shop floor.

The regimented capitalism of the early postwar years has been called the "golden age of [state] capitalism," with high and egalitarian growth. By the mid-sixties, popular activism was beginning to expose some of the long-concealed record of American history, and addressing some of its brutal legacy, again with the cooperation of a sympathetic administration.

By the early seventies, the established social order was tottering under the impact of the "Nixon shock" that undermined the postwar Bretton Woods system, stagflation, and not least, the growing threat of the popular movements that were civilizing the society. Elite concerns are well attested by major publications bracketing the mainstream spectrum of opinion.

At the left-liberal end, the liberal internationalists of the Trilateral Commission released their first publication, *The Crisis of Democracy*. The political flavor of the commission is illustrated by the fact that the Carter administration was drawn largely from its ranks. The "Crisis" that concerned them was the activism of the sixties, which was mobilizing people to press their concerns in the political arena. These "special interests," as they are called, were imposing too many pressures on the state, causing a crisis of democracy. The solution they recommended was more "moderation in democracy" by the special interests: minorities, women, the young, the old, workers, farmers, in short, the population, who are to be "spectators" not "participants," in accord with liberal democratic theory (Walter Lippmann, Harold Lasswell, Reinhold Niebuhr, and other distinguished figures).

Unspoken is a crucial premise: the "special interests" are to be "put in their place," as Lippmann advised, so that ample room is left for the "national interest" that is upheld by the "masters of mankind," Adam Smith's term for the business classes, who shape national policy so that their own interests are "most peculiarly attended to." Smith's words, which resonate loudly today.

Of particular concern to the Trilateral liberals were the failures of the institutions responsible "for the indoctrination of the young," particularly the schools and universities. That's why we see young people protesting for civil rights, women's rights, ending a criminal war of aggression, and other diversions from the proper course of passivity and conformism. Here, too, a change of course is necessary for a proper social order to be sustained, tasks that were attended to in due course.

Another concern was the media, out of control and adversarial, threatening "democracy" by raising too many questions. The commission advised that state intervention might be necessary to overcome this crisis.

That is how "the time of troubles" was perceived at the left end of the mainstream spectrum. At the right end, positions were much harsher. The most important example is the Powell Memorandum, submitted to the Chamber of Commerce by corporate lawyer (later Supreme Court Justice) Lewis Powell. Written in apocalyptic terms, the memorandum is a call to arms to the business world to defend the "American economic system" and "the American political system of democracy under the rule of law," all "under broad attack" in a manner unprecedented in American history. The attack is so powerful that the very survival of the economic system and political democracy is at stake, as "no thoughtful person can question."

Powell recommends that business rise from its traditional passivity and take strong measures to counter this "massive assault upon its fundamental economies, upon its philosophy, upon its right to continue to manage its own affairs, and indeed upon its integrity."

The business world can easily take such measures, Powell reminds it. It holds the wealth of the country and largely owns the institutions that are bent on destruction of the business world, and American democracy and freedom with it.

The measures he outlines range widely. Thus, "there should be no hesitation to attack the Naders and the Marcuses and others who openly seek destruction of the system. . . . Perhaps the single most effective antagonist of American business is Ralph Nader, who— thanks largely to the media—has become a legend in his own time and an idol of millions of Americans." The left that dominates the media is so incorrigible as to commend Nader's efforts to make cars safer, an outrageous attack on our fundamental values.

Scarcely less dangerous is Herbert Marcuse, with his enormous sway over the college campuses. These far-left bastions are "graduating scores of bright young men who despise the American political and economic system" and who then move into media and government, institutions from which business and advocates of "free enterprise" are virtually barred. As every "business executive knows, few elements of American society today have as little influence in government as the American businessmen, the corporation, or even the millions of corporate stockholders" (who the left falsely believes are skewed toward the wealthy).

In this case Powell at last provides evidence, not just rants from rightwing screeds: "Current examples of the impotency of business, and of the near-contempt with which business's views are held, are the stampedes by politicians to support almost any legislation related to 'consumerism' or to the 'environment,'" scare quotes for these absurd concoctions of the raging left.

It's not just the college campuses that must be "cured" of the pathology of despising everything American. The same holds for media, particularly TV, which must be carefully monitored and "kept under constant surveillance . . . in the same way that textbooks should be." The monitoring should be carried out by neutral and independent advocates of the American way, as determined by the business world. It is of highest importance to monitor "the daily 'news analysis,' which so often includes the most insidious type of criticism of the enterprise system."

Business has remained silent as this "assault on the enterprise system . . . has gradually evolved over the past two decades." The innocents in corporate headquarters never even dreamt of developing programs to "sell free enterprise," contrary to what scholarship documents in extensive detail.

The harshly oppressed business community will find it "difficult to compete with an Eldridge Cleaver or even a Charles Reich for reader attention," or with the "ultraliberal Jack Newfield, who wrote in the journal *New York* that the root need in our country is 'to redistribute wealth.'"

The horror, the horror!

The task of redistributing wealth even further to the very rich was undertaken soon after, in part influenced by Powell's memorandum, though the process was underway independently under the ideological leadership of Powell's major sources, notably Milton Friedman. The disarray of the seventies provided the opportunity for the neoliberal gurus to move beyond destroying the economy of Chile, as they were then doing (the crash came soon after), to applying their doctrines to the US and UK, and much of the world beyond.

Powell's memorandum provides interesting insight into the Chamber of Commerce mentality. The basic stance is that of a spoiled three-year-old who owns everything imaginable but has a tantrum if someone takes one of the marbles from a collection he had forgotten about. Having virtually everything is not enough. We cannot be deterred from the pursuit of the "vile maxim" of the masters of mankind: "All for ourselves and nothing for other people," a maxim that seems to hold "in every age of the world," as Adam Smith observed.

It didn't take long for the assault of the masters to be understood. In 1978, UAW president Doug Fraser withdrew from a Carter-organized labor-management commission, condemning business leaders for having "chosen to wage a one-sided class war in this country—a war against working people, the unemployed, the poor, the minorities, the very young and the very old, and even many in the middle class of our society," and having "broken and discarded the fragile, unwritten compact previously existing during a period of growth and progress," the golden age of fragile class collaboration.

And then on to the full-fledged class war of the neoliberal years.

The political parties adapted to the business assault and helped accelerate it. The Democrats abandoned their limited commitment to working people, becoming a party of affluent professionals and Wall Street. Moderate Republicans, who had barely been distinguishable from liberal Democrats, disappeared. Today they would not even be RINOs [Republicans In Name Only]. The party leadership understood well that they cannot gain votes on their actual policies of abject service to the super-rich and the corporate sector and must therefore shift voters' attention to what are called "cultural issues." That process began with Nixon's Southern strategy, designed to switch Southern Democrats to Republicans with racist dog whistles, which under Reagan became open shouts. They also recognized that by pretending to strenuously oppose abortion they could pick up the Evangelical and Catholic vote. Then came guns, and all the rest of the current apparatus of deception. Meanwhile, behind the curtain, the party pursued the vile maxim with a vengeance.

While the Democrats had delivered working people to their class enemy, still barriers to the assault remained. The Reaganites understood the need to deprive their enemy of any means of defense. Like Thatcher in England, their first act was a major attack on labor, opening the door for the corporate world to intensify the war against working people that had been resumed at the end of World War II. Clinton cooperated, with his policies of neoliberal globalization, designed to maximize corporate profits and undermine labor still further.

It shouldn't be necessary to review the consequences once again, from the "transfer" of some $50 trillion to the coffers of the top 1 percent to the wide range of other achievements of class war with few restraints. One revealing illustration is mortality: "from the 1980s onward, the US started falling behind its peers" in mortality, reaching over a million extra deaths by 2021. The increase in mortality in the past half-dozen years is without precedent, apart from war and pestilence. It is also since about 1980 that US health care costs began to diverge radically from comparable countries, along with some of the worst outcomes.

Other dimensions reveal similar departures from the norm—incarceration, to mention only one. In the 1970s, US incarceration rates were within the range of comparable countries. By now they are five to ten times as high, another indication of social breakdown.

During these years the Republicans virtually abandoned any pretense of being a normal parliamentary party, to an extent that arouses amazement among long-time political analysts. Thomas Mann and Norman Ornstein of the American Enterprise Institute describe the former party as a "radical insurgency" that has abandoned normal parliamentary procedures. Some go further. The veteran political analyst of the London *Financial Times* Edward Luce writes that "I've covered extremism and violent ideologies around the world over my career. Have never come across a political force more nihilistic, dangerous & contemptible than today's Republicans. Nothing close." His comment is endorsed by former CIA director Michael Hayden.

Mann and Ornstein trace the sharp decline of the GOP to Newt Gingrich's weaponization of the party, turning it into an instrument to hold power by any means. The process accelerated under Mitch McConnell, barely concealed. Obama's election provided new fodder for the white supremacist element of the campaign of diverting attention to "cultural issues," fostering the grievances of "the Great Replacement."

It is quite remarkable to see what has happened to the remnants of what was once an authentic political party. By now, qualifications for Congress are pretty much reduced to voting "No" on McConnell's command and occasional trips to Mar-a-Lago to shine Trump's shoes.

The popular base has been affected by the decline, particularly in the years of Trump worship. Some 70 percent believe that the 2020 election was stolen. Two-thirds "believe the country's demographic changes are being orchestrated by 'liberal leaders actively trying to leverage political power by replacing more conservative white voters,'" the Great Replacement theory that not long ago was restricted to a neo-Nazi fringe. Half of Republicans think that "top Democrats are involved in elite child sex-trafficking rings." The almost unbelievable story goes on.

Most ominous is the marginal concern with global warming, a reflection of obedient leadership denialism since the Koch brothers' juggernaut of 2009 that successfully terminated the mild deviation toward sanity under McCain. In this case, the shocking cowardice of the GOP leadership may do us all in if the GOP regains power—perhaps permanently, as a minority party, if their radical efforts to undermine democracy succeed. And with a deeply reactionary Supreme Court, they may.

If it does, we can guess what's in store. Trump has been very clear about his intent to "drain the swamp" by destroying the nonpartisan civil service that is the foundation of anything resembling a democracy. The recent Budapest and Dallas conferences where the Conservative Political Action Conference (CPAC)—the core of the GOP—was the star attraction made it clear enough where the organization is headed. Its guide is Viktor Orbán, whose racist Christian nationalist protofascist government was hailed as the ideal for the future. For the world, the Trump project of constructing an alliance of brutal reactionary states is likely to be consolidated. And worst of all, the world will careen to terminal disaster while profits flood the fossil fuel companies and the banks that invest in them.

Stepping back, US political parties are mainly candidate-producing organizations, with little room for popular initiative, and participation limited to pushing a lever every few years.

The current primary season provides a good illustration. A candidate organizes an event in some town, appears, and says "Here's what I'm going to do for you." Maybe a few even believe it. Then they go home and decide how to cast their vote.

Suppose we lived in a democratic society. The people in the town would have meetings in which they decided on their priorities for a coming election. They might decide to invite some declared candidate to attend a town meeting to listen to the programs they had decided on, and either accept them or not. Acceptance might mean that the candidate is now considered.

More serious steps toward democracy would go far beyond the limited political sphere, but even such small steps as these are scarcely on the horizon.

Fortunately, significant changes are well within reach in what remains a very free society by comparative standards. But opportunities have to reach consciousness, and be grasped, firmly. We cannot overemphasize the fact that now survival is literally at stake.

Republicans are much less divided on culture than Democrats. Is this why the GOP is so keen on cultural and social fights in its attempt to return to power?

The GOP has had a problem since it shed its more liberal elements and adopted the Powell-Friedman et al., neoliberal project since the early seventies, gaining power with Reagan. Put simply, one can't approach voters saying, "I'm going to rob you blind and destroy all your support systems, so vote for me." Even a political operator like Trump can't carry that off. He has to pose with a banner in one hand reading "I love you," while the other hand stabs you in the back with the actual legislative programs.

The solution is culture wars to divert attention from policies. And it is clear enough what works with the targeted population: white supremacy, Christian nationalism, no abortion, lots of guns, no more public schools that disturb white children by teaching history or basic biology, no public education altogether because it's run by sex fiends and Marxists. Or whatever will be concocted next, perhaps by QAnon, increasingly the source of "ideas" for the organization.

It doesn't take much imagination to think up ideas that work. There's a substantial store that are deeply rooted in American tradition. That's understood by the thinkers on the Roberts Court. As Justice Alito observed in his decision reversing *Roe v. Wade*, there's little to support women's rights in American history and tradition. Certainly, they were of little concern to the founders or authors of the 14th Amendment. So, the convenient forms of "originalism" that have recently become judicial doctrine provide no basis for the "egregiously wrong" *Roe* decision.

Same with much else. When I was a student at an Ivy League college seventy-five years ago, classes that brought up evolution would often begin by an admonition that you don't have to believe this, but you should know what some people think.

Recent polls have been welcomed by those who have been hoping for some progress in this domain, but the actual results tell a more complex story. One of the most detailed studies, commissioned by the pro-science People for the American Way Foundation, shows that "among the majority of Americans favoring evolution, 20 percent say schools should teach only evolution, with no mention of creationism." But not evolution—or "evolution theory," as it's called. "To put it simply, this poll shows that most Americans believe that God created evolution," said Ralph G. Neas, president of the foundation.

In this and many other respects, the US remains in many ways a pre-modern society, easily attracted to well-crafted "culture wars." That will very likely become even more so in the future as the GOP pursues its totalitarian efforts to restrict what children are allowed to read and what libraries are allowed to purchase, laws that have a broad chilling effect beyond their direct application.

Such efforts to strangle intellectual freedom are likely to be reinforced by the medieval proclivities of the current Supreme Court, revealed by recent decisions undermining the Establishment clause of the Constitution by compelling adherence to religious doctrine.

These decisions effectively adopt Justice Alito's conception that the religious are a persecuted sector in our secular society, which has to be taught to respect freedom of religion.

Perhaps the religious are as severely persecuted as the business community in the American society of Justice Powell's vivid imagination.

The effort to eliminate public education has been a core part of the broader neoliberal effort to atomize the population and destroy social bonds. It has caused severe harm to what had been a major American contribution to democracy: mass public education. Much more than education is involved. Public schools establish communities of participation for the common good, helping to create a healthy democratic society. That is not what is sought by bitter class war.

A prime way of destroying a public institution is defunding. That leads inevitably to failure and public discontent, hence susceptibility to privatization so that the institution will be under the control of unaccountable private power. With superb irony, this is called "handing the institution back to the people."

Defunding reaches to teacher's salaries. The Economic Policy Institute, which monitors such matters, reports that "in 2021, the relative teacher wage penalty—how much less teachers are paid than other college-educated professionals—grew to a record high of 23.5 percent. The financial penalty that teachers face discourages college students from entering the teaching profession. It also makes it difficult for school districts to keep current teachers in the classroom."

That is by now no small problem. The Bureau of Labor Statistics reports that "roughly 300,000 public school educators and staff left the field between Feb. 2020 and May 2022. And an alarming 55 percent of educators indicated that they could be leaving their profession or retire early, according to a survey from the National Education Association."

Harassment of teachers and school boards contributes its share to rendering the profession intolerable, and to the long-term goal of eliminating public education. That would be a further contribution to atomizing and dumbing down the population, leaving people more susceptible to control and to "indoctrination of the young," thus reducing the threat of another crisis of democracy.

The left of the Democratic party contributes in its own way to the GOP exploitation of "cultural issues." Class politics, workers' rights, even social and economic issues have been rather generally sidelined in favor of identity concerns. These are important in themselves, but we should not be oblivious to the consequences of displacement of traditional left concerns, or to the effects on the general public of how legitimate concerns are sometimes manifested.

The Republican Party's long-term relationship with Big Business is show-ing signs of deep friction over culture and social causes. How likely is it that we may become witness to a divorce between the two entities? And what might be the political ramifications of such decoupling?

Not very likely, in my opinion. I think the masters of mankind under-stand very well where their interests lie and will continue to support pro-business elements in both parties, disregarding rhetoric that they do not expect to be translated into policy. Such support can be lavish in the wake of Supreme Court decisions that place few limits on buying elections (*Buckley v. Valeo, Citizens United*), only one of the means by which the masters can ensure that their own interests "are most pecu-liarly attended to."

There has been class warfare in the US for the last forty years, and it's been a one-sided fight. However, there are political developments under-way over the last few years indicating that it is no longer a one-sided class war. Do you agree with this overall assessment of class politics in the US?

Class war is unceasing, but there are variations in how one-sided it is. For many historical reasons, the US has had a highly class-conscious and unusually powerful business class, the underlying reason for the violence and brutality of its labor history and the lack of social bene-fits, by now extreme in comparative terms. The New Deal period was a break, lasting into the transitional 1970s, leading to resumption of class war in force. In the past few years there has been a renewed popular commitment to some form of social democracy, in part under Bernie Sanders's highly effective leadership, in part through popular move-ments that have arisen on their own. These developments have some-what ameliorated the savagery of the neoliberal class war, but, so far at least, there has not been a major breakthrough. Even such popularly supported initiatives as joining the rest of the world in providing health care, a bare minimum for a civilized society, have not been able to over-come relentless business pressures.

Such pressures sometimes reach astonishing levels. A current illustration is the legislation in GOP-run states to punish banks that seek to save human society from destruction by curtailing investment in fossil fuels. It is hard to find appropriate words for such cases of capitalist frenzy going totally berserk.

However reluctantly, segments of the business world are taking some measures that reflect popular concerns about survival. Still, I think it is not enough to cause a break between the masters and the political organization that has mostly loyally served them.

The Schumer-Manchin reconciliation bill, which Biden signed into law, reaffirmed the idea that transformational policies are extremely difficult under the two-party system even when Democrats are in control and humanity's future is at stake. On the other hand, of course, the US remains in many respects a conservative nation to the point that Democrats believe that they have to be moderate otherwise they will die. Your thoughts on the political situation in connection with the Inflation Reduction Act?

It was observed long ago that the US is basically a one-party state: the business party, with two factions, Democrats and Republicans. Now there is one faction: the Democrats. The Republicans hardly qualify as an authentic parliamentary party. That's fairly explicit under McConnell's rule. When Obama took office, McConnell made it clear that his primary goal was to ensure that Obama could achieve virtually nothing, so that Republicans could return to power. When Biden was elected, McConnell reiterated that position even more strongly. And he's lived up to it. On virtually every issue, the GOP is 100 percent opposed, even when they know that the legislation is popular and would be very valuable for the population. With a handful of right-wing Democrats joining the uniform GOP opposition, Biden's platform has been cut down very sharply. Perhaps he could have done more, but he's being unfairly blamed, I think, for the failure of what would have been constructive programs, badly needed. That includes Biden's climate program, inadequate but far better than anything that preceded it, and if enacted, a stepping stone for going further.

There is a lot wrong with the whole electoral system, but in this case, I don't see how Biden had many options. The final bill—the Inflation Reduction Act—was passed with Joe Manchin's agreement, while he was laughing all the way to the bank. Kyrsten Sinema also had to throw in her two cents for the benefit of the mostly predatory private equity industry.

The act has some good features. It's better than nothing, perhaps much better, some credible analysts believe.

The political situation is ugly, and very likely to get much worse in November if the GOP manages to take over. It is likely to get so much worse that it will literally threaten survival, "as no thoughtful person can question," to quote the estimable Justice Powell.

Noam Chomsky

SIX MONTHS INTO WAR, DIPLOMATIC SETTLEMENT IN UKRAINE IS STILL POSSIBLE

August 24, 2022

C. J. Polychroniou: *It's been six months since Russia's invasion of Ukraine, yet there is no end to the war in sight. Putin's strategy has backfired in a huge way, as it not only failed to take down Kyiv but also revived the Western alliance while Finland and Sweden ended decades of neutrality by joining NATO. The war has also caused a massive humanitarian crisis, brought higher energy prices, and made Russia into a pariah state. From day one, you described the invasion as a criminal act of aggression and compared it to the US invasion of Iraq and the Hitler-Stalin invasion of Poland, in spite of the fact that Russia felt threatened from NATO's expansion to the east. I reckon that you still hold this view, but do you think that Putin would have had second thoughts about an invasion if he knew that this military adventure of his would end up in a prolonged war?*

Noam Chomsky: Reading Putin's mind has become a cottage industry, notable for the extreme confidence of those who interpret the scanty tea leaves. I have some guesses, but they are not based on better evidence than others have, so they have low credibility.

My guess is that Russian intelligence agreed with the announced US government expectations that conquest of Kyiv and installation of a puppet government would be an easy task, not the debacle it turned out to be. I suppose that if Putin had had better information about the Ukrainian will and capacity to resist, and the incompetence of the Russian military, his plans would have been different. Perhaps the plans would have been what many informed analysts had expected, what Russia now seems to have turned to, a Plan B: trying to establish firmer control over Crimea and the passage to Russia, and to take over the Donbas region.

Possibly, benefiting from better intelligence, Putin might have had the wisdom to respond seriously to the tentative initiatives of Macron for a negotiated settlement that would have avoided the war, and might have even proceeded to Europe-Russia accommodation along the lines of proposals by de Gaulle and Gorbachev. All we know is that the initiatives were dismissed with contempt, at great cost, not least to Russia. Instead, Putin launched a murderous war of aggression which, indeed, ranks with the US invasion of Iraq and the Hitler-Stalin invasion of Poland.

That Russia felt threatened by NATO expansion to the East, in violation of firm and unambiguous promises to Gorbachev, has been stressed by virtually every high-level US diplomat with any familiarity with Russia for thirty years, well before Putin. To take just one of a rich array of examples, in 2008 when he was ambassador to Russia and Bush II recklessly invited Ukraine to join NATO, current CIA director William Burns warned that "Ukrainian entry into NATO is the brightest of all redlines for the Russian elite (not just Putin)." He added that "I have yet to find anyone who views Ukraine in NATO as anything other than a direct challenge to Russian interests." More generally, Burns called NATO expansion into Eastern Europe "premature at best, and needlessly provocative at worst." And if the expansion reached Ukraine, Burns warned, "There could be no doubt that Putin would fight back hard."

Burns was merely reiterating common understanding at the highest level of government, back to the early nineties. Bush II's own secretary of defense Robert Gates recognized that "trying to bring Georgia and Ukraine into NATO was truly overreaching, . . . recklessly ignoring what the Russians considered their own vital national interests."

The warnings from informed government sources were strong and explicit. They were rejected by Washington from Clinton on. In fact, on to the present moment. That conclusion is confirmed by the recent comprehensive *Washington Post* study of the background to the invasion. Reviewing the study, George Beebe and Anatol Lieven observe that "the Biden administration's efforts to avert the war altogether come across as quite lacking. As Foreign Minister Sergey Lavrov put it during the weeks preceding the invasion, for Russia 'the key to everything is the guarantee that NATO will not expand eastward.' But nowhere in the *Post*'s account is there any mention that the White House considered offering concrete compromises regarding Ukraine's future admission into NATO." Rather, as the State Department had already conceded, "the United States made no effort to address one of Vladimir Putin's most often stated top security concerns—the possibility of Ukraine's membership into NATO."

In brief, provocations continued to the last minute. They were not confined to undermining negotiations but included expansion of the project of integrating Ukraine into the NATO military command, turning it into a "de facto" member of NATO, as US military journals put it.

The glaringly obvious record of provocation is, presumably, the reason for the tacit rule that the Russian assault must be called "unprovoked," a term otherwise scarcely if ever used but required in this case in polite society. Psychologists should have no problem explaining the curious behavior.

Though the provocations were consistent and conscious over many years, despite the warnings, they, of course, in no way justify Putin's resort to "the supreme international crime" of aggression. Though it may help explain a crime, provocation provides no justification for it.

As for Russia's becoming a "pariah state," I think some qualifications are in order. It is surely becoming a pariah state in Europe and the Anglosphere, to an extent that has amazed even seasoned cold warriors. Graham Fuller, one of the top figures in US intelligence for many years, recently commented that:

> I don't think that I've ever seen—in my entire life—such a dominant American media blitz as what we're seeing regarding Ukraine today. The US isn't only pressing its *interpretation* of events—the US is also engaging in full-scale *demonization* of Russia as a state, as a society, and as a culture. The bias is extraordinary—I never saw anything like this when I was involved in Russian affairs during the Cold War.

Picking up those tea leaves again, one might perhaps surmise that as in the required reference to the "unprovoked" invasion, some guilt feelings are not too well concealed.

That is the stance of the US and to varying degrees its close allies. Most of the world, however, continues to stand aloof, condemning the aggression but maintaining normal relations with Russia, just as Western critics of the US-UK invasion of Iraq maintained normal relations with the (entirely unprovoked) aggressors. There is also considerable ridicule of the pious proclamations on human rights, democracy, and "sanctity of borders" issued by the world champions in violence and subversion—matters the Global South knows about well from ample experience.

Russia claims that the US is directly involved in the Ukraine war. Is the US fighting a "proxy war" in Ukraine?

That the US is heavily involved in the war, and proudly so, is not in question. That it is fighting a proxy war is widely held outside of the Europe-Anglosphere domain. It is not hard to see why. Official US policy, open and public, is that the war must go on until Russia is so severely weakened that it cannot undertake further aggression. The policy is justified by exalted proclamations about a cosmic struggle between democracy, freedom, and all good things versus ultimate evil bent on global conquest. The fevered rhetoric is not new. The fairy tale style reached comical heights in the major Cold War document NSC 68 and is commonly found elsewhere.

Taken literally, official policy entails that Russia must be subjected to harsher punishment than Germany was at Versailles in 1919. Those targeted are likely to take explicit policy literally, with obvious consequences as to how they may react.

The assessment that the US is dedicated to a proxy war is reinforced by common Western discourse. While there is extensive discussion of how to fight Russian aggression more effectively, one finds hardly a word about how to bring the horrors to an end—horrors that go far beyond Ukraine. Those who dare to raise the question are usually vilified, even such revered figures as Henry Kissinger—though, interestingly, calls for a diplomatic settlement pass without the usual demonization when they appear in the major establishment journal.

Whatever terminology one prefers to use, the basic facts about US policy and plans are clear enough. To me, "proxy war" seems a fair term, but what matters are the policies and plans.

As was to be expected, the invasion has also led to a prolonged propaganda war on the part of all sides involved. On that note, you said recently that, with the banning of RT and other Russian media venues, Americans have less access to the official adversary than Soviets had in the 1970s. Can you elaborate a bit on this, especially since your statement about censorship in the US over the war in Ukraine was totally distorted, leaving readers to think that what you implied is that censorship in the US today is worse than it was under communism in Russia?

On the Russian side, the domestic propaganda war is extreme. On the US side, while there are no official bans, it's hard to deny Graham Fuller's observations.

Literal censorship in the US and other Western societies is rare. But as George Orwell wrote in 1945 in his (unpublished) introduction to *Animal Farm*, the "sinister fact" about free societies is that censorship is "largely voluntary. Unpopular ideas can be silenced, and inconvenient facts kept dark, without the need for any official ban," generally a more effective means of thought control than overt force.

Orwell was referring to England, but the practice goes far beyond, in revealing ways. To take a current example, the highly respected Middle East scholar Alain Gresh was censored by French TV because of his critical comments on Israel's latest terrorist crimes in occupied Gaza.

Gresh observed that "this form of censorship is exceptional. On the question of Palestine, it is rarely presented in such an obvious manner." A more effective form of censorship is exercised by careful selection of commentators. They are acceptable, Gresh concludes, if they "regret the violence" while adding that Israel has "the right to defend itself" and stress the need to "fight extremists on both sides," but "it seems there is no room for those who radically criticise Israel's occupation and apartheid."

In the United States, such means of silencing unpopular ideas and keeping inconvenient facts dark have been honed to a high art, as one would expect in an unusually free society. By now there are literally thousands of pages documenting the practices in close detail. Fine organizations of media critique like FAIR in the US and Media Lens in England pour out more on a regular basis.

There is also extensive discussion in print about the advantages of Western models of indoctrination over the crude and transparent measures of totalitarian states. The more sophisticated devices of free society instill doctrines by presupposition, not assertion, as in the case Gresh describes. The rules are never heard, just tacitly assumed. Debate is allowed, even encouraged, but within bounds, which are unexpressed and rigid. They become internalized. As Orwell puts it, those subjected to subtle indoctrination, with a good education for example, have instilled into them the understanding that there are certain things "it wouldn't do to say"—or even to think.

The modes of indoctrination need not be conscious. Those who implement them already have internalized the understanding that there are certain things "it wouldn't do to say"—or even to think.

Such devices are particularly effective in a highly insular culture like that of the US, where few would dream of seeking foreign sources, particularly those of a reviled enemy, and where the appearance of limitless freedom offers no incentive to go beyond the established framework.

It's in this general context that I mentioned the case of banning of Russian sources such as *RT*—"exceptional" as Gresh pointed out. Though there was no time to elaborate in a few brief remarks in a long interview on other topics, the direct banning brought to mind an interesting topic I had written about thirty years ago. Like much other work, the article reviewed many cases of the usual modes of silencing unpopular ideas and suppressing unwanted facts in free societies, but it also reported government-academic studies seeking to determine where Russians were getting their news in the seventies: the late Soviet period, pre-Gorbachev. The results indicated that despite the rigid censorship, a remarkably high percentage of Russians were accessing such sources as BBC, even illegal samizdat, and may well have been better informed than Americans.

I checked at the time with Russian émigrés who related their own experiences of evading the intrusive but not very efficient censorship. They basically confirmed the picture, though they felt that the numbers reported were too high, possibly because the samples might have been skewed to Leningrad and Moscow.

Direct banning of the publications of adversaries is not only illegitimate but also harmful. Thus, it would be important for Americans to have been aware that immediately before the invasion, the Russian Foreign Minister was emphasizing that "the key to everything is the guarantee that NATO will not expand eastward" to Ukraine—the firm redline for decades. Had there been any concern to avoid horrible crimes and to move to a better world, this could have been an opening to explore.

The same is true of Russian government pronouncements when the invasion was already underway; for example, Lavrov's statement on May 29 that:

we have goals: to demilitarise Ukraine (there should be no weapons threatening Russia on its territory); to restore the rights of the Russian people in line with the Constitution of Ukraine (the Kiev regime violated it by adopting anti-Russia laws) and the conventions (in which Ukraine takes part); and to denazify Ukraine. Nazi and neo-Nazi theory and practice have deeply permeated daily life in Ukraine and are codified in its laws.

It might be useful for Americans to have access to such words by a flip of the switch on TV, at least those Americans with some interest in ending the horrors rather than plunging into the apocalyptic battle conjured up from the tea leaves to cage the rampaging bear before it devours all of us.

Peace negotiations between Russia and Ukraine have stagnated since early spring. Apparently, Russia wants to enforce peace on its own terms, while Ukraine seems to have adopted the position that there can be no negotiations until Russia's prospects on the battlefield become dim. Do you see an end to this conflict any time soon? Is negotiating to end the war an appeasement, as those who oppose peace talks claim?

Whether negotiations have stagnated is not entirely clear. Little is reported, but it seems possible that "talks to end the war are back on the agenda: A meeting between Ukraine, Turkey and the UN shows that Kyiv may be warming to the idea of discussions with Moscow," and that "Given Russian territorial advances," it may be that Ukraine "has softened its opposition to considering a diplomatic end to the war." If so, it's up to Putin to show whether his "avowed zeal for negotiations is really a bluff," or has some substance.

What's happening is obscure. It brings to mind the "Afghan trap" that we discussed earlier, when the US was fighting a proxy war with Russia "to the last Afghan," as Cordovez and Harrison put it in their definitive study of how the UN managed to arrange for a Russian withdrawal despite US efforts to prevent a diplomatic settlement. That was the period when Carter's National Security Adviser Zbigniew Brzezinski, who claimed credit for instigating the Russian invasion, applauded the outcome even though it came at the cost of some "agitated Muslims."

Are we witnessing something similar today? Perhaps.

No doubt Russia wants to enforce peace on its own terms. A negotiated diplomatic settlement is one that each side tolerates while relinquishing some of its own demands. There's only one way to find out whether Russia is serious about negotiations: try. Nothing is lost.

On the battlefield prospects, there are confident and sharply conflicting claims by military experts. I have no such credentials; I think it's fair to conclude from the spectacle that the fog of war has not lifted. We do know what the US position is, or at least was last April at the Ramstein Air Base conference of NATO powers and other military leaders that the US. organized: "Ukraine clearly believes it can win and so does everyone here." Whether it was actually believed then, or is now, I don't know, and know of no way to find out.

For what it's worth, I personally respect the words of Jeremy Corbyn published on the day after the Ramstein war conference opened, words that contributed to his being virtually expelled from the Labour Party: "There must be an immediate ceasefire in Ukraine followed by a Russian troop withdrawal and agreement between Russia and Ukraine on future security arrangements. All wars end in a negotiation of some sort—so why not now?"

Noam Chomsky

TWENTY-FIRST-CENTURY US FOREIGN POLICY IS SHAPED BY FEARS OF CHINA'S RISE

August 4, 2022

C. J. Polychroniou: *Noam, Western powers are responding to China's rise as a dominant economic and military power with ever-increasing calls in favor of bellicose diplomacy. US general Mark Milley, chairman of the Joint Chiefs of Staff, said during a recent trip to the Indo-Pacific that China has become more aggressive in the region and the Biden administration has described it as a "pacing threat." Rishi Sunak, currently the leading candidate to replace outgoing prime minister Boris Johnson, said China is the UK's "biggest threat." Sunak has promised to ban Confucius Institutes, learning centers funded and run by an organization affiliated with the Chinese government, from the UK if he becomes the next prime minister. Why is the West so frightened of a prospering China and what does it say about imperialism in the twenty-first century?*

Noam Chomsky: It may be useful to take a brief but broader look, first at the record of the fears, then at the geostrategic circumstances of their current manifestations. We are speaking here of the West in a narrow sense, specifically the Anglo-American "special relationship," which since 1945 has been the United States, with Britain a junior partner, sometimes reluctant, sometimes eager to serve the master, strikingly in the Blair years.

The fears are far-reaching. In the case of Russia, they go back to 1917. Secretary of State Robert Lansing warned President Wilson that the Bolsheviks were appealing "to the proletariat of all countries, to the ignorant and mentally deficient, who by their numbers are urged to become masters . . . a very real danger in view of the present social unrest throughout the world."

Lansing's concerns were reiterated in different circumstances by Secretary of State John Foster Dulles forty years later, when he lamented that the US is "hopelessly far behind the Soviets in developing controls over the minds and emotions of unsophisticated peoples." The basic problem, he elaborated, is the Communist "ability to get control of mass movements . . . something we have no capacity to duplicate. . . . The poor people are the ones they appeal to and they have always wanted to plunder the rich."

These are recurrent fears of the privileged, in one form or another, throughout history.

Scholarship substantially agrees with Lansing's concerns. The acknowledged dean of Cold War scholarship, John Lewis Gaddis, traces the Cold War back to 1917, with the Bolshevik challenge "to the very survival of the capitalist order . . . a profound and potentially far-reaching intervention by the new Soviet government in the internal affairs, not just of the West, but of virtually every country in the world." The Bolshevik intervention was what Lansing recognized: working people around the world might take note and react, the feared domino effect, a dominant theme in planning. Gaddis goes on to argue that the Western (including US) invasion of Russia was a justified act of self-defense against this intolerable challenge to what is right and just, what is now termed "the rule-based international order" (in which the US sets the rules).

Gaddis was appealing to a concept that the US War Department in 1945 called "logical illogicality," referring to the postwar plans for the US to take control of most of the world and surround Russia with military force, while denying the adversary any comparable rights. The superficial observer might regard that as illogical, but it has a deeper logic, the War Department recognized—a logic called "imperialism" by the unkind.

The same doctrines of logical illogicality reign today as the US defends itself from Eurasian threats. At the Western border of Eurasia, the US defends itself by expanding to the Russian border the aggressive military alliance it runs, NATO. At the Eastern border, the US defends itself by establishing a ring of "sentinel states" to "encircle" China, armed with high precision weapons aimed at China, backed with huge naval military exercises (RIMPAC [Rim of the Pacific]) aimed not very subtly at China. All of this is part of the more extensive efforts at encirclements, jointly with "subimperialist" Australia, which we have discussed earlier, borrowing Clinton Fernandes's term and analysis. One effect might be to increase the incentive for China to attack Taiwan in order to break out of the encirclement and have open access to the oceans.

Needless to say, there are no reciprocal rights. Logical illogicality.

Always the actions are in "self-defense." If there was a violent power in history that wasn't acting in "self-defense," it would be helpful to be reminded of it.

Fear of China is more visceral, drawing from the deep racist currents that have poisoned American society since its origins. In the nineteenth century, Chinese people were kidnapped and brought to work as virtual slaves to build railroads as the nation expanded to its "natural borders"; the slur that was applied to them ("coolie") was an import from Britain, where Chinese workers also served as virtual slave laborers generating Britain's wealth. Chinese people who tried to settle were subjected to vicious racist attacks. Chinese laborers were banned entry for ten years in the 1882 Chinese Exclusion Act, and Chinese were banned entirely in the racist 1924 immigration act, aimed primarily at Italians and Jews (sending many to gas chambers when entry to the US was denied).

"Yellow peril" hysteria was reawakened in the 1950s, after China's stunning defeat of [Douglas] MacArthur's army in Korea. The fears resonate often, ranging widely in nature. At one level, Lyndon Johnson warned that without superior air power, unless we stop "them" in Vietnam, "they" will sweep over us and take all "we" have. At another level, when Congress breaks its GOP-imposed logjam to pass legislation to reconstruct collapsing infrastructure and the crucial chip industry, not because the US needs them but to overcome the challenge of China's development.

There are others who pose imminent threats to our survival. Right now, Russia. The chair of the House Permanent Select Committee on Intelligence, Adam Schiff, draws on deeply rooted cultural maladies when he warns that unless we stop them in Ukraine, they'll be attacking our shores.

There is never a dearth of terrifying enemies, but the "heathen Chinese" have always conjured up special fears.

Let's turn from understandable paranoia about the poor who want to plunder the rich to the second topic: world order and imperialism in the twenty-first century, and the intense US-UK geopolitical concerns about an emergent China.

It's useful to recall the experience of our predecessor in global dominance. An island off the coast of Europe, Britain's primary concern was to prevent unification of Europe into a force beyond its control. Similarly, though magnified far beyond, the US and its Western hemisphere domains can be regarded as an "island" off the coast of the Eurasian land mass—which is the basis for world control, according to the "heartland theory" of Halford Mackinder, a founder of modern geopolitics, whose thoughts are now being revived by global strategists.

Extending the logic of imperial Britain, then, we would expect the US to be seeking to prevent unification of the "heartland" as an independent force, not subject to US domination. The self-defense operations at the western and eastern ends of the heartland also fall into place.

Conflict over heartland unification has been a significant theme in post–World War II history. During the Cold War years, there were some European initiatives to construct a unified Europe incorporating Russia that would be an independent force in world affairs. Such ideas were advanced most prominently by Charles de Gaulle, with echoes in Germany. They were beaten back in favor of the Atlanticist system, NATO-based, largely run from Washington.

Heartland unification took on new prominence with the collapse of the Soviet Union. The idea of a "common European home" from Lisbon to Vladivostok was advanced by Mikhail Gorbachev, who looked forward to transition to social democracy in Russia and its former domains, and to a coequal partnership with the US in creating a world order based on cooperation rather than conflict. These are topics of substantial scholarship, explored in unusual depth by historian Richard Sakwa.

Predictably, the US—the island off the coast of Eurasia—strongly opposed these initiatives. Throughout the Cold War, they were not much of a problem, given power relations and prevailing doctrine about the Kremlin conspiracy to conquer the world. The task took new forms with the collapse of the Soviet Union. With some wavering at the margins, the US quickly adopted the policy of "enlargement" of the Atlantic power system, with Russia participating only on subordinate terms. Coequal partnership proposals continued to be put forth during the Putin years, until quite recently. They were "anathema to those who believe in enduring hegemony of the Atlanticist power system," Sakwa observes.

Putin's invasion of Ukraine, after dismissing tentative French and German efforts to avert the tragic crime, have settled the issue, at least for now. For now, Europe has succumbed to the Atlanticist doctrine, even adopting the formal US goal of "weakening Russia" severely, whatever the cost to Ukraine and well beyond.

For now. Without integration, German-based Europe and Russia will very likely decline. Russia, with its enormous natural resources, is likely to continue to drift into the massive China-based Eurasian development project, the Belt and Road Initiative (BRI), now expanding to Africa and even Latin America.

The temptation for Europe to join the BRI system, already strong, will likely intensify. The German-based integrated production system in Europe, stretching from the Netherlands to Russia's former Eastern European satellites, has become the most successful economic system in the world. It relies heavily on the huge export market and investment opportunities in China, and on Russia's rich natural resources, even including metals needed for transition to renewable energy. Abandoning all of that, along with access to the expanding global BRI system, will be quite a price to pay for hanging on to Washington's coattails. Such considerations will not be absent as the world system takes shape in the wake of the COVID crisis and Russia's invasion of Ukraine.

The question of Eurasian integration in a common European home falls within a more general framework, which cannot be forgotten for a moment. Either the great powers will cooperate to face ominous global crises or they will march to oblivion together.

With the bitter antagonisms of today, it may seem impossible to imagine such cooperation. But it need not be an unattainable idea. In 1945 it seemed no less impossible to imagine that France, Germany, England, and smaller European powers could cooperate in a Western Europe without borders and with some common institutions. They are not without internal problems, and Britain has recently pulled out, dooming itself to becoming a probably fading US satellite. Nonetheless, it is a stunning reversal of centuries of savage mutual destruction, peaking in the twentieth century.

Taking note of that, Sakwa writes, "What for one generation is a sad delusion, for another becomes a realistic and necessary project." A project that is essential if a livable world is to emerge from today's chaos and violence.

China-Russia ties have deepened after Russia's invasion of Ukraine, though there are probably limits to the partnership. In any case, is there something else in this strategic relationship between two autocratic nations besides the concern for limiting US power and influence? And to what extent could the US take advantage of potential strains and divisions in the Sino-Russian relationship as it did during the Cold War era?

The record during the Cold War is instructive. Even when Russia and China were close to war, the US kept insisting on the immense threat posed by the imagined "Sino-Soviet alliance." Something similar was true of North Vietnam. Its leaders recognized that their real enemy was China: the US could devastate Vietnam with its incomparable means of violence, but it would go away. China would always be there, a permanent threat. US planners refused to hear.

Kissinger's diplomacy belatedly recognized the facts and exploited China-Russia conflicts. I don't think that carries lessons for today. Circumstances are very different.

Putin and associates appear to have visions of a Russian sphere occupying an independent place between the Atlanticist and China-based global systems. That does not seem very likely to transpire. More likely, China will accept Russia as a subordinate, providing raw materials, advanced weapons, scientific talent, maybe more.

The Atlanticist powers, along with their Asian subimperial associates, are becoming isolated in the world scene. The Global South is mostly standing aloof, not joining in sanctions against Russia or breaking commercial and other relations. Though it has serious internal problems, China keeps moving ahead with its vast development, investment, loan programs abroad, and technological progress at home. It is far in the lead in the fast-growing sustainable energy sector and has just surprised the world by creating a super-advanced chip, still probably years short of production but a central part of the modern advanced economy.

There are many uncertainties, but it seems a fair guess that these tendencies will persist. If there is a break, it may be unwillingness of German-based Europe to continue to suffer the effects of subordination in the Atlanticist system. The advantages of a common European home may well become increasingly tempting, with major consequences for world order.

India is being wooed by China, Russia, and the US. Does India have anything to worry about in a strong Sino-Russian partnership? Can the Quad rely on India for full cooperation in connection with its mission and objectives in the Indo-Pacific region?

Before discussing India's foreign policy concerns, let's not forget some stark facts. South Asia is facing major catastrophe. Summer heat is already at a level that is barely survivable for the vast poor majority, and much worse is coming. India and Pakistan must cooperate on this and related crises, like management of dwindling water resources. Instead, each is devoting scarce resources to unwinnable wars, for Pakistan an intolerable burden.

Both states have severe internal problems. In India, PM Modi has been leading an effort to destroy India's secular democracy, which, with all its flaws, is still one of the great achievements of the post-colonial era. His program is aimed at creating a racist Hindu ethnocracy. He is a natural associate in the growing alliance of states with similar characteristics: Hungary along with Israel and its Abraham Accord partners, closely linked with the core sectors of the GOP. That's aside from the brutal repression of Kashmir, reportedly the most militarized territory in the world and the scene of harsh repression. The occupation of foreign territory again qualifies him for association with the Abraham Accords, which bring together the other two cases of criminal annexation and occupation, Israel and Morocco.

All of that is part of the background for addressing the serious questions of India's international relations.

India is engaged in a difficult balancing act. Russia remains by far its major source of arms. It is engaged in a long and worsening border dispute with China. It therefore must eye with concern a deepening Russia-China alliance. The US-run Quad (US-Japan-Australia-India) is intended to be a core part of the encirclement of China, but India is a reluctant partner, unwilling to fully adopt the subimperial role. Unlike the other members of the Quad, it joins the rest of the Global South in refusing to become embroiled in what they see as a US-Russia proxy war in Ukraine. India cannot however move too far in alienating the US, which is also a natural ally, particularly so in the framework of the emerging GOP-centered alliance of reactionary states.

Altogether, a complex situation, even overlooking the enormous internal problems facing South Asia.

The US is a country in political and social turmoil and possibly in the midst of a historic transition. Its influence in the world has been weakening in recent years, and its institutions are under severe attack from dark and reactionary forces. Indeed, with US democracy in sharp decline, there is even talk of a radical plan for the restructuring of the federal government in the event that Donald Trump returns to power in 2024. To what extent has imperial overstretch contributed to the decline of the domestic society, and to what degree can domestic politics have an effect on foreign policy decision-making? In either case, is a declining US less or more likely to represent a threat to global peace and security?

There has been much talk of US decline for decades. There is some truth to it. The peak of US power, with no historical parallel, was in 1945. That obviously couldn't last and has been declining since, though by some measures US power remains about as it was then, as Sean Kenji Starrs shows in his important studies of control of wealth by transnationals.

There is a great deal to say about this general topic, discussed elsewhere. But keeping to the narrower question raised, recent US decline is mostly from internal blows. And it is severe. One crucial measure is mortality. The headline of one recent study reads: "America Was in an Early-Death Crisis Long before COVID." The study goes on to show that "even before the pandemic began, more people here were dying at younger ages than in comparably wealthy nations." The data are startling, going well beyond even the "deaths of despair" phenomenon among working-age white Americans that has led to increasing mortality, something unheard of, apart from war and pestilence. That is only one striking indication of how the country has been falling apart socioeconomically and politically since the neoliberal assault took shape with Reagan-Bush, Clinton, and their successors.

The "radical plan" to undermine the remnants of American democracy was announced a few days before the November election, and quickly forgotten in the ensuing turmoil. It was revealed only recently in an *Axios* investigation. The basic idea is to reverse the programs since the nineteenth century to create an apolitical civil service, an essential foundation for a functioning democracy. Trump issued an executive order giving the president (intended to be him, or maybe more accurately Him) the authority to fill the top ranks of the civil service with loyalists, a step toward the fascist ideal of a powerful party with a Maximal Leader that controls the society. Biden reversed the order. Congressional Democrats are seeking to pass legislation to bar such a direct attack on democracy, but Republicans are unlikely to go along, anticipating that their many current initiatives to establish their permanent rule as a minority party will bear fruit. The reactionary Roberts court might well approve.

More may be in store. The court decided to take up an outlandish case, *Moore v. Harper*, which, if the court approves, would permit state legislatures, mostly Republican because of well-known GOP structural advantages, to pick electors who reject the popular vote and keep to party loyalty. This "independent state legislature theory" does have some constitutional basis but has been considered so outrageous that it has been dismissed—until now, as the GOP hurtles forward in its campaign to hold on to power no matter what the irrelevant population wants.

It doesn't seem to me that the GOP campaign to undermine democracy results from imperial overstretch. There's a good deal of valuable scholarship about its nature and roots, which seem to lie elsewhere, primarily in search for power.

It's not clear what the impact would be on foreign policy. Trump himself is a loose cannon, with no clear idea in his head apart from ME! He also has a penchant for wrecking whatever anyone else has helped construct—while always adhering very closely to the primary principle: enrich the super-rich and corporate power, at least that part that doesn't veer to some criticism of his august majesty. His GOP competitors are in such awe and fear of his power over the mass voting base that they say very little.

The general implications for global peace and security seem clear enough. Trump's triumphs in this domain were to greatly enhance the two major threats to survival of organized human society: environmental destruction and nuclear war. Neither were spared his wrecking ball. He pulled out of the Paris agreements on impending climate catastrophe and did what he could to eliminate regulations that somewhat mitigate the effects on Americans. He carried forward the GOP program (started by G. W. Bush) to dismantle the arms control regime that has been laboriously constructed to reduce the threat of terminal nuclear war. He also wrecked the joint agreement with Iran on nuclear policy (JCPOA [Joint Comprehensive Plan of Action), violating the UN Security Council endorsement of the agreement, again enhancing global threats.

What he might do on particular issues is anyone's guess. Perhaps what he had just heard on Fox News.

The idea that the future of the world might soon again be in such hands almost surpasses belief.

There's no shortage of vital tasks ahead.

Noam Chomsky

US GOVERNMENT'S NONRESPONSE TO CLIMATE CRISIS HAS HISTORICAL PRECEDENT

July 22, 2022

C. J. Polychroniou: *Noam, the United States, by all accounts, is doing a horrendous job at tackling the climate crisis. The Environmental Performance Index, developed by Yale and Columbia Universities, ranks the US 43rd among 180 nations on performance indicators covering climate change and environmental health, and ecosystem vitality. In fact, the US is the only major economy without a national climate change policy, and Biden's push for a clean energy program is all but dead, thanks to the determination of a single senator to protect his own portfolio investment over the future of the planet. On top of that, the Supreme Court has restricted the EPA's authority to regulate greenhouse gas emissions. Clearly, then, the US is not going to meet the target of achieving a 50 [to] 52 percent reduction from 2005 levels of greenhouse gas emissions in 2030. So, the question of paramount importance, in my own humble view, is this: Why is the US so uniquely bad in confronting the climate crisis? There has got to be more to the story besides the influence of the fossil fuel industry, no?*

Noam Chomsky: A lot more. Some indications about what is underway were given in the Supreme Court EPA decision. In the first place, there was no reason at all for the court to take up this case, which had to do with a 2015 proposal that was never implemented and is not in force. Presumably, the court went out of its way to select the case as part of a long-term campaign to undermine the "administrative state"—that is, to undermine public capacity to restrict rapacious, and in this case destructive, private power. Or to put it more vividly, as we've discussed before, the capacity to restrict what Adam Smith called the "vile maxim": "All for ourselves and nothing for other people," the maxim that seems to guide "the masters of mankind . . . in every age of the world."

In his age, the masters were the merchants and manufacturers of England; in ours, the private institutions that have become increasingly concentrated and obscenely wealthy during the neoliberal assault against the global population. The fossil fuel companies are among them, but others in the economic stratosphere will be beneficiaries of dismantling of the administrative state, a substantial intensification of the neoliberal class war. That's what we are likely to see in the days ahead if the GOP, with its extreme subordination to private wealth and corporate power, extends its already substantial hold over the society.

It will be a short-term victory, however. There are good reasons why in past years the business world regularly called for regulation and other forms of state intervention to protect itself from the ravages of uncontrolled markets. The not-very-hidden principle underlying the vile maxim is that you, the "unpeople" of the world, are to be thrown into the market to find some way to survive. We, the masters, demand and receive ample protection from the nanny state.

The need for a "visible hand" is vastly more urgent now as the world hurtles toward destruction of organized human life, with the narrow window for survival being closed by the masters and their servants in the political system, basking in the applause of the most enthusiastic proponents of the vile maxim.

That leaves unanswered the deeper question: Why is the US so "uniquely bad"? It hasn't always been so. That's important to remember. What is happening today is chillingly reminiscent of the 1930s, when the global state capitalist system was collapsing, with many "morbid symptoms." Gramsci's phrase, writing in Mussolini's prison cells. Then the US was a beacon of hope. While Europe was descending into fascist darkness, the US was paving the way to social democracy under the impact of a revived and militant labor movement, with a sympathetic administration.

To be sure, much of the business world was strenuously opposed to these developments, biding its time for the opportunity to restore the business rule that has been unusually strong in the US, for historical reasons that we have discussed before. World War II put the conflicts in the background. When the war ended, the campaign to dismantle social democratic heresies was undertaken with vigor, but didn't become triumphant until the neoliberal years, aided by neoliberal ideologues fresh from their service in Pinochet's vicious dictatorship.

The fate of Biden's energy program carries lessons as well. While nowhere near sufficient, the program was a long step beyond anything that preceded, as a result of major activist campaigns and the Sanders movement. The final blow was indeed delivered by coal baron Joe Manchin, who had been chipping away at the program steadily and finally declared that he'd accept nothing meaningful.

Manchin gave reasons: his concern over the deficit and inflation. Hardly credible. On the deficit, one way to address it is by reversing the radically regressive tax cuts of the neoliberal years, culminating in Trump's one legislative achievement: the "Donor Relief Act of 2017," as Joseph Stiglitz called it, a huge gift to the very rich and corporate sector, stabbing everyone else in the back. For the GOP, that is a red line that can't be touched (along with funding the IRS to enable it [to] catch wealthy tax cheats). Manchin goes along. No taxes on the rich. We have to preserve one of the great achievements of the neoliberal programs: for the first time in a century, billionaires pay taxes at a lower rate than workers.

What about inflation? There's no credible argument that relates Biden's climate program to the worldwide inflation. And if Manchin had concerns about this, he'd be calling for a windfall tax on corporate profits, cutting the bloated Pentagon budget, reversing the sharply regressive tax changes of the neoliberal years, and lots more.

Most Democrats are deeply dissatisfied with Biden's overall approach to
the climate crisis, according to a Pew Research Center report released just
last week. This is especially so among young Americans, which leaves room
for hoping that the course of the country can change in the near future. In
any case, couldn't the case be made that the Democrats' sweeping plan to
tackle the climate crisis was destined to fail if they tried to accomplish this
through backroom deals rather than taking the cause directly to people
and communities across the land?

Biden is unfairly blamed for this and other failures of his legislative program. The prime reason for the failure is the Mitch McConnell strategy:
block anything that might help the country, blame the harsh outcomes
on the Democrats, retake power and intensify the harm for the population while enriching still more the constituency that counts. It works.

A popular-based party committed to the common good would
have organized throughout the country, at the grassroots. That's not
the modern Democratic Party. Would it have made any difference?
It's hard to say. Could it, for example, have touched the Republican
voting base, now in thrall to their denialist leadership and the divine
Trump? Recall the recent polls that show that given a choice of twenty-nine issues of concern for the coming election, moderate Republicans picked climate change as twenty-eighth, the rest twenty-ninth.
That's not easy to break through.

Not easy, but not necessarily impossible. It's useful to recall the
Yellow Vest slogan: "You privileged people are worried about the end
of the world, we're worried about the end of the month." When people
are concerned about how to survive in their precarious lives, there's
not much use telling them that scientists, whom they distrust anyway,
are predicting dire consequences down the road.

Certainly, that message should never be suppressed. People care
about their grandchildren. But it should be accompanied by showing
how you can get a better life and better jobs right now by shifting from
destruction of the environment that sustains life to creating a better
one. Right now. I can refer again to Bob Pollin's outstanding work,
both scrupulous analysis and direct engagement on the ground.

President Joe Biden said he will use his presidential powers to tackle the climate emergency. Every president since Washington has used executive powers in various ways, but it is unclear what Biden has in mind with regard to climate policy. For instance, he can issue an executive order to stop approvals of all new fossil fuel infrastructure projects and ban federal fossil fuel leasing and drilling. Yet, he has been pushing all along for more oil production and approved more permits for oil and gas leasing on federal lands in 2021 than Trump did in the first year of his presidency. So, whom is he kidding when he talks about using the executive order power to tackle the climate emergency?

On approving more production and permits, there is an excuse: It was ordered by the right-wing judiciary. Whether the excuse is valid or a pretext, one can debate. The reaction to Russia's invasion of Ukraine should move the minute hand of the Doomsday Clock even closer to midnight by reversing the limited efforts to move toward sustainable energy. Again, one can debate to what extent that choice was forced. The range of executive orders is limited, and the court might again resort to its "major questions" doctrine to accelerate the race to catastrophe, as it did in *West Virginia v. EPA*.

There is one conclusion that we can draw with fair confidence. Unless a mass popular movement develops that is powerful enough to break through the many barriers, humanity is facing a bitter fate.

The Pew Research Center report cited earlier reveals that an overwhelming majority of America favors planting a trillion trees to absorb carbon emissions and providing a tax credit to businesses for developing technology to capture and store carbon emissions. This confirms similar public views on climate policy captured by Pew surveys in past years, which seems to indicate that the vision of the Green New Deal has yet to make inroads into mainstream America. If this is the case, what has gone wrong? And what does it say about the prospect of implementing a Global Green New Deal, which was first launched by the United Nations Environmental Project in 2009?

The two favored policies have a common feature: no reduction in fossil fuel use—or reduction in profits for the fossil fuel conglomerate (the producers, the banks, the corporations otherwise involved in poisoning the atmosphere). The much harder message to get across is that we have to make serious moves right now to face the looming challenge, which is right in front of our eyes these scorching days. The longer we delay, the more forbidding the obstacles, the greater the cost and suffering. We can see what's gone wrong. There's no secret about how to steer the *Titanic* away from the icebergs. There's still time.

I'll reiterate something so obvious it shouldn't even have to be articulated. This must be a common effort, everywhere. Crucially, that means a common effort of the great powers, hard as this may be to conceive at the moment. It means concern for the most miserable and tortured victims, who are not responsible for the crisis that has been created by the rich in the rich societies but will be punished more severely than anyone else. It means concern for the species that enrich the Earth and are being destroyed by our foolishness and cruel disregard for what we are doing to our common home.

Noam Chomsky

BIDEN'S MIDDLE EAST TRIP CONTAINS ECHOES OF TRUMP'S POLICIES

July 15, 2022

C. J. Polychroniou: *US foreign policy under Joe Biden is barely distinguishable from that of Trump's, as you pointed out just a few months after Biden took office. Indeed, as a presidential candidate, Biden had called Saudi Arabia a "pariah" state following the killing of journalist Jamal Khashoggi, but as president he is warming up to its de facto and murderous leader Mohammed bin Salman (MBS). What do you think is the purpose of his visit to Saudi Arabia?*

Noam Chomsky: It is surely a mistake to carry out a sadistic assassination of a journalist for the *Washington Post*, particularly one who was hailed as "a guardian of truth" in 2018 when he was chosen as Person of the Year by *Time Magazine*.

That's definitely bad form, particularly when done carelessly and not well concealed.

US relations with the family kingdom called "Saudi Arabia" have always proceeded amicably, undisturbed by its horrifying record of human rights abuses, which persists. That's hardly a surprise in the case of "a stupendous source of strategic power, and one of the greatest material prizes in world history . . . probably the richest economic prize in the world in the field of foreign investment," as the State Department described the prize in the mid-1940s, when the US wrested it from Britain in a mini-war during World War II. More generally, the Middle East was regarded at a high level as the most "strategically important area in the world," as President Eisenhower said. While assessments have varied over eighty years, the essence remains.

The same is true with regard to countries that do not rise to this impressive level. The US has regularly provided strong support for murderous tyrants when it was convenient, often to the last minute of their rule: [Ferdinand] Marcos, [François] Duvalier, [Nicolae] Ceausescu, Suharto, and a long string of other villains, including Saddam Hussein until he violated (or maybe misunderstood) orders and invaded Kuwait. And, of course, the US is simply following in the path of its imperial predecessors. Nothing new, not even the rhetoric of benevolent intent.

The most revealing examples are when the intent really is benevolent, not unconcealed Kissingerian cynicism ("realism"). An instructive case is Robert Pastor's explanation of why the Carter Human Rights administration reluctantly had to support the [Anastasio] Somoza regime, and when that proved impossible, to maintain the US-trained National Guard even after it had been massacring the population "with a brutality a nation usually reserves for its enemy," killing some forty thousand people.

The Latin America specialist of the [Jimmy Carter] administration and a genuine liberal scholar, Pastor was doubtless sincere in voicing these regrets. He was also perceptive in providing the compelling reasons: "The United States did not want to control Nicaragua or the other nations of the region, but it also did not want developments to get out of control. It wanted Nicaraguans to act independently, *except* when doing so would affect US interests adversely" (his emphasis).

We sincerely want you to be free—free to do what we want.

It's much the same with Saudi Arabia. We wish they were more polite, but first things first.

In the case of Biden's visit, first things presumably include renewed efforts to persuade MBS to increase production so as to reduce high gas prices in the US. There would be other ways, for example, a wind-fall tax on the fossil fuel industries that are drowning in profits, with the revenues distributed to those who have been gouged by the neo-liberal class war of the past forty years, which has transferred some $50 trillion to the pockets of the top 1 percent. That, however, is "polit-ically impossible."

Politically even more impossible in elite calculations would be the feasible measures to try to stave off catastrophe by moving rapidly to cut off the flow of these poisons. These need not, however, be the cal-culations of those who have some interest in leaving a decent world to their children and grandchildren. Time is short.

There are broader considerations in Biden's Middle East tour. One goal surely is to firm up Trump's one great geopolitical achievement: the Abraham Accords, which raised tacit relations among the most brutal and criminal states of the Middle East–North Africa (MENA) region to formal alliance. The accords have been widely hailed as a contribution to peace and prosperity, though not all are delighted. Not, for example, Sahrawis, handed over to the Moroccan dicta-torship to secure its agreement to join the accords—in violation of international law, but in conformity to the "rules-based international order" that the US and its allies prefer to the archaic and unacceptable UN-based order.

Sahrawis can join Palestinians and Syrian Druze, whose territo-ries have been annexed by Israel in violation of the unanimous orders of the Security Council, now endorsed by the US. And they can also join other "unpeople," not least the Palestinian victims of Israel's bru-tal and illegal occupation in areas not officially annexed.

Celebration of these diplomatic triumphs will presumably also be heralded as one of the achievements of Biden's visit, though not exactly in these terms.

Israel may be the only country in the world where Biden is less popular than Trump, and one cannot, of course, forget the numerous times that he had been humiliated by former Israeli Prime Minister Bibi Netanyahu. Is there anything that Biden aims to accomplish with his visit to Israel other than reaffirm US support and deepen the role of the alliance between the two countries in the region? After all, the Biden administration proceeded with whitewashing Israel's killing of Palestinian American journalist Shireen Abu Akleh in advance of the president's visit to the Middle East.

As in the Khashoggi case, the handling of Abu Akleh's killing was bad form. Not just the killing—or, quite likely, assassination. It's not wise, in front of TV cameras, to allow the IDF [Israel Defense Forces] to attack a funeral procession and even the pallbearers, forcing them to almost drop the coffin. The brazenness of the assault is a revealing illustration of the drift of Israel to the right and the confidence that the boss will accept virtually anything. The confidence is not entirely misplaced, particularly after the four Trump years of lavish gifts and kicking Palestinians in the face.

I haven't seen polls, but it wouldn't be much of a surprise to find that Trump is also popular in Hungary's "illiberal democracy," praised by Trump and virtually worshipped by media star Tucker Carlson on the far right. Orbán's Hungary is now becoming a close ally of Israel on the basis of shared racist attitudes and practices and shared grievances about being unappreciated by soft-hearted liberals in the West.

It's an open question how much domestic capital Biden will win with his expected professions of eternal love for Israel. That stance has become less popular among his liberal base than it used to be as Israel's criminal behavior becomes harder to gloss over. All-out support for Israel has shifted to Evangelicals and the right, sectors of which believe Biden is not the elected president and a substantial contingent of which believes Biden and other top Democrats are grooming children for sexual abuse. But there will still probably be some domestic gains. And it will show the hawkish elements that run foreign policy that he's committed to containment of Iran by an Israel-Saudi alliance, to borrow prevailing doctrine.

Biden may hope to firm up the alliance, but they scarcely need his help. Rhetoric aside, the alliance has been firm since 1967.

In brief, at the time, there was a sharp conflict in the Arab world—in fact, an actual war in Yemen—between Saudi-based radical Islam and Egypt-based secular nationalism. Like Britain before it, the US tended to support radical Islam, seeing it as less of a threat to imperial dominance. Israel settled the matter for the time being by handing the victory to Saudi Arabia. It was at that point that US support for Israel took the extreme form that has since prevailed, as part of a Middle East strategy based on three pillars: Israel, Saudi Arabia, Iran (then under the Shah). Technically, the three were at war. In reality, they were tacit allies, very close allies in the case of Israel and Iran.

The Abraham Accords raise the alliance to a formal level, now with a slightly different cast of characters. It seems to be proceeding well on its own on the basis of shared interests. It's not clear that Biden can do much beyond expressing US support, which in any event is hardly in doubt.

Do you see any reason why Palestinian leaders should meet with Biden? Can they accomplish anything else by doing so other than have their pictures taken with the president of the United States?

Failure to do so will evoke a stream of hostile propaganda, the last thing the beleaguered Palestinians need right now. Doing so will achieve little or nothing, but it's the least bad option, it seems.

On this narrow question, that is. Palestinian hopes lie elsewhere.

It may seem strange to say this, in the light of the colossal and unprecedented US support for Israel since its demonstration of its military strength in 1967, but Palestinian hopes may lie in the United States. There are cracks in the formerly solid support for Israeli actions. Liberal opinion has shifted toward support for Palestinian rights, even among the Jewish community, as Norman Finkelstein documented a decade ago. The increasingly brutal torture of the 2 million inhabitants of Gaza's open-air prison has had particularly dramatic effects.

These shifts have not yet influenced policy, but they are likely to become more pronounced as Israel continues its drift to the right and the almost daily crimes become harder to conceal or explain away. If Palestinians can overcome their sharp internal divisions and effective solidarity movements develop in the US, changes can come, both at the people-to-people level and in government policy.

There's a background. In the 1970s, Israel made a fateful decision to choose expansion over security, rejecting opportunities for peaceful settlement along the lines of a growing international consensus. That compelled reliance on the US, which also entails submission to US demands. Such demands were made by every president before Obama, and however reluctantly, Israel has to obey. Changing US government policy, if significant, cannot fail to influence the array of policy options for Israel.

That could be a path toward the elusive goal of a just peace in the former Palestine, and even for regional accords that will not merely reflect the interests of repressive power structures but of the people of the region, who have repeatedly struggled for a more decent fate.

Noam Chomsky

HUMANITY FACES TWO EXISTENTIAL THREATS. ONE IS NEARLY IGNORED.

July 13, 2022

C. J. Polychroniou: *Noam, Russia's invasion of Ukraine has triggered several unexpected and unintended consequences. One of them, which is not as widely discussed as it should be, is that the use of nuclear arsenals, perhaps with lower yields, has been almost normalized. Indeed, in the course of this war, we have heard of several scenarios for how Russia might use nuclear weapons, and, in the early days of the invasion, Russian president Vladimir Putin even ordered his country's nuclear forces on a higher alert. And, just last month, he said that Russia will use nuclear weapons to defend its sovereignty and stressed that the "era of the unipolar world" has ended. On the other hand, we have people like Francis Fukuyama saying that the possibility of a nuclear war "is not something anyone should be worrying about" because there are many stopping points before we get to that point. How did we get to a stage where people are having such a nonchalant attitude about nuclear weapons?*

Noam Chomsky: Before turning to the important issues raised, we should keep firmly in mind one overriding concern: the great powers will find a way to cooperate in addressing today's critical problems, or the wreckage of human society will be so extreme that no one will care.

227

All else fades alongside of recognition of that fundamental fact about the contemporary world, very possibly the last stage in human history. It cannot be reiterated too often or too strongly.

In the *Toronto Star*, the veteran journalist and political analyst Linda McQuaig wrote that she had just heard "what struck me as possibly the most foolish remark ever uttered on TV. And I know that's a high bar."

McQuaig was referring to "the celebrated U.S. political scientist Francis Fukuyama" and the comment of his that you just quoted. Put simply, "there's no need to be concerned about nuclear war. Take my word for it."

In defense of "possibly the most foolish remark ever uttered on TV," we might argue that it is not only commonly voiced, but in fact is implicit in official US policy. Last April, Defense Secretary Lloyd Austin said that Washington's goal in Ukraine is "to see Russia weakened to the degree that it can't do the kinds of things that it has done in invading Ukraine." He was reprimanded by the president, but "officials acknowledged that was indeed the long-term strategy, even if Mr. Biden did not want to publicly provoke Mr. Putin into escalation."

The long-term strategy, then, is to keep the war going in order to weaken Russia, and to a degree considerably harsher than the treatment of Germany at Versailles a century ago, which did not succeed in the proclaimed goal.

The long-term strategy was reaffirmed clearly enough in the recent North Atlantic Treaty Organization (NATO) summit, providing a new "Strategic Concept" based on a core principle: no diplomacy on Ukraine, only war to "weaken Russia."

It takes no great insight to see that this approximates what may be the most foolish remark ever uttered. The tacit assumption is that while the US and its allies are proceeding to weaken Russia sufficiently, Russian leaders will stand by quietly, refraining from resorting to the advanced weapons we all know Russia has.

Take our word for it.

Perhaps so, but quite a gamble, not only with the fate of Ukrainians but far beyond.

In further defense of this colossal foolishness, we might add that it is prevailing common sense. It is commonly just taken for granted that we can disregard the shocking record of the past seventy-five years, which demonstrates with brilliant clarity that it is a near miracle that we have escaped nuclear war—terminal war if major powers are involved.

Illustrations are everywhere. To take one, some of the most careful and sophisticated studies of public opinion on major issues are carried out by the Yale University Program on Climate Change Communication. Though climate is the main focus of their concerns, the studies range much more broadly.

The most recent study, just released, poses twenty-nine major current issues and asks subjects to rank them in terms of significance for the upcoming November election. Nuclear war is not mentioned. The threat is severe and increasing, and it's easy to construct all-too-plausible scenarios that would lead up the escalation ladder to terminal destruction. But our leaders and "celebrated political scientists" assure us, either directly or implicitly: "No need for concern, take our word for it."

What is omitted from the study is terrifying enough. What is included is hardly less so. "Of 29 issues we asked about," the directors of the poll report, "registered voters overall indicated that global warming is the 24th most highly ranked voting issue."

It is only the most important issue that has ever arisen in human history, alongside of nuclear war.

It gets worse on a closer look. Republicans may well take Congress in a few months. Their leadership is not concealing their intent to find ways to hold on to virtually permanent political power, independent of the popular will, and might succeed with the help of the ultra-reactionary Supreme Court. The party—to dignify it with that word—has been 100 percent denialist on global warming since it succumbed to the Koch conglomerate onslaught in 2009, and the leadership has carried along the voting base. In the Yale study, moderate

Republicans ranked global warming as twenty-eighth among the twenty-ninth options offered. The rest ranked it twenty-ninth.

The two most important issues in human history, issues of literal survival, may soon be off the agenda in the most powerful state in human history, carrying forward the grim experience of the four Trump years.

Not completely off the agenda, of course. There are voices of sanity, some with considerable prestige and experience. A decade ago, four of them—William Perry, Henry Kissinger, George Shultz, and Sam Nunn—wrote an op-ed in the *Wall Street Journal* calling for "reversing the world's reliance on nuclear weapons, to prevent their proliferation into potentially dangerous hands, and ultimately ending them as a threat to the world."

They are not alone. Last month (June 21–23), the first meeting was convened of states-parties to the 2017 Treaty on the Prohibition of Nuclear Weapons (TPNW). Citing "increasingly strident nuclear rhetoric," the TPNW states-parties issued the Vienna Declaration, which condemns all threats to use nuclear weapons as violations of international law, including the UN Charter. The declaration demands "that all nuclear-armed states never use or threaten to use nuclear weapons under any circumstances."

The nuclear states have refused to join the treaty, but that can change under popular pressure, as we have often seen before.

In August, the tenth review conference of the Nuclear Nonproliferation Treaty (NPT) will convene. That could offer an opportunity for an organized public to demand adherence to its provisions, which call for "good faith" efforts to remove the scourge of nuclear weapons from the Earth, and while pursuing these efforts, to sharply reduce the enormous threats they pose.

That will not happen if the two most important issues in human history are removed from attention, one almost completely while the other barely reaches a fraction of the concern it requires if there is to be a livable world.

We need not be passive observers, content to be mere instruments in the hands of the powerful. That is a choice, not a necessity.

Recently, Ukrainian president Volodymyr Zelenskyy warned in an interview with CNN that the world should take seriously the possibility that Russia might use nuclear weapons in Ukraine. However, on various occasions, he himself has hinted at the idea of Ukraine developing nuclear weapons even though the country is a signatory to the Nuclear Nonproliferation Treaty. I don't know if Ukraine has the capabilities to proceed with the development of a nuclear weapons program, but wouldn't it be absolutely suicidal to do so?

Completely suicidal. Even the first tentative efforts would lead to harsh retaliation, and then up the escalatory ladder. But in the light of the level of sanity exhibited by the leaders of the world, is it unthinkable?

Putin has openly stated that Russia is open to dialogue on nuclear nonproliferation, but the perspective on the part of the US appears to be that Russia's invasion of Ukraine has subverted the Nuclear Nonproliferation Treaty. I'd like your comments on this issue.

Let's recall the overriding concern: the great powers will find a way to cooperate in addressing today's critical problems, or the wreckage of human society will be so extreme that no one will care.

It follows that every option for dialogue should be seriously considered, and where at all feasible, pursued. Dialogue can, in fact, be pursued in an international setting at the upcoming NPT review conference. Or the option can be simply dismissed as unthinkable, adopting the stance of the West at the G20 conference last week, where Russian foreign minister, Sergey Lavrov, was treated "like a skunk at the tropical resort party, shunned by many, though by no means all."

The final qualification is of no slight significance. Those who did not join the West in shunning the skunk included the Indonesian hosts, who welcomed him, and a number of others: China, India, Brazil, Turkey, Argentina, and others, along with Indonesia. That raises once again the question of just who is being isolated in the new world order that is taking shape.

232 A LIVABLE FUTURE IS POSSIBLE

That is no idle question, and it is not ignored. There are some serious reflections about it close to the centers of power. One case is an
analysis of the evolving world order by Graham Fuller, former vice
chair of the National Intelligence Council at [the] CIA with responsibility for global intelligence estimates. His analysis raises issues that
merit close attention.

Fuller has no illusions about the nature and roots of the war. Prime
responsibility falls on the agents of the criminal aggression, Putin and
his circle. That should be beyond controversy. But "secondary con-
demnation belongs to the U.S. (NATO) in deliberately provoking a
war with Russia by implacably pushing its hostile military organization, despite Moscow's repeated notifications about crossing red
lines, right up to the gates of Russia. This war did not have to be if
Ukrainian neutrality, à la Finland and Austria, had been accepted.
Instead, Washington has called for clear Russian defeat."

Fuller sees the conflict not as a "Ukrainian-Russian war but an
American-Russian war fought by proxy to the last Ukrainian.... And
most of the rest of the world—Latin America, India, the Middle East
and Africa—find few national interests in this fundamentally American war against Russia."

Those who refused to shun Russia at the G20 conference strongly
condemned the invasion but did not take too seriously the professed
outrage of the US and its allies. Very likely, they were asking whether
the US was shunned as a pariah after carrying out its many violent
criminal exploits, which there is no need to review. For many, the
memories are heightened by vivid and ugly direct experience. How
can they be expected to pay attention to the protestations of high
principles from the leading violators of these principles, always with
immunity from anything more than occasional mild reprimands?

Europe is already suffering badly, Fuller continues, and will,
sooner or later, have to "return to the purchase of inexpensive Russian
energy." It has little realistic choice. "Russia lies on the doorstep and a
natural economic relationship with Russia will possess overwhelming
logic in the end." Beyond that, "Europe can even less afford to blunder into confrontation with China—a 'threat' perceived primarily by

Washington yet unconvincing to many European states and much of the world." It will cost Europe dearly to isolate itself from China's Belt and Road Initiative, "perhaps the most ambitious economic and geopolitical project in world history," which runs right through Russia and "is already linking China with Europe by rail and sea. . . . The end of the Ukraine war will bring serious reconsideration in Europe about the benefits of propping up Washington's desperate bid to maintain its global hegemony."

Another consequence of this desperate bid is that

> Russia's geopolitical character has very likely now decisively tilted towards Eurasia. . . . Russian elites now no longer possess an alternative to accepting that its economic future lies in the Pacific where Vladivostok lies only one or two hours away by air from the vast economies of Beijing, Tokyo, and Seoul. China and Russia have now been decisively pushed ever more closely together specifically out of common concern to block unfettered US freedom of unilateral military and economic intervention around the world. That the US can split US-induced Russian and Chinese cooperation is a fantasy. Russia has scientific brilliance, abundant energy, rich rare minerals and metals, while global warming will increase the agricultural potential of Siberia. China has the capital, the markets, and the manpower to contribute to what becomes a natural partnership across Eurasia.

Fuller is far from alone. "The Idea of Eurasia Is Once Again the Subject of Geopolitics," reads a headline in the London *Economist*. The report reviews the renewed attention to the principle of the founder of modern geopolitics, Halford Mackinder, that control of the central Asian heartland is key to world control. These conceptions are taking new form as the Ukraine war reshapes the global strategic landscape in ways that may turn out to be profound.

The "utter corruption" of the media, Fuller writes, is one of the most disturbing features of the current crisis: "In the midst of a virulent anti-Russian propaganda barrage whose likes I have never seen during my Cold Warrior days, serious analysts must dig deep these days to gain some objective understanding of what is actually taking place in Ukraine."

That is sensible advice. There is more. The tendencies that are shaping world order are not immutable. Human agency has not ended. That crucially encompasses the agency of an organized public that demands an end to cynical posturing and a serious commitment to grasp the opportunities that exist for dialogue and accommodation. The alternatives are too grim to contemplate.

The campaign for nuclear disarmament goes back to the late 1950s. Yet the prospects for nuclear disarmament are dim, if not nonexistent. Nuclear disarmament requires that nation-states trust each other, which is a zero-probability event in the real world, but it is also extremely doubtful that the nuclear knowledge genie can ever be put back in the bottle. So, what is to be done? What are the most realistic ways to avoid nuclear war?

There are realistic ways to reduce the likelihood of terminal war—once again, the appropriate term for nuclear war involving great powers. The most immediate is a serious arms control regime. Elements of such a regime had been laboriously constructed since Eisenhower's Open Skies proposals in 1955—dismantled by Trump in May 2020 when he was wielding his wrecking ball. There were other important steps forward, among them the Reagan-Gorbachev Intermediate-Range Nuclear Forces Treaty (INF) in 1987, which significantly reduced the threat of outbreak of terminal war in Europe—and, we should not forget, was impelled by enormous popular anti-nuclear protests in Europe and the US. Another step was the 1972 Anti-Ballistic Missile Treaty (ABM), which both sides recognized to be a "substantial factor in curbing the race in strategic offensive arms."

The Anti-Ballistic Missile Treaty was dismantled by George W. Bush, the INF treaty by Trump.

At the end of the Trump years, very little was left beyond the New START treaty, which Biden was able to rescue from demolition literally by a few days. It was due to expire shortly after his inauguration.

There is more, such as Trump's destruction of the joint agreement (JCPOA) on Iranian nuclear programs in violation of the UN Security Council, which had endorsed it, another contribution of the modern GOP to global destruction.

One of the great tragedies of the Ukraine war is that these means for reducing the threat of terminal war are being cast out the window. The US cannot deign to descend to agreements with the skunk at the party. The tragedy is enhanced by the impending return to full power of the party of the wreckers.

Nonetheless, the same kinds of mass mobilization that helped bring about earlier steps toward sanity can be effective again. That means first resurrecting the tattered arms control regime, and then moving well beyond.

Other steps could be taken right now if sufficient popular pressures were mounted. In the coming weeks, in fact, at the August NPT conference. Beyond moves to advance the TPNW and the professed goals of the NPT itself, there are further possibilities. One crucial issue that is likely to be raised again at the conference is a nuclear weapons–free zone (NWFZ) in the Middle East. That could be a significant step toward international security. Popular pressures could help bring it to realization.

Establishment of a Middle East NWFZ has come up regularly at NPT review sessions, primarily at the initiative of the Arab states, who have even threatened to withdraw from the NPT if moves are not taken to implement it. It has almost unanimous global support, but is always blocked by Washington, most recently by Obama at the 2015 conference.

To review the basic facts once again, the call for a Mideast NWFZ is backed by the Arab states, Iran, and the Global South, G-77, now expanded to 134 countries, the large majority of the world. Europe raises no objections. The unilateral US veto is accompanied with various pieties, easily dismissed. The real reasons are well understood: the massive Israeli nuclear weapons system, the only one in the region, must not be subject to international regulation. That is off the table, a the *New York Times* editors made clear recently in calling for a "Nuclear-Weapons-Free Persian Gulf"—*Persian Gulf*, not Middle East. A Persian Gulf NWFZ, the editors say, would be "One Way Forward on Iran," which is causing troubles once again by adhering to the unanimous consensus (minus the Master).

The US refuses to officially acknowledge Israel's nuclear weapons facilities, presumably because to do so would call into question the legality of all US aid to Israel, under US law. That's a door that both political parties have insisted on keeping tightly shut, but as public opinion on the matter has been visibly shifting, there are some breaks in rigid discipline. Congressional Representative Betty McCollum, for one, has aroused much ire for sponsoring legislation to bar Israel from using US military aid to attack Palestinian children.

Establishment of NWFZs is an important step toward reducing the nuclear weapons threat, even apart from the symbolism of global rejection of these monstrous achievements of human ingenuity. More accurately, it would be an important step if these could be implemented. Unfortunately, they are blocked by US insistence on maintaining nuclear weapons facilities within them, matters we have reviewed before.

All of this could be on the agenda, right now, as ways of addressing the terminal threat.

Beyond that, there is the overriding concern: to repeat again, the great powers will find a way to cooperate in addressing today's critical problems, or nothing else will matter.

Noam Chomsky

THE "HISTORIC" NATO SUMMIT IN MADRID SHORED UP US MILITARISM

July 6, 2022

C. J. Polychroniou: *Noam, as was expected, the war in Ukraine domi-nated the recent NATO summit in Madrid and produced some extraordi-nary decisions that will lead to the "NATO-ization of Europe," as Russia was declared "the most significant and direct threat" to its members' peace and security. Turkey dropped its objections to Finland and Sweden joining the alliance after it managed to extract major concessions, NATO's east-ern flank will receive massive reinforcement, additional defense systems will be stationed in Germany, Italy, and elsewhere, and the US will boost its military presence all across European soil. Given all of this, is it Russia that represents a threat to Europe, or NATO to Russia? And what does the "NATO-ization" of Europe mean for global peace and security? Is it a prelude to World War III?*

Noam Chomsky: We can dismiss the obligatory boilerplate about high principles and noble goals, and the rank hypocrisy: for exam-ple, the lament about the fate of the arms control regime because of Russian-Chinese disruption, with no mention of the fact it is the US that has torn it to shreds under W. Bush and particularly Trump. All of that is to be expected in "historic" pronouncements of a new Strategic Concept for NATO.

The Ukraine war did indeed provide the backdrop for the meeting of NATO powers—with bitter irony, just after the conclusion of the first meeting of the states that signed the Treaty on the Prohibition of Nuclear Weapons (TPNW), which passed unnoticed.

The NATO summit was expanded for the first time to include the Asian "sentinel states" that the US has established and provided with advanced high-precision weapons to "encircle" China. Accordingly, the North Atlantic was officially expanded to include the newly created Indo-Pacific region, a vast area where security concerns for the Atlanticist powers of NATO are held to arise. The imperial implications should be clear enough. There's a good deal more to say about this. I will return to it.

US policy toward Ukraine and Russia was strongly affirmed in the Strategic Concept: no negotiations, only war to "weaken Russia."

This has been steady policy since George W. Bush's 2008 invitation to Ukraine to join NATO, vetoed by France and Germany, who agreed with high-level US diplomats for the past thirty years that no Russian government could tolerate that, for reasons too obvious to review. The offer remained on the agenda in deference to US power.

After the Maidan uprising in 2014, the US began openly to move to integrate Ukraine into the NATO military command, policies extended under Biden, accompanied by official acknowledgment after the invasion that Russian security concerns, meaning NATO membership, had not been taken into consideration. The plans have not been concealed. The goals are to ensure full compatibility of the Ukrainian military with NATO forces in order to "integrate Ukraine into NATO de facto."

Zelenskyy's efforts to implement a diplomatic settlement were ignored, including his proposals last March to accept Austrian-style neutralization for the indefinite future. The proposals, which had indications of Russian support, were termed a "real breakthrough" by UN Secretary-General António Guterres, but never pursued.

The official Russian stance at the time (March 2022) was that its military operations would end if Ukraine too were to "cease military action, change its constitution to enshrine neutrality, acknowledge Crimea as Russian territory, and recognize the separatist republics of Donetsk and Lugansk as independent states."

There was a considerable gap between the Ukrainian and Russian positions on a diplomatic settlement, but they might have been narrowed in negotiations. Even after the invasion, it appears that there may have remained some space for a way to end the horrors.

France and Germany continued to make overtures toward diplomatic settlement. These are completely dropped in the recent Strategic Concept, which simply "reaffirms" all plans to move toward incorporating Ukraine (and Georgia) into NATO, formally dismissing Russian concerns.

The shifts in the European stance reflect Europe's increasing subordination to the US. The shift was accelerated by Putin's choice of aggression after refusing to consider European initiatives that might have averted the crime and possibly even opened a path toward Europe-Russia accommodation that would be highly beneficial to all—and highly beneficial to the world, which may not survive great power confrontation.

That is not a throw-away line. It is reality. The great powers will either find a way to cooperate, to work together in confronting imminent global threats, or the future will be too grim to contemplate. These elementary facts should be kept firmly in mind while discussing particular issues.

We should also be clear about the import of the new Strategic Concept. Reaffirming the US program of de facto incorporation of Ukraine within NATO is also reaffirming, unambiguously, the refusal to contemplate a diplomatic settlement. It is reaffirming the Ramstein declarations a few weeks ago that the war in Ukraine must be fought to weaken Russia, in fact to weaken it more severely than the Versailles treaty weakened Germany, if we assume that US officials mean what they say—and we can expect that adversaries take them at their words.

The Ramstein declarations were accompanied by assurances that Ukraine would drive Russia out of all Ukrainian territory. In assessing the credibility of these assurances, we may recall that they come from the sources that confidently predicted that the US-created Iraqi and Afghan armies would resist ISIS [also known as Daesh] and the Taliban, instead of collapsing immediately, as they did, and that the Russian invasion would conquer Kyiv and occupy Ukraine in three days.

The message to Russia is: "You have no escape. Either surrender, or continue your slow and brutal advance, or, in the event that defeat threatens, go for broke and destroy Ukraine, as of course you can."

The logic is quite clear. So is the import beyond Ukraine itself. Millions will face starvation, the world will continue to march toward environmental destruction, the likelihood of nuclear war will increase.

But we must pursue this course to punish Russia severely enough so that it cannot undertake further aggression.

We might pause for a moment to look at the crucial underlying premise: Russia is bent on further aggression, and must be stopped now, or else. Munich 1938. By now this has become a Fundamental Truth, beyond challenge or inquiry. With so much at stake, perhaps we may be forgiven for breaking the rules and raising a few questions.

Inquiry at once faces a difficulty. There has been little effort to establish the Fundamental Truth. As good a version as any is presented by Peter Dickinson, editor of the prestigious Atlantic Council's UkraineAlert service. The heart of Dickinson's argument is this:

> Putin has never made any secret of the fact that he views the territory of modern Ukraine as historically Russian land. For years, he has denied Ukraine's right to exist while claiming that all Ukrainians are in fact Russians ("one people"). The real question is which other sovereign nations might also fit Putin's definition. He recently set off alarm bells by commenting that the entire former Soviet Union was historically Russian territory.
>
> Nor is it clear if Putin's appetite for reclaiming Russian lands is limited to the 14 non-Russian post-Soviet states. Im-

perial Russia once also ruled Finland and Poland, while the Soviet Empire after World War II stretched deep into Central Europe and included East Germany. One thing is clear: unless he is stopped in Ukraine, Putin's imperial ambitions are certain to expand.

That is clear, requiring no further argument.

The totality of evidence is given in the linked article. But now another problem arises. In it, Putin says nothing remotely like what set off the dramatic alarm bells. More like the opposite.

Putin says that the old Soviet Union "ceased to exist," and he wants "to emphasise that in recent history we have always treated the processes of sovereignisation that have occurred in the post-Soviet area with respect." As for Ukraine, "If we had had good allied relations, or at least a partnership between us, it would never have occurred to anybody [to resort to force]. And, by the way, there would have been no Crimea problem. Because if the rights of the people who live there, the Russian-speaking population, had been respected, if the Russian language and culture had been treated with respect, it would never have occurred to anybody to start all this."

Nothing more is quoted. That's the totality of evidence Dickinson presents, apart from what has become the last resort of proponents of the thesis that unless "stopped in Ukraine, Putin's imperial ambitions are certain to expand": musings of no clear import about Peter the Great.

This is no minor matter. On this basis, so our leaders instruct us, we must ensure that the war continues in order to weaken Russia, and beyond Ukraine itself, to drive millions to starvation while we march on triumphantly toward an unlivable Earth and face increasing risk of terminal nuclear war.

Perhaps there is some better evidence for what is so "clear" that we must assume these incredible risks. If so, it would be good to hear it.

Putin's cited remarks, as distinct from the fevered constructions, are consistent with the historical and diplomatic record, including the post-invasion Russian official stance just quoted, but much farther back.

The core issue for thirty years has been Ukraine's entry into NATO. That has always been understood by high US officials, who have warned Washington against the reckless and provocative acts it has been taking. It has also been understood by Washington's most favored Russian diplomats. Clinton's friend Boris Yeltsin objected strenuously when Clinton began the process of NATO expansion in violation of firm promises to Gorbachev when the Soviet Union collapsed. The same is true of Gorbachev himself, who accused the West and NATO of destroying the structure of European security by expanding its alliance. "No head of the Kremlin can ignore such a thing," he said, adding that the US was unfortunately starting to establish a "mega empire," words echoed by Putin and other Russian officials.

I am unaware of a word in the record about plans to invade anyone outside the long-familiar red lines: Ukraine and Georgia. The only Russian threats that have been cited are that if NATO advances to its borders, Russia will strengthen its defenses in response.

With specific regard to Ukraine, until recently Putin was calling publicly for implementation of the Minsk II agreement: neutralization of Ukraine and a federal arrangement with a degree of autonomy for the Donbas region. It is always reasonable to suspect dark motives in great power posturing, but it is the official positions that offer a basis for diplomacy if there is any interest in that course.

On Crimea, Russia had made no moves until it was about to lose its sole warm water naval base, in the Crimean Peninsula. The background is reviewed by John Quigley, the US State department representative in the OSCE [Organization for Security and Co-operation in Europe] delegation that considered the problem of Ukraine after the collapse of the Soviet Union.

Crimea, he reports, was a particular focus of attention. His intensive efforts to find a solution for the problem of Crimea faced a "dilemma." Crimea's population "was majority Russian and saw no reason to be part of Ukraine." Crimea had been Russian until 1954, when, for unknown reasons, Soviet Communist Party Chair Nikita Khrushchev decided to switch Crimea from the Soviet Russian republic to the Soviet Ukrainian republic. As Quigley notes, even after 1954, Crimea was effectively governed more from Moscow than from Kyiv. When the Soviet Union was dissolved, Crimea's population suddenly found itself a minority in a foreign country. Ukraine accepted a need for a certain degree of self-rule, but Crimea declared independence as what it called the Crimean Republic. Over Ukraine's objection, an election for president was called in the declared Crimean Republic, and a candidate was elected on a platform of merger with Russia. At the time, however, the Russian government was not prepared to back the Crimeans.

Quigley sought a compromise that would provide autonomy for Crimea under a Ukraine-Crimea treaty, with international guarantees to protect Crimea from Ukrainian infringement. The "treaty went nowhere, however. . . . Ukraine cracked down on the Crimean Republic, and the conflict remained unresolved. Tension simmered until 2014, by which time Russia was prepared to act to take Crimea back. Crimea was then formally merged into the Russian Federation."

It's not a simple matter of unprovoked Russian aggression, as in the received US version.

Like many others familiar with the region, Quigley now calls for a diplomatic settlement and wonders whether the current US goal "is less to force Russia out of Ukraine than to fight Russia to the last Ukrainian."

Is there still an option for diplomacy? No one can know unless the possibility is explored. That will not happen if it is an established Fundamental Truth that Putin's ambitions are insatiable.

Apart from the question of Putin's ambitions, there is a small matter of capability. While trembling in fear of the new Peter the Great, Western powers are also gloating over the demonstration that their firm convictions about Russia's enormous military power were quickly dispelled with the Russian debacle in its attack on Kyiv. US intelligence had predicted victory in a few days. Instead, tenacious Ukrainian resistance revealed that Russia could not conquer cities a few miles from its border defended by a mostly citizens' army.

But no matter: the new Peter the Great is on the march. Lack of evidence of intention and official proposals to the contrary are as irrelevant to Fundamental Truth as lack of military capacity.

What we are observing is nothing new. Russian devils of incomparable might aiming to conquer the world and destroy civilization have been a staple of official rhetoric, and obedient commentary, for seventy-five years. The rhetoric of the critical internal document NSC-68 (1950) is a striking illustration, almost unbelievable in its infantile crudity.

At times, the method has been acknowledged. From his position as "present at the creation" of the Cold War, the distinguished statesman Dean Acheson recognized that it was necessary to be "clearer than truth" in exercises (like NSC-68) to "bludgeon the mass mind" of government into obedience with elite plans. That was in fact "NSC-68's purpose."

Scholarship has also occasionally recorded the fact. Harvard professor of government and long-time government adviser Samuel Huntington observed that "you may have to sell [intervention or other military action] in such a way as to create the misimpression that it is the Soviet Union that you are fighting. That is what the United States has been doing ever since the Truman Doctrine."

Today's formula is no innovation.

We often tend to forget that the US is a global power. Planning is global: what is happening in one part of the world is often replicated elsewhere. By focusing on one particular manifestation, we often miss the global tapestry in which it is one strand.

When the US took over global hegemony from Britain after World War II, it kept the same guiding geopolitical concepts, now greatly expanded by a far more powerful hegemon.

Britain is an island off the coast of Europe. A primary goal of British imperial rule was to prevent a unified hostile Europe.

The US-run Western hemisphere is an "island" off the coast of the Eurasian land mass, with far grander imperial objectives (or "responsibilities," as they are politely termed). It must therefore make sure to control it from all directions, North being a new arena of conflict as global warming opens it up to exploitation and commerce. The NATO-based Atlanticist system is the Western bulwark. The Strategic Concept and its ongoing implementation places this bulwark more firmly in Washington's hands, thanks to Putin.

With virtually no notice, there are similar developments on the Eastern flank of the Eurasian land mass as NATO extends its reach to the Indo-Pacific region under the new Concept. NATO is deepening its relations with its island partners off the coast of China—Japan, Australia, South Korea, New Zealand—even inviting them to the NATO summit, but much more significant, enlisting them in the "encirclement" of China that is a key element of current bipartisan US strategy.

While the US is firming up its control of the western flank of the Eurasian landmass at the NATO Summit, it is carrying out related exercises at the eastern flank: the Rim of the Pacific (RIMPAC) programs now underway. Under the direction of the US Navy, these are "the grandest of all war games," Australian political scientist Gavan McCormack writes, "the largest air, land, and sea war manoeuvres in the world. They would assemble a staggering 238 ships, 170 aircraft, 4 submarines and 25,000 military personnel from 26 countries. . . . To China, scarcely surprisingly these exercises are seen as expression of an anti-China 'Asian NATO design.' They are war games, and they are to include various simulations engaging 'enemy forces,' attacking targets and conducting amphibious landings on Hawaii Island and in Hawaiian waters."

RIMPAC is supplemented by regular US naval missions in China's Exclusive Economic Zone (EEZ). These are merely "innocent passage" in accord with the principle of "freedom of navigation;" the US protests when China objects, as does India, Indonesia, and many others. The US appeals to the Law of the Sea—which bars threat or use of force in these zones. Quietly, the US client state Australia, of course, in coordination with Washington, is engaged in "military espionage" in the EEZ, installing highly sophisticated sensing devices "so that the US can more effectively destroy Chinese vessels as quickly as possible at the start of any conflict."

These exercises on the eastern flank are accompanied by others in the Pacific Northeast region and, in part, in the Baltic region, with participation of new NATO members Finland and Sweden. Over the years, they have been slowly integrated into the NATO military system and have now taken the final step, pleading "security concerns" that are scarcely even laughable but do benefit their substantial military industries and help drive the societies to the right.

The empire doesn't rest. The stakes are too high.

In official rhetoric, as always, these programs are undertaken for benign purposes: to enforce "the rules-based international order." The term appears repeatedly in the Strategic Concept of the NATO Summit. Missing from the document is a different phrase: "UN-based international order." That is no accidental omission: The two concepts are crucially different.

The UN-based international order is enshrined in the UN Charter, the foundation of modern international law. Under the US Constitution (Article VI), the UN Charter is also "the supreme law of the land." But it is unacceptable to US elite opinion and is violated freely, with no notice, by US presidents.

The Charter has two primary flaws. One is that it bans "the threat or use of force" in international affairs, apart from designated circumstances that almost never arise. That means that it bans US foreign policy, obviously an unacceptable outcome. Consequently, the revered Constitution can be put aside. If, unimaginably, the question of observing the Constitution ever reached the Supreme Court, it would be dismissed as a "political question."

The rules-based international order overcomes this flaw. It permits the threat and use of force freely by the master, and those he authorizes. Illustrations are so dramatically obvious that one might think that they would be difficult to ignore. That would be a mistake: they are routinely ignored. Take one of the major international crimes: annexation of conquered territory in violation of international law. There are two examples: Morocco's annexation of Western Sahara in violation of the ruling of the International Court of Justice, and Israel's annexation of the Golan Heights in Syria and Greater Jerusalem in violation of unanimous Security Council orders. All have been supported by the US for many years, and were formally authorized by the Trump administration, now by Biden. One will have to search hard for expressions of concern, even notice.

The second flaw is that the UN Security Council and other international institutions, like the World Court, set the rules. That flaw is also overcome in the rules-based international order, in which the US sets the rules and others obey.

It is, then, easy to understand Washington's preference for the rules-based international order, now forcefully affirmed in the NATO Strategic Concept, and adopted in US commentary and scholarship.

Turning elsewhere, we do find serious commentary and analysis. Australian strategic analyst Clinton Fernandes discusses the matter in some depth in his book *Sub-Imperial Power* (Melbourne 2022).

Tracing the concept to its western origins in British imperial rule, Fernandes shows that

> the rules-based order differs sharply from the United Nations–centred international system and the international order underpinned by international law. The United States sits at the apex of the system, exercising control over the sovereignty of many countries. The United Kingdom, a lieutenant with nuclear weapons and far-flung territories, supports the United States. So do subimperial powers like Australia and Israel. The rules-based international order involves control of the effective political sovereignty of other countries, a belief in imperial benevolence and the economics of comparative advantage. Since policy planners and media commentators cannot bring themselves to say "empire," the "rules-based international order" serves as the euphemism.

"The economics of comparative advantage," as Fernandes discusses, is another euphemism. Its meaning is "stay in your place," for the benefit of all. It is often advised with the best of intentions. Surely that was the case when Adam Smith advised the American colonies to keep to their comparative advantage in agriculture and import British manufactured goods, thus "promoting the progress of their country toward real wealth and greatness."

Having overthrown British rule, the colonies were free to reject this kind advice and to resort to the same kinds of radical violation of orthodox free trade principles that Britain used in becoming the world's great center of manufacturing and global power. That pattern has been replicated with impressive consistency. Those that adopted the favored principle, usually under force, became the third world. Those that violated it became the wealthy first world, including the one country of the South that resisted colonization, Japan, and thus was able to violate the rules and develop, with its former colonies in tow.

The consistency of the record is close to axiomatic. After all, development means changing comparative advantage.

In short, the rules-based order confers many advantages on the powerful. One can easily understand why it is viewed so favorably in their domains, while the UN-based order is dismissed except when it can be invoked to punish enemies.

Turkey continues to resist joining sanctions against Russia and acts, in fact, as a sanctions "safe haven" for Russian oligarchs. Yet it is treated by the US and the NATO alliance in general as a reliable strategic ally, and everyone ignores the fact that Erdoğan's regime is as blatantly authoritarian and oppressive as that of Putin. In fact, following his somersault vis-a-vis Saudi Arabia, the Biden administration is now warming up to Erdoğan and wants to upgrade Turkey's fleet of American-made F-16 fighter jets. How should we interpret this anomalous situation within the NATO alliance? Yet another instance of Western hypocrisy or the dictates of Realpolitik?

What is anomalous is that Erdoğan is playing his own game instead of just obeying orders. There's nothing anomalous about his being "blatantly authoritarian and oppressive." That's not a concern [for the US], as in numerous other cases. What is a concern is that he's not entirely a "reliable strategic ally." Turkey was actually sanctioned by the US for purchasing a Russian missile defense system. And even after the invasion of Ukraine, Erdoğan left open whether he would purchase Russian arms or depart from his "friendship" with Mr. Putin. In this particular regard, Turkey is acting more like the Global South than like NATO.

Turkey has departed from strict obedience in other ways. It delayed the accession of Sweden and Finland into NATO. The reason, it seems, is Turkey's commitment to intensify its murderous repression of its Kurdish population. Sweden had been granting asylum to Kurds fleeing Turkish state violence—"terrorists" in Turkish official lingo. There are legitimate concerns that an ugly underground bargain may have been struck when Turkey dropped its opposition to full Swedish entry into NATO.

The background should not be overlooked. Brutal repression of the Kurds in Turkey has a long history. It reached a crescendo in the 1990s, with a state terror campaign that killed tens of thousands of Kurds, destroyed thousands of towns and villages, and drove hundreds of thousands from their homes, many to hideous slums in barely survivable corners of Istanbul. Some were offered the opportunity to return to what was left of their homes, but only if they publicly blamed Kurdish PKK guerrillas. With the amazing courage that has been the hallmark of the Kurdish struggles for justice, they refused.

These terrible crimes, some of the worst of the decade, were strongly supported by the US, which poured arms into Turkey to expedite the atrocities. The flow increased under Clinton as the crimes escalated. Turkey became the leading recipient of US arms (apart from Israel-Egypt, a separate category), replacing Colombia, the leading violator of human rights in the Western hemisphere. That extends a long and well-established pattern. As usual, the media cooperated by ignoring the Turkish horrors and crucial US support for them.

By 2000, the crimes were abating, and an astonishing period began in Turkey. There was remarkable progress in opening up the society, condemning state crimes, advancing freedom and justice. For me personally, it was a great privilege to be able to witness it firsthand, even to participate in limited ways. Prominent in this democratic revolution were Turkish intellectuals, who put their

Western counterparts to shame. They not only protested state crimes but carried out regular civil disobedience, risking and often enduring harsh punishment, and returning to the fray. One striking example was Ismail Beşikçi, who as a young historian was the first non-Kurdish academic to document the horrific repression of the Kurds. Repeatedly imprisoned, tortured, abused, he refused to stop his work, continuing to document the escalating crimes. There were many others.

By the early 2000s, it seemed that a new era was dawning. There were some thrilling moments. One unforgettable experience was at the editorial offices of Hrant Dink, the courageous journalist who was assassinated with state complicity for his defense of human rights, particularly the rights of the Armenian community that had been subjected to genocidal slaughter, still officially denied. With his widow, I was standing on the balcony of the office, observing an enormous demonstration honoring Hrant Dink and his work, and calling for an end to ongoing crimes of state, no small act of courage and dedication in the harshly repressive Turkish state.

The hopes were soon to wane as Erdoğan instituted his increasingly brutal rule, moving to restore the nightmare from which Turkey had begun to emerge. All similar to what happened a few years later in the Arab Spring.

Turkey is also extending its aggression in Syria, aimed at the Kurdish population who, in the midst of the horrendous chaos of the Syrian conflicts, had managed to carve out an island of flourishing democracy and rights (Rojava). The Kurds had also provided the ground troops for Washington's war against ISIS in Syria, suffering over ten thousand casualties. In thanks for their service in this successful war, President Trump withdrew the small US force that served as a deterrent to the Turkish onslaught, leaving them at its mercy.

There is an old Kurdish proverb that the Kurds have no friends but the mountains. There is just concern that Turkish-Swedish NATO maneuverings might confirm it.

The NATO summit reached the interesting conclusion that China represents a "security challenge" to the interests and security of its member states, but it is not to be treated as an adversary. Semantics aside, can the West really stop China from exercising an ever-increasing role in global affairs? Indeed, is a unipolar power system a safer alternative to world peace than a bipolar or multipolar system?

The US is quite openly seeking to restrict China's role in global affairs and to impede its development. These are what constitute the "security challenge." The challenge thus has two dimensions, roughly what is called "soft power" and "hard power."

The former is internal development of industry, education, science, and technology. This provides the basis for the expansion of China's arena of influence through such projects as the Belt and Road (BRI) initiative, a massive multidimensional project that integrates much of Eurasia within a Chinese-based economic and technological system, reaching to the Middle East and Africa, and even to US Latin American domains.

The US complains, correctly, that Chinese internal development violates the rules-based international order. It does, radically. China is following the practices that the US did, as did England before it and all other developed societies since. China is rejecting the policy of "kicking away the ladder": first climb the ladder of development by any means available, including robbery of higher technology and ample violence and deceit, then impose a "rules-based order" that bars others from doing the same. That is a staple of modern economic history, now formalized in the highly protectionist investor-rights agreements that are masked under the cynical pretense of "free trade."

The "security challenge" also has a military dimension. This is countered by the program of encircling China by heavily-armed sentinel states, and by such projects as the massive RIMPAC exercises now underway, defending the US off the coasts of China. No infringement on US domination of the "Indo-Pacific" region can be tolerated, even a threat that China might set up its second overseas military base in the Pacific Solomon Islands (the first is in Djibouti).

Digressing briefly to criminal "whataboutism," we might mention
that the US has eight hundred bases worldwide, which, along with
their very prominent role in "defense" (aka imperial domination),
enable hundreds of "low-profile proxy wars" in Africa, the greater
Middle East, and Asia.

Washington, along with concurring commentary in the media and
journals of opinion, are quite correct in charging China with violation of the rules-based order that the US upholds, now with even more
firm European support than before. They are also correct in deplor-
ing severe human rights violations in China, but that is not a concern
of the rules-based order, which easily accommodates and commonly
vigorously supports such violations.

The question of how best to enhance world peace does not arise in
this connection. Everyone is in favor of "peace," even Hitler: on their
own terms. For the US, the terms are the rules-based international
order. Others have their own ideas. Most of the world is the proverbial
grass on which the elephants trample.

*The climate crisis was also on the agenda at the three-day summit in
Madrid. In fact, it was recognized as "a defining challenge of our time"
and NATO general-secretary Jens Stoltenberg informed the world that the
organization will "set the gold standard on addressing the security implications of climate change." Personally, I sure feel better now knowing that
militarism can be added to the methods of tackling the climate crisis. How
about you?*

How encouraging that NATO will address "the security implications of
climate change," where "security" has the usual meaning that excludes
the security of people.

The issues raised here are the most important of all and are the
most easily summarized. The human species is advancing toward a
precipice. Soon irreversible tipping points will be reached, and we will
be falling over the precipice to a "hothouse Earth" in which life will be
intolerable for those remnants that survive.

Military expenses make a double contribution to this impending disaster: first, in their enormous contribution to destroying the conditions for tolerable existence, and second, in the opportunity costs—what *isn't* being done with the huge resources devoted to undermining any hope for the future.

Putin's aggression in Ukraine made the same double contribution: destruction and robbery of the resources that must be used to avert environmental destruction. All of this couldn't have happened at a worse time. The window for constructive action is closing while humanity persists on this mad course.

All else pales into insignificance. We will find ways to cooperate to avert disaster and create a better world, as we still can. Or we will bring the human experiment to an inglorious end.

It's as simple as that.

INDEX

midterm elections influenced by,
109–10
rentier, 22
shocks in, 113–14
education, attacks on, 23–24, 25,
26, 183–84, 190–91
Eisenhower, Dwight, 3, 29, 222, 234
Eizenstat, Stuart, 20
election denialism, 187
of authoritarian movements, 115,
141–42
and social disorder, 114
elections. *See* midterm elections
Ellsberg, Daniel, 105, 108, 154
emissions. *See* carbon emissions;
net-zero emissions
employment, 53–54
energy, access to, 50, 121, 125–26,
129–30
"Energy Discrimination Elimination" laws, 91
energy efficiency, 50
Energy Information Administration, 50
energy transition. *See also* clean
renewable energy; just transition
cheaper energy resulting from, 50
Chinese technologies for, 5, 210
in communities, 11–12
economic benefits of, 124–26
financing, 54–56, 126–27
investment in, 55–56, 125, 126
job creation and, 7, 13, 50, 122,
129
and job loss, 7–10, 122
to net-zero emissions by 2050,

49–50, 120–21, 123–24
rich countries paying for, 13–15,
55, 124
engineering, science and, 31
the Enlightenment, 71–72
Environmental Protection Agency
(EPA), 215–16
Epstein, Gerald, 45, 89
Erdoğan, Recep Tayyip, 248–49,
250
Eurasia, 233, 251
Europe. *See also* European Union
(EU)
China and, 18, 82, 208–9,
232–33
Concert of, 19
German-dominated, 208–9, 210
NATO-ization of, 237
nuclear threat in, 109
Old *vs.* New, 62–63, 132
Russia as part of, 85, 167, 208–9
US influence in, 167, 239
European Union (EU), 1
Cuba sanctions and, 20
democracy troubled in, 21, 24,
25–26
emissions of, 12, 123–24
Green Deal in, 9
Iran sanctions and, 98–99
just transition policies in, 8–9
life satisfaction declining in, 21
price cap on Russian oil by, 162
Russia and, 82, 102, 166–67,
208–9, 210, 232, 239
UK leaving, 209
evangelical churches, 69, 141
evolution, 190

global warming and, 74
inherited from UK, 19, 244
Iran and, 97–98, 151–52
Russia and, 208, 233
sanctions and, 20–21
United States military
bases of, worldwide, 252
budget of, 126
carbon emissions of, 169
United States Supreme Court,
140–41, 188, 190, 192, 213,
215–16, 229
Universal Declaration of Human
Rights, 6–7
USS Fallujah, 63–64
US Strategic Command (STRAT-
COM), 104, 105, 108, 154

Versailles Treaty, 19, 199, 228, 239
Vieira, Liszt, 68
Vienna Declaration, 230
Vietnam War, 131, 134, 168, 207,
210

wages, growth in, 110–11
wage slavery, 53
war. *See* Iraq, US invasion of;
nuclear war, threat of; Ukraine,
Russian invasion of
war crimes, 63–66, 86
water scarcity, 170
Watumull, Jeffrey, 39
wealth, redistribution of, 185
weapons systems, 16–17
West Virginia, just transition in,
9–10, 11
West Virginia v. EPA, 219

white Christian nationalism, 26
Whitehouse, Sheldon, 127, 128
white supremacy, 112
white working class
death rates in, 113, 212
Democrats losing, 90
wildfires, 165
Wilkinson, Richard, 22
Willow project, 51
Wilson, Woodrow, 53, 181, 205
wind power, 123, 176–77. *See also*
clean renewable energy
Wittgenstein, Ludwig, 169
Wolfers, Justin, 111
women
education of, 6
in Iran, 94, 96–97
workers. *See* labor movement
World Bank, 2, 14, 70, 129
World Meteorological Organization, 107
World Social Forum, 79
World Trade Organization (WTO),
20
World War II, 2–3, 44, 95
and labor movement, 217
"logical illogicality" following,
205–6
and Munich Agreement, 240

Yale Program on Climate Change
Communication, 77, 229–30
"yellow peril," 206–7
Yellow Vests, 218
Yeltsin, Boris, 85, 242
Yemen, 225
Young, Stephen, 105

ABOUT THE AUTHORS

Noam Chomsky is Institute Professor (emeritus) in the Department of Linguistics and Philosophy at the Massachusetts Institute of Technology and Laureate Professor of Linguistics and Agnese Nelms Haury Chair in the Program in Environment and Social Justice at the University of Arizona. His work is widely credited with having revolutionized the field of modern linguistics. Chomsky is the author of numerous bestselling political works, which have been translated into scores of languages. Recent books include *What Kind of Creatures Are We?*, as well as *Optimism Over Despair, Notes on Resistance*, and *Chronicles of Dissent*.

C. J. Polychroniou is a political economist/political scientist who has taught and worked in universities and research centers in Europe and the United States. His main research interests are in European economic integration, globalization, the political economy of the United States, and the deconstruction of neoliberalism's politico-economic project. He is a regular contributor to *Truthout* as well as a member of *Truthout*'s Public Intellectual Project. He has published several books, and his articles have appeared in a variety of journals, magazines, newspapers, and popular news websites. Many of his publications have been translated into several foreign languages, including Arabic, Croatian, French, Greek, Hungarian, Italian, Japanese, Portuguese, Russian, Spanish, and Turkish.

ALSO AVAILABLE FROM HAYMARKET BOOKS

Chronicles of Dissent: Interviews with David Barsamian
David Barsamian and Noam Chomsky

Consequences of Capitalism: Manufacturing Discontent and Resistance
Noam Chomsky and Marv Waterstone

Fateful Triangle: The United States, Israel, and the Palestinians
Noam Chomsky, foreword by Edward W. Said

Gaza in Crisis: Reflections on the US-Israeli War Against the Palestinians
Noam Chomsky and Ilan Pappé

Illegitimate Authority: Facing the Challenges of Our Time
Noam Chomsky, edited by C.J. Polychroniou

Masters of Mankind: Essays and Lectures, 1969-2013
Noam Chomsky, foreword by Marcus Raskin

Notes on Resistance
David Barsamian and Noam Chomsky

Optimism over Despair: On Capitalism, Empire, and Social Change
Noam Chomsky and C.J. Polychroniou

The Precipice: Neoliberalism, the Pandemic, and the Urgent Need for Radical Change
Noam Chomsky and C. J. Polychroniou

Propaganda and the Public Mind
David Barsamian and Noam Chomsky

Turning the Tide: U.S. Intervention in Central America and the Struggle for Peace
Noam Chomsky

ABOUT HAYMARKET BOOKS

Haymarket Books is a radical, independent, nonprofit book publisher based in Chicago. Our mission is to publish books that contribute to struggles for social and economic justice. We strive to make our books a vibrant and organic part of social movements and the education and development of a critical, engaged, and internationalist Left.

We take inspiration and courage from our namesakes, the Haymarket Martyrs, who gave their lives fighting for a better world. Their 1886 struggle for the eight-hour day—which gave us May Day, the international workers' holiday—reminds workers around the world that ordinary people can organize and struggle for their own liberation. These struggles—against oppression, exploitation, environmental devastation, and war—continue today across the globe.

Since our founding in 2001, Haymarket has published more than nine hundred titles. Radically independent, we seek to drive a wedge into the risk-averse world of corporate book publishing. Our authors include Angela Y. Davis, Arundhati Roy, Keeanga-Yamahtta Taylor, Eve L. Ewing, Aja Monet, Mariame Kaba, Naomi Klein, Rebecca Solnit, Olúfẹmi O. Táíwò, Mohammed El-Kurd, José Olivarez, Noam Chomsky, Winona LaDuke, Robyn Maynard, Leanne Betasamosake Simpson, Howard Zinn, Mike Davis, Marc Lamont Hill, Dave Zirin, Astra Taylor, and Amy Goodman, among many other leading writers of our time. We are also the trade publishers of the acclaimed Historical Materialism Book Series.

Haymarket also manages a vibrant community organizing and event space in Chicago, Haymarket House, the popular Haymarket Books Live event series and podcast, and the annual Socialism Conference.